FRANCIS BACON AND RENAISSANCE PROSE

Published by the Syndics of the Cambridge University Press
Bentley House, P.O. Box 92, 200 Euston Road, London, N.W. 1
American Branch: 32 East 57th Street, New York, N.Y. 10022

Standard Book Number: 521 06709 X

Printed in Great Britain
at the University Printing House, Cambridge
(Brooke Crutchley, University Printer)

for
ILSE-RENATE

CONTENTS

ILLUSTRATIONS

ACKNOWLEDGMENTS

In terms of the fundamental necessity of obtaining texts and criticism I am heavily indebted to the resources of the Cambridge University Library and to its staff, who make those resources available with courtesy and speed. I shall always be grateful to the Master and Fellows of Churchill College for electing me to a research fellowship on the basis of an earlier version of this study; one which was also read by Joan Bennett, Anne Righter, and Leo Salingar, who offered advice and—that most necessary commodity to the research student—encouragement. In a later form it was a doctoral dissertation, and I must thank my examiners, Professors Geoffrey Bullough and Lionel Knights, for their kind and shrewd criticism which has helped much in the process of turning it into a book. My greatest debt is to my supervisor, Robert Bolgar, who gave very generously of his unrivalled knowledge of classical and Renaissance literature, and who delivered his criticisms, from corrections of the most banal slip to suggestions which made me rethink whole sections of the work, with unfailing good humour. To my wife I owe thanks for her patient typing and retyping, and above all for the love and support which made the work possible.

For the errors, prejudices, and confusions still remaining I am entirely responsible.

B. W. V.

Downing College
Cambridge

BIBLIOGRAPHICAL NOTE

All references to Bacon are to the *Works* edited by James Spedding, R. L. Ellis, and D. D. Heath (London, 14 volumes, 1857–74), and are given in abbreviated form, e.g. Volume 3, page 375: (3. 375).

References to secondary material concerning Bacon are set out in full in the analytical Bibliography (pp. 307–12), and are cited elsewhere by the item number; thus 'B 51' refers to Jones, R. F., *Ancients and Moderns*, and 'B, §iv' refers to section iv of the Index to Subjects (e.g. 'Philosophy', 'Sources'), p. 312.

THUS have I concluded this portion of learning touching Civil Knowledge; and with civil
knowledge have concluded Human Philosophy; and with human philosophy, Philosophy in General. And being now at some
pause, looking back into that I have passed
through, this writing seemeth to me, (*si nun-
quam fallit imago*) as far as a man can judge of
his own work, not much better than that noise
or sound which musicians make while they are
tuning their instruments; which is nothing
pleasant to hear, but yet is a cause why the
music is sweeter afterwards. So have I been
content to tune the instruments of the muses,
that they may play that have better hands.

The Advancement of Learning, Book 2

CHAPTER I

THE QUESTION OF STYLE

Few literary reputations have oscillated so extremely as that of Francis Bacon. As a scientist he dominated the seventeenth century to an extent which has still to be fully realised, despite the admirable study by Richard Foster Jones (B 51). His European reputation in the seventeenth and eighteenth centuries was hardly less brilliant, and, though his star fell somewhat in England after Newton and Locke, it rose again very powerfully for the Romantics (Coleridge and Shelley in particular had an almost personal relationship with his work), and to the Victorians he once again became an object of serious philosophical investigation, in particular for his concept of induction (B, §v). But it is hard not to think that both extremes of his reputation were excessive. In the seventeenth century men were inspired by his call for a rebirth of science based on observation, experiment, and co-operation. This general appeal was, historically, correct and well formulated, but it was only a leitmotiv in Bacon's thought, and the more detailed exposition of his theories of induction, negative instances, the laborious collection of natural data before any attempt at evaluating them—theories to which he devoted the bulk of his work and time in the last ten years of his life—these were almost totally ignored in the seventeenth century, and rightly so. Modern investigation of his sources (B, §iv)[1] has shown not only the expected result, that he was derivative (we have yet to be shown how he consistently reapplied old ideas to new purposes) but that he was contradictory to an extent unusual even in that age of contradictions: he castigates other scientists' natural histories for including legendary material which has not been tested by experiment and then does the same thing himself. He attacks Aristotle, but is in fact dependent on him for many ideas and methods, and his concept of magic and alchemy is fundamentally medieval.

The closer we look at Bacon's performance as a scientist, the more disappointed we become. Bacon was unaware of many of the new developments of his age[1] and when he did hear of them he rejected them out of hand to return to the traditional theories—so he was either ignorant of or indifferent to the work of Kepler, Copernicus, Galileo, Napier's logarithms, Harvey's discovery of the circulation of the blood, and William Gilbert's *De Magnete*, one of the few pieces of empirical research in the Renaissance, which he rejected scornfully. Gilbert, he said, 'hath made a philosophy out of the observations of a loadstone' (3. 293). F. R. Johnson has shown that Bacon knew less about astronomy than Donne[2] (though his ignorance of mathematics was probably more serious), and it is no wonder that accounts of seventeenth-century science tend increasingly to abandon Bacon as a figure of serious interest.[3] It is a commonplace of criticism that the inductive process as he formulated it undervalued the hypothesis and was incapable of playing any valuable part in scientific development: the significance of this theory was also overvalued in the nineteenth century, and it was left to C. D. Broad, speaking in Cambridge at a celebration of the tercentenary, to provide a witty and elegant exposure of its weaknesses.[4] More balanced estimates of Bacon's place in the history of thought have been provided by Hiram Haydn (B45), and by N. W. Gilbert, who in his study of Renaissance methodology (B37) insists that credit must be given to Bacon in that 'the notion of experimentation begins to be formulated expressly' by him first of all. Even more impressive is the testimony of Hardin Craig, who in his classic study of 'The Elizabethan Mind in Literature' (B22) gives Bacon a high place, not only as a witness to contemporary thinking, but as a man who has completely digested it—he writes at one point that 'Bacon, as usual, sees the situation with great clarity; he always discovers or re-discovers the truth'. The reassessment of Bacon in our time has produced reliable expositions of his thought from a purely philosophic point of view by F. H. Anderson (B3), and from a more technological position by B. Farrington (B27), though one could wish that both writers had devoted less space to the sum-

2

mary, and more to the discussion and criticism of Bacon's views. Other aspects of Bacon's work have been well handled: Karl Wallace continues his useful studies of Bacon's theory of rhetoric (B93-6), and John L. Harrison has provided an excellent defence of Bacon's much-abused references to poetry (B44). But with the exception of Anne Righter's sensitive though necessarily limited paper (B77) there has been no extended discussion of Bacon's style—indeed with this one praiseworthy exception what has been done is either unsympathetic or inaccurate, or both.[1]

If we can no longer estimate Bacon the scientist very highly, justice has certainly yet to be done to him as a writer. This situation is not only the excuse for writing a book on him, but points to a deeper truth: one cannot ascribe Bacon's remarkable hold over men's minds in the seventeenth century and after to any other source but his ability as an imaginative writer. Bacon himself defined 'the duty and office of Rhetoric' with a clear grasp of the psychology of persuasion: 'to apply Reason to the Imagination for the better moving of the Will' (3. 409), and his own theory of rhetoric is both highly detailed and original. In effect, his whole life's work was dedicated to persuasion, and he shows himself to be very aware of the importance of persuasive writing, interpreting a proverb of Solomon in *The Advancement of Learning* as 'signifying that profoundness of wisdom will help a man to a name of admiration, but that it is eloquence that prevaileth in an active life' (3. 409).[2] His normal references to his work and its style do not range beyond modest descriptions of it as 'clear' or 'not harsh or unpleasant' (3. 352; 4. 42), but in the letter to Playfere proposing a Latin translation of the *Advancement* Bacon recognises metaphorically the need for his scientific programme to reach and persuade as wide an audience as possible, and he visualises the process in terms of sowing a seed, lighting a fire, and ringing a bell, all powerful images for ideal communication. To 'excite men's wits' the sooner, he writes, he intends to utter his ideas 'as seeds' rather than wait for them to mature further; he will distribute them even better, in the words of the proverb:

by sowing with the basket, than with the hand. Wherefore, since I have only taken upon me to ring a bell to call other wits together, (which is the meanest office) it cannot but be consonant to my desire, to have that bell heard as far as can be. And since that they are but sparks, which can work but upon matter prepared, I have the more reason to wish that those sparks may fly abroad, that they may the better find and light upon those minds and spirits which are apt to be kindled. (10. 300–1.)

Another more famous metaphor for this process of communication is that of himself as the trumpeter heralding a new age, the 'buccinator novi temporis'.

The trumpet was heard, the sparks caught fire, and the results belong to the history of thought. But the nature of this communication, the literary creativeness which produced such a remarkable effect, have yet to be analysed. Not that their power has not been felt—indeed it is remarkable how many studies of Bacon[1] pay incidental tribute to his literary art, to 'the marvellous language in which Bacon often clothes his thoughts. His utterances are not infrequently marked with a grandeur and solemnity of tone, a majesty of diction, which renders it impossible to forget, and difficult even to criticise them. He speaks as one having authority, and it is impossible to resist the magic of his voice.' Even an unsympathetic writer speaks of 'Bacon's gorgeous rhetoric', and a study of his place in the 'counter-Renaissance' finds the distinction between his confidence and the bombastic egotism of men like Paracelsus, in Bacon's 'superior mastery of words, his truly wonderful capacity to keep his trumpet clean of overly brassy notes' and the ability to sound 'the sonorous peal of genuine dignity', in hearing which 'we are captured and acquiescent'. The power in Bacon's writing which moves his commentators to such eloquence derives initially from a strong imagination capable of presenting abstract ideas in a concrete but flexible form. D. G. James has accurately described 'the recoil, in Bacon's mind, from abstraction; his imagination did not go on to grasp firmly a world which lent itself to mathematical treatment; instead, it clung to a mode of apprehension that would ordinarily be called more poetical'. Indeed the whole end of his philosophy is a non-rational

4

vision of man's unlimited capacity to dominate the universe, a vision which Harold Fisch rightly defines as a 'fundamentally religious and poetical view of the world', created by 'the transference of the energies of Faith into the region of technology. Bacon makes Physics not a technique but a religion, and Induction becomes for him not so much a useful mechanism for the discovery of certain limited axioms, but rather a mystic path, an ultimate revelation and a millennial hope.'

II

Given the potency of this poetic vision a stylistic analysis—which, with certain limitations, is a valid critical approach to any writer—becomes an urgent necessity for Bacon, for I think it could be said that the disparity between the meagre, confused and inaccurate contents of his scientific programme and its overwhelming effect can only be explained by his mastery of style (though not thereby discredited for, as both H. Fisch and A. N. Whitehead point out, 'Bacon's Faustian dream of magical power over the world continues to drive us on'). However, the concept of style, and the most profitable way of analysing it are topics of considerable complexity, and I think it right that this study, which works on certain principles of method that have been gradually developed, should at one point announce what these principles are, and discuss the theoretical issues involved. Indeed the failure to state one's principles may be misleading, while the deliberate withholding of them can have sinister implications. I have tried to benefit from the most enlightened modern discussions of stylistic analysis that I could find[1] and, although I may seem to be embracing an impossibly wide field, the task seems worth while. However, the study of style is still a complex and indeed a confused topic, with much overlapping and repetition, and as an attempt to introduce some clarity I have therefore extracted what I take to be some essential stylistic principles and organised a brief discussion around each of them, juxtaposing what seem to me erroneous approaches with more enlightened ones. The principles are set out not with the generalising intent of the analytical theorist such as Aristotle or I. A. Richards but for more humble reasons, partly to clarify my own ideas and partly to expose the kinds of choices and alignments that I have made. They are informative, heuristic, and do not aspire to the profundity of fixed laws: it would be easy to quarrel with them, for they perhaps raise more questions than they answer, but that would be to mistake the spirit in which they are offered. Some working clarification of stylistic method seems necessary, but inevitably other assumptions have to be left un-analysed—this is hardly the place to attempt to define what we mean by 'literary values'.

The concept of 'style' itself should, I think, be as broad as possible (in practice, it is usually as narrow as its opponents care to make it) and to a literary student it should certainly include the concept of structure—so a linguist's complaint that 'to consider structure a *component* of style, except perhaps in a short poem, stretches the meaning of the term "style" to its limits' (Ohmann, 8, p. 425[*]) means simply that we must use a broader definition. My own working definition, which does not claim to be exclusive, would assume that a writer's style is an individual selection from the language available at the time (either in the widest sense or in the more limited form of 'literary' language); that his choice is made either subconsciously, so showing some habitual tendencies which may be significant, or consciously, that is according to a variety of principles which will depend at one level on his attitude to his reader and at the other on his concepts of the proper nature of (and the connections between) form, meaning and language in the developing work of art. I think that our analysis of style should go far beyond its commonly accepted aim, that merely initial stage of determining the individualising characteristics of a writer, and should consider the relation between the style of a particular passage and, loosely speaking, the argument or overall intention of the whole work, and indeed its degree of excellence. This is a functional view of stylistics, and above all a literary one, as what follows will explain.

[*] For sources given in full see pp. 267–8 n. 1.

The Question of Style

My first principle is that the study of a writer's style is only one of several possible critical approaches: this may seem unexceptionable if stated so, but even discursive reading in this field will show that many 'stylisticians' regard their approach as being the best if not the only way of dealing with a literary text. The attitude shown here is often connected with the apparently inevitable methodological split between form and content, and usually such critics affirm that the approach through style leads from form to content by the best possible route. So, for Leo Spitzer,

> language is only one outward crystallization of the 'inward form', or, to use another metaphor: the life-blood of the poetic creation is everywhere the same, whether we tap the organism at 'language' or 'ideas', at 'plot' or at 'composition'. (*16*, p. 18.)

R. A. Sayce says much the same thing, though with less vivid images: by studying style

> We shall in fact be studying the content, but instead of approaching it from the outside, more or less superficially, we shall come to it from the inside, through the texture and substance of the writing, in a word through the medium of the artist...Viewed in this light, the study of style should not be an accidental appendage but the first and most important stage in the total assessment of the work (*13*, pp. 6, 134).

This is certainly true of many literary works (and, one might suppose, of most great ones), but there are, equally, those where other approaches are not only prior, but more important. In some cases (Shakespeare's *Coriolanus*, say) the analysis of the artist's creative adaptation of his sources may be a more valuable clue to his intentions and implicit valuations than the work's styles. In others the presentation of a human situation and the interrelation between characters and their moral and psychological states is clearly the dominant artistic achievement and is not much dependent on the particular details of language. Such considerations may even apply to a whole genre—as René Wellek says, 'Many novels seem not to require any close attention to style' (Sebeok, *15*, p. 416).

I do not want to deny the validity of an approach through style

7

—far from it, for I think that it is a potentially valuable approach which has been neglected. Indeed, in the majority of extant criticism, as Floyd Gray has said:

On s'attache plus aux idées des écrivains qu'à leur façon de les faire vivre, sans toujours se rendre compte que l'art commence aux confins de l'idée, qu'on est écrivain non pour ce qu'on écrit, mais parce qu'on sait écrire. (*3*, p. 9.)

That may be too bluntly put, but it does point to one important aspect of literary art which the stylistic critic undertakes to evaluate. His task is more sensitively stated by Paul Valéry:

En somme l'étude dont nous parlions aurait pour objet de préciser et de développer la recherche des effets proprements littéraires du langage, l'examen des inventions expressives et suggestives qui ont été faites pour accroître le pouvoir et la pénétration de la parole. (Quoted, Sayce, *13*, p. 7, from *Introduction à la poétique* (Paris, 1938), pp. 12–13.)

It seems to me undeniable that a study of the *effets proprements littéraires* can help our appreciation of a work of art, but I do not want to elevate this discipline to a superior position, and would prefer to conclude more modestly, with Amado Alonso, that 'every study which contributes to the better comprehension and interpretation of a literary work is legitimate' (*1*, p. 489), and that stylistics is certainly one such approach. However, even within this discipline there will be variations, for 'like other high-order abstractions the concept of style has many facets' (Ullmann, *17*, p. 1) and so the critic should not impose one method only—hence it is unwise of R. Ohmann to complain that there are too many 'critical methods', all apparently defective, and which should all be replaced by 'Generative grammar' (*8*, 423–5 *et seq.*).

The second principle is that the study of style is a literary, not a scientific discipline, and thus the choice of material for analysis, the conduct of the analysis, and the evaluation of the results should be conditioned not by ease of availability or adaptability to 'scientific' manipulation, but by a framework of literary values. Some linguists want to elevate stylistics to a science and disparagingly compare the 'unscientific' and 'impressionistic' method of a critic like Spitzer to the accuracy of 'rigorous and exhaustive

8

linguistic analysis', such as 'the kind of inventory of linguistic items that forms the basis of modern structuralism' (Enkvist, 2, pp. 7–9, a technical-looking sentence which means no more than 'the counting of heads'). Certainly stylistic analysis, if performed with conscientious detail, should be one of the most objective of critical approaches, and with it (unlike some other methods) the data referred to will be available for checking; but the interpretations put on these data, the relating of them to aesthetic evaluation, is a critical process which is hardly susceptible to scientific methods. The linguist may be concerned with the single process of stylistic definition, but the literary critic will want to go on from there to make judgments of value; and despite the linguist's *caveat* (Riffaterre, *10*, p. 163) the critic may have started from these value judgments, for he will only be undertaking stylistic analysis if he is convinced that the work concerned is either aesthetically valuable in itself, or of historical significance. And any literary reader of modern linguistic discussions of style is bound to be depressed by the way in which linguists, in order to illustrate their principles, frequently retreat into the pre-linguistic stage of signs and symbols ('AR', 'SB', for examples, or 'Vt + NP', 'Be + Adj', 'O – I', 'MHQ', etc.), or to a few simple sentences which can be endlessly manipulated ('Dickens wrote *Bleak House*', say, or 'John loves Mary'), or at best to a highly simplified scale of utterance (American Folk-Tale narrative, Marathi baby-talk, or Californian suicide-notes). I am not wanting to score easily off the methods of linguistics: I realise that the first two groups consist of attempts at conventional representations of concepts, but they are in practice given too much attention at the expense of any literary analysis, and the poverty of imaginative resources available in the third group is symptomatic both of the crisis in linguistics, which is still producing conflicting theories of language so quickly that few of them seem to get developed in much practical detail, and perhaps even more of the fundamental difficulty of applying 'rigorous and exhaustive' linguistic analysis to literature—the concepts and methods evolved with such theoretical rigour are just too simple and too rigid to admit of any varied and flexible application to the endlessly subtle phenomenon of literary language. It may well be that linguistics will develop adequate methods for analysing complex styles, but in its self-limitation to scientific description it must always be regarded as the servant of literary criticism.

Another discipline which approaches the study of style in a scientific way is psychology, and here again the results so far achieved show how wide the gap is between the carefully formulated scientific method and its possible application to a complex literary text. So one psychologist in a paper entitled 'Vectors of Prose Style' (Sebeok, *15*, pp. 283–92) performed an experiment in reading, asking 8 different judges to comment on 150 passages of about 300 words each, according to 29 different criteria, but his 'laborious calculations', as René Wellek says, 'lead only to such obvious results as that the "humorous–serious" distinction is more reliable than the "good–bad" or "weak–strong" distinction, (Wellek, *20*, p. 409). Other psychological papers at this conference produced equally predictable results, albeit now established statistically—so a study of suicide notes showed that such notes 'contain more *mands*', that is demands, pleas, requests such as 'take care of the house', 'bury me' in this or that cemetery, and more 'distress-expressing' phrases than other letters (*ibid.*—what else would one expect?), and the author of the paper records with some surprise the result of an experiment to differentiate genuine suicide notes from false ones (that is, where the writers had not actually killed themselves): his team of subjects correctly assigned only half of the sample, whereas he and his co-investigator, who had been working on the project for some time, spotted nearly all of them, so suggesting that they had 'picked up a feeling for the suicidal style' (Sebeok, *15*, p. 304). The literary student finds this quite a normal event, and wonders how the psychologist would have gone on to analyse this 'feeling', or to account for it statistically.

The desire for quantification dominant in modern psychology joins up with the wish to make stylistics a science, complete with experimentally verifiable procedures, which seems to have affected linguists too. This we see from the example of Michael Riffaterre, who had performed in 1957 an excellent stylistic analysis *in propria persona*, as it were (*9*), but in 1959, now wishing to promote 'the development of stylistics as a science' (*10*, p. 159), went on to formulate a laboratory technique which would eliminate the possible subjectivity of the literary critic by employing an 'average reader', who apparently can be counted on to perceive significant elements of style, and whose responses are then monitored by an 'analyst':

In the linguistic message, more or less perceived, the passage from potential to actual style is a twofold phenomenon: first, the stylistic unit and then, the aroused attention of the reader. It follows that stylistic investigation will have to use *informants*. These will provide us with reactions to the text: for instance, a native endowed with consciousness of the object language will read the text and the stylistician will draw from him his reactions. The segments of the text which cause his reactions, the informant will call in turn beautiful or unaesthetic, well or poorly written, expressive or flavorless; but the analyst will use these characterizations only as clues to the elements of the relevant structure. The analyst will not consider whether or not they are justified on the level of aesthetics. (*10*, p. 162.)

Several obvious objections can be made to this account: the use of an 'informant' only pushes the process of judging back one stage; the informant has no great literary sensitivity ('a native endowed with consciousness of the object language'), and is thus dependent on the experimenter's taste and principles of selection; perhaps most damning, the categories used ('well or poorly written') are (*a*) vague, and (*b*) limited to simple descriptions, such as can be entered on punched cards and statistically evaluated. From that description (and I have quoted it fully in order to give its author a fair hearing) we can see to what absurdities linguistic 'stylisticians' are driven by their fear of a reader being influenced by 'ephemeral fashions or prejudiced aesthetic beliefs' (*ibid.* p. 163). As a corrective to it we might quote the words of a nineteenth-century grammarian which remain as a pertinent stress on an aspect totally ignored by the scientists:

La stylistique est l'étude de la langue comme art; pour la traiter, il faut posséder le sens artistique, le talent de se pénétrer des sentiments des autres... (W. Meyer-Luebke, quoted Ullmann, *19*, p. 99.)

And two distinguished modern students of style describe similar abilities needed by a successful practitioner: 'it requires a combination of artistic gifts and scholarly qualities' (Ullmann, *19*, p. 100), such unscientific attributes as 'talent, experience, and faith' (Spitzer, *16*, p. 27). These are qualities not susceptible to laboratory analysis, and the literary student may continue to believe (without being accused of complacency) that a critic of Spitzer's sensitivity is worth a million 'average readers' and their attendant analysts. Literary criticism is now, as always, characterised by the higher development of its practical techniques over its theoretical apparatus and, although it could in time acquire scientific objectivity, until then we may, like Wellek (who seems to me to have made some of the most penetrating comments on style), 'be content to think of literary criticism as a discipline that studies the structures and values of literature and uses gratefully the help of linguistics and psychology' (*20*, p. 411). But I do not foresee many literary critics using linguistics if the development of 'future style analysis' is really as Mr Riffaterre sees it, to that ideal scientific state of being mensurable: 'since devices can be reduced to the level of the context, any concept of an intrinsic stylistic value is void (e.g. the expressivity "inherent to" iterative verbal forms, superlatives, etc.). In its place, the leveling function is distributional in nature and therefore measurable' (*12*, p. 217).

I do not (of course) want to suggest that linguists are automatically excluded from making any contribution to the study of style, and that literary critics are *per se* authorities here, for under the third of my principles we can find examples of the identical split between theory and practice being made by literary critics. This is again one that may seem quite unexceptionable: stylistic criticism must be directed at specific individual texts, and can only generalise about 'schools' or 'movements' after widespread and sensitive reading. The particular case relevant to Bacon (to draw this discussion a little nearer the subject of my study) is the question of schools of style in England in the sixteenth and seventeenth centuries. The theory of Morris W. Croll that Bacon as a prose-writer is a terse, gnomic 'Senecan' opposing the more expansive

'Ciceronian' style will be considered in detail below (chapter 4), but I should like to bring out here one feature of this theory as it is developed by George Williamson in *The Senecan Amble: A Study in Prose Form from Bacon to Collier* (London, 1951); that is the attempt to define particular schools of style not on the basis of an analysis of the authors concerned (indeed, as I show below, the alignment of Bacon with Senecanism is based on amazingly brief reference) but on the rhetorical figures which are supposed to characterise them. The categories as formulated by Croll were relatively loose, but Williamson tries to apply them in detail, thus producing extremely contorted attempts to distinguish between so-called 'schools', as in this passage from the end of a long consideration of what constitutes Euphuistic, Ciceronian and Isocratean styles:

It would be easy to say that Euphuism was a new name for the Isocratic, but less easy to accept the consequences for Ascham and Lyly. Perhaps if we divide the Gorgian figures into schemes of rhythm and schemes of point, we can argue that in contradistinction the Ciceronian and Isocratean, the Isocratean and Euphuistic, overlap in their use of isocolon and parison; the Euphuistic and Senecan overlap in their use of antithesis and paromoion. For the accurate definition of a prose style it is necessary to determine not only what figures are used but how they are used. Ascham the Ciceronian, Isocratean, and Euphuist in turn—and all by virtue of his figures of language or *schemata verborum*—is a case in point. How would the *Ciceronianus* have classified him? At least we may assume that Echo would not have answered 'Attic'.[1]

The categories are of course far too vague for this sort of definition, and the sight of the critic struggling so with a self-imposed classification does not inspire confidence. René Wellek seems at one point to accept Croll's theories in so far as they apply to the Baroque, and also to grant that a literary movement can be defined in terms of 'few specific figures' used by it (*21*, pp. 98–101), but he goes on to abandon the idea: 'One must acknowledge that all stylistic devices may occur at almost all times' (p. 102)—indeed, to take a specific example, the rhetorical figures singled out by Croll and Williamson as characteristic of 'the Baroque' could be found in every writer influenced by

rhetoric, from Cicero to Dr Johnson. Croll himself never thought
that movements—let alone single authors—could be defined in
these fragmented terms, and he drew attention to the fallacious
application of the figure of antithesis as a defining factor: 'it is a
pity to use as the test of style a figure which may lead to the
identification—and, alas, still does lead to it—of styles so different
in kind as that of Browne and that of Lyly' (quoted Williamson,
p. 62 n. 1). The further issue is whether one is justified in dealing
with wholesale descriptions of writers' styles in advance of any
actual analysis, and Williamson seems to think that he is, writing at
one point that 'In this study I am concerned necessarily with the
species of style rather than with individual styles' (p. 37 n. 1). But
surely we can only rise to defining a species after we have analysed
the individual styles which are said to compose it; otherwise we
construct a childishly circular argument. The process of stylistic
analysis is essentially an inductive one (though not ignoring hypothesis), still more so when we begin to generalise outwards in
a historical context. Traditional 'species' must be forgotten until a
series of individual analyses can be freshly redisposed—and in fact
most of the accepted 'schools' of style in the English Renaissance
seem to me to be superficially, if not wrongly, defined.

My fourth principle is that a writer's work can be quite satisfac-
torily studied on its own or with reference to his own theory of
style in so far as he consciously expresses it, but that such a study
can gain much from viewing its subject in historical terms: that is,
by considering the development of particular aspects of style as
seen in preceding and contemporary theory and practice. W. K.
Wimsatt prefaced his study of Dr Johnson's prose style by explaining that he had attempted first to arrange Johnson's 'statements
relevant to a theory of composition' into a partial system, and
then to establish 'relation between this system and Johnson's
actual practice. The last must be the ultimate aim in the study of a
writer's theory, for his theory and his writing are but different
manifestations of the same thing, a preference, and if a writer is
aware of his preference and is honest, his expressed theory should
somehow square his practice' (Wimsatt, *23*, p. xii). I have worked

on the same principle in this study of Bacon, and have discovered what is, I believe, a common enough phenomenon, that Bacon's stylistic practice is certainly based on his theories but far exceeds them in range and subtlety. Similarly with the writer's relation to his predecessors and contemporaries, as Mr Wimsatt says, 'A study of style need not involve historical considerations but can find its complement in them' (*ibid.*). Thus I have tried to fill in something of the background to Bacon's theories and practice in terms of the particular stylistic devices which seem important for him, but this part of each section is inevitably limited—to discuss precedent and contemporary practice adequately would require a full history of sixteenth-century prose. In trying to discover what theories influenced prose style in this period I have made use of classical rhetorics and their Elizabethan counterparts: I have not discussed medieval rhetoric, nor have I made use of such continental recensions as those by Susenbrotus and Trapezuntius (except in so far as their classifications or definitions were incorporated into English rhetoric books), for neither source seems to offer a fundamental reinterpretation of Aristotle, Cicero and Quintilian. Again such sources of influence will not on their own 'account for' the nature, let alone the excellence or clumsiness, of a particular writer, but, given such a style-conscious period as the Renaissance, and one where education was fairly standardised throughout England, with rhetoric playing the dominant part in both schools and universities, it would be foolish not to consider such an important source of stylistic theory.

Likewise, to pass on to my fifth principle, it seems to me unwise not to consider any relevant biographical circumstances of a writer's career or possible formative influences (e.g. education, profession). A writer does not work in a vacuum (some may be approaching this stage now, but few did so in the Renaissance), and we must consider the prevailing styles and conventions which operated in the social or intellectual milieu within which he thought and wrote. In Bacon's case the relevant milieu is that of his professions, and I believe that I have discovered evidence of his concept of literary structure having been deeply influenced by his study and practice of the law, and strengthened by his lifelong activity in parliament. The stylistic critic cannot neglect any external evidence which may be valuable, least of all (and this must surely be an incontrovertible principle) such key documents as the writer's revisions of his work. In his study of Gobineau, Michael Riffaterre states cogently the value of such evidence:

La première question que pose l'étude du style est de savoir dans quelle mesure celui-ci est conscient, voulu, travaillé en conséquence; de savoir jusqu'à quel point, au contraire, il reste instinctif et l'expression, à travers ou malgré le travail de l'écrivain, du naturel de l'homme. La manière la plus efficace de répondre à cette question est l'étude des variantes du texte, des corrections apportées à la première version: le seul nombre des variantes indique si l'on a affaire à un écrivain hâtif ou à un artiste qui, tel Flaubert, remettait cent fois son ouvrage sur le métier; l'étude des tendances de ces variantes, tendances vers la concision, par exemple, tendance, au contraire, vers l'enrichissement du vocabulaire, révèle le style en formation, son point de départ, c'est-à-dire l'état natif, le plus proche de la psychologie de l'auteur, et son procès vers le résultat, le seul élément que connaisse le lecteur, mais dont les racines sont dès lors révélées. (*9*, p. 26.)

Mr Riffaterre goes on to list many examples of such studies (pp. 26–7), to which we might add such valuable analyses as have been made of the revisions of Montaigne or Pope, Proust or Yeats. The detailed alterations which Bacon made in the *Essays* and the *Advancement of Learning* have never been studied, though they are often referred to, and in chapter 7 I try to show that all the types of stylistic revision made there confirm the tendencies within his style which I have analysed earlier.

One clause in Mr Riffaterre's account ('l'état natif, le plus proche de la psychologie de l'auteur'—he himself goes on to study the *tics* or psychological obsessions shown in Gobineau's repetitions, pp. 116–22) brings us to my next principle, the extent to which the critic is justified in extrapolating from his stylistic analysis hypotheses as to the psychology of the author: the principle I have worked on is that such psychological guess-work is more likely to produce abuse than insight. This was the stylistic method advocated by Leo Spitzer, though not limited to him. Spitzer began by asking himself the question 'can one distinguish the *soul* of a particular French writer in his particular language?' (*16*, p. 11), and then applied to stylistics the 'circle of understanding' method of Dilthey and Schleiermacher, which works from a basic intuition as to the relevance of a detail within the whole and then seeks confirmation for it: so Spitzer would notice significant details in the work of art, 'then, grouping these details and seeking to integrate them into a creative principle which may have been present in the soul of the artist' (*ibid.* p. 19), he would reread the text to find conclusive evidence. The dangers of this approach— mainly that it might begin with an insignificant detail, or with a psychological deduction and seek linguistic support, or would follow one clue and ignore all the others—have been well exposed by a number of style critics (Riffaterre, *10*, pp. 163–4; Wellek and Warren, *22*, pp. 183–4; Ullmann, *19*, pp. 121–6), and indeed Spitzer himself came to realise the flaws in his method, both from a historical and from an absolute viewpoint: on the first, he admitted that psychological linguistics applies

only to writers who think in terms of the 'individual genius', of an individual manner of writing, that is, to writers of the eighteenth and later centuries; in previous periods the writer (even a Dante) sought to express objective things in an objective style. Precisely the insight that 'psychological stylistics' is not valid for earlier writers (Montaigne being a glaring exception) has reinforced in me another tendency which was present in my work from the beginning, that of applying to literary art a structural method that seeks to define their unity without recourse to the personality of the author. (Quoted, Wellek and Warren, *22*, p. 183.)

Certainly this *caveat* applies to sixteenth-century prose-writers as a whole, who are not given to personal subjective revelation, and particularly to Bacon, who seems to be extremely 'objective' in that he is interested in the outside world to the exclusion of himself, and for this and other reasons I have not made guesses about his psychology.

But, as I try to show, Bacon is seldom if ever neutral, being concerned throughout his whole career to convince the reader of a definite viewpoint, whether in law or politics, science or moral philosophy. The general stylistic considerations behind the presence of 'feeling' in prose have been usefully set out by Richard Ohmann:

Style adds the force of personality to the impersonal forces of logic and evidence, and is thus deeply involved in the business of persuasion...Emotion enters prose not only as disguises for slipping into the reader's confidence, but as sheer expression of self. Complete honesty demands that the writer not only state his ideas accurately, but also take an emotional stance. A proposition is never held altogether dispassionately, nor can it be expressed without some indication of feeling. (7, p. 21.)

As I argue below, certain stylistic devices of Bacon's (such as repetition and variation in syntax, all varieties of imagery) express very clear emotional positions. If we were to work back from these to Bacon's psychology we should only discover that he felt such-and-such about certain topics—and this he has expressed. Otherwise I find no evidence in his style which either contradicts his thought and attitudes, or points to aspects of which he was himself unaware. (These are favourite ploys in modern criticism, particularly, it seems, in Victorian studies.) But even if we were to find such psychological obsessions in a style, we are not entitled to give them any aesthetic status. This weakness of psychological stylistics on the absolute scale was again best seen by Spitzer himself:

Even where the critic has succeeded in connecting one aspect of an author's work with some personal experience, some *Erlebnis*, it does not follow, it would even be wrong to assume, that such correspondence between life and work will always contribute to the artistic beauty of the latter. After all, the *Erlebnis* is no more than the raw material of the work of art, in the same way as are, for example, its literary sources. (Quoted and translated, Ullmann, *19*, p. 125.)

So Spitzer abandoned this method for a 'structural' approach where 'stylistic analysis is subordinated to an interpretation of the work of art as a poetic organism in its own right, without any recourse to psychology' (*ibid.*). This is certainly the approach which promises most for stylistics but, though we must applaud

Spitzer's courage in admitting the weaknesses of his system, we must remember that in his hands it produced some brilliant analyses. Could any other method have achieved, for example, his remarkable demonstration of the accelerating syntactical and emotional progressions of Diderot? (*16*, pp. 135–91).

Granted that the style critic will not use his analysis to construct hypotheses about his writer's psychology, how is he justified in neglecting a work's whole 'content' to focus on its 'form'? This is a question which has much exercised students of style: it seems to me that some temporary separation is unavoidable but that the critic should always be trying to see how one informs the other. Amado Alonso reminds us of the essential principle that the two are interdependent and mutually defining: the 'contents' of a work of art, he writes, 'have a qualitative interplay in the form or construction itself. For it is impossible to think of the very same form with different contents; the contents, with their characteristic nature, are formative in themselves' (*1*, p. 491). As N. Enkvist says, the familiar concept of style as something which is 'added' to thought postulates such an impossibility as 'the existence of prelinguistic thought or prestylistic expression' (*2*, p. 13), and Stephen Ullmann would take this principle still further: 'Language and thought are not only indissolubly intertwined, but they may actually stimulate each other, and there are cases, especially in poetry, where language precedes and to some extent predetermines the idea which it is supposed to express' (*19*, p. 152). (Certainly in Bacon's use of imagery, the image often seems to run ahead of, and possibly even predetermine, the thought.) W. K. Wimsatt traces the historical growth of this concept of the identity of style and meaning, quoting Cardinal Newman's dictum that 'Matter and expression are parts of one: style is a thinking out into language' (*23*, pp. 1–2), adding rightly that 'It is hardly necessary to adduce proof that the doctrine of identity of style and meaning is today firmly established. This doctrine is, I take it, one from which a modern theorist hardly can escape, or hardly wishes to' (*ibid.*), and later giving a sensitive definition of style as 'the last and most detailed elaboration of meaning' (*ibid.* p. 63). But, although this doctrine may be accepted in the literary world, it is a linguist (significantly so in view of my earlier argument) who complains that studies of figurative language 'embrace only a small, though important, part of style, and liberally mixed with content, at that' (Ohmann, *8*, p. 424)—as if this were a sin (of course the presence of meaning in language is something of an embarrassment to a scientific stylistician). He goes on to reject the concept of the interdependence of form and content ('This austere doctrine has a certain theoretical appeal', p. 427), which seems surprising in view of his earlier and quite admirable statement that 'a dichotomy between thought and emotion, though useful, is artificial. A writer's characteristic way of manipulating experience is organically related to his feelings about coming to know; his attitude toward the reader and toward the process of communicating is also part of the whole' (*7*, p. 29).

But, although nearly everyone accepts the identity of style and meaning, the methodological problem remains. I would suggest that if the critic is discussing a mimetic fictive form, such as the novel or the drama, he will have to study style primarily within the work's self-sufficient structure, in terms of the writer's development of individual characters' speech and relationships to one another. This is a very complex business, and is perhaps for that reason seldom performed. If he is studying a non-mimetic fictive form such as the lyric poem, he will clearly have to relate its style to the poem's subject, and the poet's attitude to the subject. If the critic is studying an imaginative work which exists at a non-fictive level, such as Montaigne's *Essais*, or indeed Bacon, then he will have to relate the style to the argument or attitude being developed (for this reason I have always tried to place a stylistic example in its context by summarising Bacon's argument at that point). But in all these examples the stress will have to be temporarily more on the style than on the content and, if the balance is disturbed here, then given the organic unity of style and meaning, the reader should return to the content with a sharper perception. This seems the only feasible method of proceeding, and the intolerable limitations of a system which would deny this temporary separation are acutely exposed in René Wellek's criticism of Croce's aesthetics from this viewpoint:

> In Croce's system, which is completely monistic, no distinction can be made between state of mind and linguistic expression. Croce consistently denies the validity of all stylistic and rhetorical categories, the distinction between style and form, between form and content, and ultimately, between word and soul, expression and intuition. In Croce, this series of identifications leads to a theoretical paralysis: an initially genuine insight into the implications of the poetical process is pushed so far that no distinctions are possible. It now seems clear that process and work, form and content, expression and style, must be kept apart, provisionally and in precarious suspense, till the final unity: only thus are possible the whole translation and rationalization which constitute the process of criticism. (Wellek and Warren, *22*, p. 184.)

That would seem to be an authoritative statement of the need for this impermanent divorce.

My ninth principle rejects such apparently 'objective' ways of analysing style as that of 'deviation from a linguistic norm' or 'frequency of linguistic devices' in favour of the study of the individual context in relation to the whole work's artistic development. Some theorists still believe that 'All concepts of style involve a consciousness of norms and the possibility of departures from them' (Gregory and Spencer, *3*, p. 102), and this was formerly widely accepted (e.g. Ullmann, *19*, p. 154; several writers listed in Riffaterre, *10*, p. 167 n. 19). The two main objections to it—that it would reduce the analysis of style to a simple plus–minus procedure which ignores the function of what is actually there in the text, and that it is in any case impossible to establish the norm—are well stated by Wellek and Riffaterre. The former makes the first objection:

> The danger of linguistic stylistics is its focus on deviations from, and distortions of, the linguistic norm. We get a kind of counter-grammar, a science of discards. Normal stylistics is abandoned to the grammarian, and deviational stylistics is reserved for the student of literature. But often the most commonplace, the most normal, linguistic elements are the constituents of literary structure. (Wellek, *20*, pp. 417–18.)

Wellek's pungent phrase 'a science of discards' (which recalls the words of a proponent of this deviational stylistics who described it as 'la science des "écarts"'—Ch. Bruneau, quoted Ullmann, *19*, p. 154) points to the purely negative aspect of this definition by exclusion. Riffaterre's destruction of the concept on linguistic grounds (*10*, pp. 167–9) seems to me conclusive: after surveying other objections, he attacks it for more fundamental reasons,

namely not so much that the linguistic norm is virtually unobtainable, but that it is irrelevant. It is irrelevant because the readers base their judgments (and the authors their devices) not on an ideal norm, but on their individual concepts of what is the accepted norm (e.g. what the reader 'would have said' in the author's place). These multiple norms are given some common traits by normative grammar. Can we at least evaluate them with some approximation to accuracy? An overall norm, even for a short period of history and for a single social class, will not do, because even a relatively stable state of the language is the theater of transformations that style is likely to reflect. Aside from the author's milieu, we have to take into account his readings, his literary affiliations and probably a second standard, the written norm...All these norms should be taken into account and our task should be done over for each generation of readers. (Pp. 167–8.)

Although few critics will even think that a whole style can be defined in terms of its deviations, I would nevertheless reserve this approach for a limited function—that is, for individual contexts, where the writer has deliberately violated some well-known convention of grammar or genre—linguistic decorum does exist, although not easily defined.

To the second of these apparently objective methods, that using statistical analysis of frequency patterns, the same conclusion applies: it is occasionally valuable as supporting evidence but it should never be thought to give the whole 'definition' of a style. Even as supporting evidence it needs to be applied carefully, and to specifically literary ends—I confess to not being very happy about the way W. K. Wimsatt compares the frequency of certain devices in Johnson, Addison, and Hazlitt by reducing them to 'quotients per hundred words' (*23*, e.g. pp. 26, 29–30, 34, 44). Such measurable things as sentence- or clause-lengths, frequency of nouns to adverbs, rhythmic patterns of cadences, and so

on, may undoubtedly be useful in defining habitual characteristics of an author's style, especially for doubtful or anonymous
works, or to establish an author's chronology (though here they
must be used with caution), but, inasmuch as they do not consider
questions of meaning or artistic imagination, they have no literary
value: 'A purely linguistic analysis of a work of literature will
yield only linguistic elements' (Riffaterre, *10*, p. 154). Whereas
linguists still seem to accept this criterion (e.g. Enkvist, *2*, pp. 28,
41, etc.; Ohmann, *7*, pp. 13–14) and to apply it (Stephen Ullmann
uses it too frequently for my liking in his books on the French
novel—*17*, p. 18—though he later shows himself aware of its
hazards, *19*, pp. 118–20), literary critics distrust it. Again Mr
Wellek has expressed our objections most forcibly:

> Statistical frequency necessarily ignores the crucial aesthetic problem, the use of
> a device in its context. No single stylistic device, I believe, is invariable: it is
> always changed by its particular context. Literary analysis begins where
> linguistic analysis stops. (*20*, p. 417; also *22*, p. 182.)

Another speaker at this conference placed the emphasis on the
nature of a literary idea, which 'simply is not a literary idea until it
has become a constituent element of a work of art. When we try
to restate it in a propositional or conceptual form, it ceases to be a
literary idea'. So that 'in their fullest sense stylistic elements cannot
be dealt with in a mensurated manner. They can be counted, but
the numbers don't really mean very much' (Sebeok, *15*, p. 429).
Clearly the critic must study individual stylistic devices in their
relation to the complete work of art and with the appropriate
aesthetic method.

My last principle holds that the choice of which stylistic factors
have literary significance and can therefore be a valuable basis for
analysis is one which will vary from writer to writer and from
work to work; categories must not be imposed from without, and
are in any case not fixed. A useful introduction to this topic is
provided by W. K. Wimsatt, who in discussing how we estimate
the aesthetic value of particular stylistic contexts relates the idea to
that of relative frequency, and develops the paradox that:

The greatest obstacle to recognizing the expressive value of rhetorical devices is the fact that they recur. One notices that Cicero uses a *litotes* or a *praeteritio* several times in a few pages, or so many hundreds of balances are counted in the *Ramblers* of Johnson. This suggests play with words, disregard of meaning. One is likely to reflect: if these devices express something, then the author must be expressing, or saying, much the same thing over and over—which is useless; therefore the author is really not trying to say anything; he is using words viciously, for an inexpressive purpose. (*23*, p. 12.)

Nevertheless, nobody thinks 'that sentences because they recur are artificial, that they say the same thing over or say nothing'. Both forms are expressive: 'The so-called "devices", really no more devices than a sentence is a device, express more special forms of meaning, not so common to thinking that they cannot be avoided, like the sentence, but common enough to reappear frequently in certain types of thinking and hence to characterize the thinking, or the style.' This seems the most fruitful way of approaching this problem, provided that one remembers that the 'device' is not in fact a constant: as Wellek observed, it is always changed by its context (see also Wellek and Warren, *22*, p. 178, and Riffaterre's approach to Gobineau, *9*, pp. 18, 22)—within the period of this study, for example, Renaissance rhetoricians taught that the same rhetorical figure could be applied to a variety of emotional moods.[1] But inasmuch as I often use the term 'device' in connection with Bacon, I should like to agree with Mr Wimsatt's final reservation: 'It might be better if the term "device" were never used, for its use leads almost immediately to the carelessness of thinking of words as separable practicably from meaning' (*ibid.*). However, as with the 'form–content' dichotomy, there seems to be no practical alternative—at least the reader will know that I am aware of the problem.

For the actual choice of significant factors we must again avoid being dogmatic. As stylistic analysis should start from an examination of the text, it is impossible to predict which elements will be important. They may seem quite minor details: for examples of successful analysis based on small-scale phenomena (and to go no further than the work used in this discussion) one might take

Ullmann on the sudden use of imagery in *l'Étranger* (*19*, pp. 121, 194–5); Ohmann on the distinction between 'embedded' sentences in Henry James and 'kernel' sentences in Lawrence (*8*, pp. 436–8); Riffaterre on the French Symbolist poets' use of nouns ending in *-ance* (*10*, p. 165). But, however minor these details may seem, they must be there: that is, one must not bring ready-made categories from outside. Leo Spitzer has recorded his dissatisfaction with those who begin studies of imagery in a particular author 'because it hasn't been done yet' (*16*, p. 171) and he goes on to urge that 'Imagery should be considered not *per se*, but according to the particular function that the author ascribes to it in his different works.' (Within Renaissance prose one might add that the study of Hooker's imagery, say, would be far less rewarding than that of his sentence and paragraph structure; or that an analysis of Greene's vocabulary is much less valuable than the same technique applied to Ben Jonson.) Nor must the stylistic critic be seduced by the particular nature of his method to ignore other aspects of style. The interest of *Senecan Amble*, for instance, is almost entirely in sentence structure and sound patterns, divorced from meaning or the writer's imaginative vision: such an approach would work equally well on writing of no literary value, or even on nonsense (this last remark does not seem far-fetched when we read the perfectly serious statement of a linguist bent on 'measuring the style' of a passage by comparing its linguistic frequencies with those from similar literary contexts, that 'Contextually distant norms would be, e.g., Gray's *Anatomy* or the London Telephone Directory of 1960'—Enkvist, *2*, p. 29). Another critic who applies a highly specialised method is R. Ohmann, using 'generative grammars with transformational rules' for the purpose of analysing sentence structures (and it seems that this is the only purpose to which such grammars could be put), who concludes his account with this condescending remark: 'Finally, though syntax seems to be a central determinant of style, it is admittedly not the whole of style. Imagery, figures of speech, and the rest are often quite important' (*8*, p. 438).

'I must repeat that we should observe stylistic procedures by taking the concrete work of art as the point of departure, not some *a priori* standpoint outside of the work' (Spitzer, *16*, p. 172). This attempt to impose an exterior category on the analysis is precisely what mars the work of so many linguists: Mr Ohmann trying to make transformational grammar *fit* stylistics: Mr Enkvist proposing a more eclectic and more elaborate series of categories to be applied to a literary work (*2*, pp. 30–1); Mr Riffaterre, in his later papers at least, trying to erect a purely linguistic framework for the analysis of style. Mr Riffaterre is indeed the most penetrating of these linguists and, despite the flaws and prejudices inherent in his desire to make this a scientific process, he is to be congratulated for rejecting many false methods and for narrowing the essential stage down to the analysis of individual stylistic contexts (*10*, pp. 169–73; *12*, *passim*). He works from the indisputably valid basis of the author's intentions and the reader's sense of development, but limits the latter to the experience of a pattern being set up and then being unexpectedly broken: so 'the context begins at the point where the reader perceives the existence of any continuous pattern' (*12*, p. 213); for 'Since stylistic intensification results from the insertion of an unexpected element into a pattern, it supposes an effect of rupture which modifies the context' (*10*, p. 170), hence 'the effectiveness of the contrast is in direct proportion to its degree of unpredictability' (*12*, p. 209; also *10*, p. 158).

This diagnosis certainly accounts for one familiar literary effect (though it could have been arrived at in a less laborious way), but it ignores the equally valid contrary process, by which the writer will prefigure an event so that we know for some time that it will occur, and, when it finally does, produces a very powerful effect: such is the dramatic function of the prologues of Euripides, or those many preparatory hints which Shakespeare will drop from the beginning of a play, pointing towards future development (especially to forecast the probable behaviour of a person caught in a plot—Hal on Falstaff, Iago on Othello). Furthermore, Mr Riffaterre's theory leads him to simplify possible events in literature:

so by a rigorous chain of reasoning he arrives at the conclusion that the patterns of movement from context to the surrounding literary areas 'imply that there is no such thing as an intrinsically stylistic device (e.g., an hyperbole in an hyperbolic context will pass unnoticed)' (*10*, p. 172). But whoever failed to notice any one of the hyperboles spoken by Shakespeare's Troilus, say, either in his fulsome praise of Cressida at the beginning of the play (i. i. 7–103) or in his equally intense agony after her betrayal (v. ii. 135–58)? Again Mr Riffaterre shows the linguist's all-too-familiar disregard for 'content' in describing as a 'microcontext' this fragment from Emily Dickinson: '*Or fame erect her siteless citadel*', which he takes as 'a case of self-sufficient style, since this isolated line was found noted on the flap of an envelope, indicating the writer's desire to preserve a form rather than a content' (*12*, p. 210). The literary reader might respond that, if anything, the poet seemed more inclined to preserve the content, but obviously we cannot separate the two like the white and the yolk of an egg.

Surely the example of the simplifications and *non sequiturs* created by such intelligent scholars as these linguists can only strengthen our conviction that the only way to analyse a literary text is to give it a careful and sensitive reading, without preconceptions, and to develop gradually the implications of the significant stylistic factors. The older school of literary-style critics were much nearer to the essential processes of reading than any of their more scientific successors, and it is not surprising to find that the best description of the truly literary process (although it is of course 'subjective' and 'impressionistic') remains that of Leo Spitzer:

Why do I insist that it is impossible to offer the reader a step-by-step rationale to be applied to a work of art? For one reason, that the first step, on which all may hinge, can never be planned: it must already have taken place. This first step is the awareness of having been struck by a detail followed by a conviction that this detail is connected basically with the work of art; it means that one has made an 'observation',—which is the starting point of a theory, that one has been prompted to raise a question—which must find an answer. To begin by omitting this first step must doom any attempt at interpretation... (*16*, pp. 26–7.)

And throughout the whole process the reader is engaged in a peculiar dialectic with the text, part active, part passive, for

> reading at its best requires a strange cohabitation in the human mind of two opposite capacities: contemplativity on the one hand and, on the other, a Protean mimeticism. That is to say: an undeflected patience that 'stays with' a book until the forces latent in it unleash in us the recreative process. (*Ibid*. p. 38.)

That profound statement of the essentially recreative process of reading is central to the whole process of literary criticism, and it is one which the scientific stylists would do well to consider.

Having thus benefited from the work of a number of great scholars and critics (the collocation is not accidental: it seems to me almost fatal to be the one without the other, and certainly the student of style must be both scholarly and critical), and having— I hope—sufficiently exposed the principles on which it has been built, the real business of this book can proceed. What follows, then, is an analysis of the significant particulars of Bacon's style arranged as separate discussions of these features, and, although it may seem unfortunate that it does not discuss whole works (in fact, Book 1 of the *Advancement of Learning* is a focal point and is handled in detail, as are some of the *Essays*), it has the advantage of exposing clearly the various planes of literary resource which operate through all of Bacon's writing, starting at the lowest level with the general structure of the works, moving up to the particular and important device, the aphorism, and from there to the greater emotive potential of symmetrical syntax and to his major imaginative resource, imagery, which is handled from two complementary directions. Nor of course does this analytical approach preclude further synthetic ones; indeed a study of the development of Bacon's style would seem to me an urgent consideration. In each case the use of a device is briefly put into the context of his own theories, and as far as possible into that of English Renaissance prose. Bacon's relation to the tradition is always important, though variable: sometimes he will take over traditional stylistic devices without altering them, but using their expressive power fully (as with imagery and syntactical symmetry); at other times he will take a traditional technique and either delimit its scope (as with his selection of *partitio* from the normal five or seven parts of an oration) or give it a significance of his own (as with the aphorism). But always he is using the full resources of English prose at a point in time (after the freedom from inarticulacy in the 1570s and before the drastic cutting-back of the 1660s) where it achieved a scope and flexibility not attained before or since, and within a very rich medium Bacon seems to me one of the outstanding writers. As I have made it plain that I believe in evaluation, not mere description, I have frequently proceeded to value-judgments— sometimes, it may seem, too boldly. But I hope that the reader will go back to Bacon to test the validity of my analysis, and that he will ultimately agree with my estimate. For—to apply one last artificial but necessary dichotomy—I feel justified in studying Bacon purely as a writer in that he appeals with great power to the intellect, but first and last through the imagination.

CHAPTER 2

ORGANISATION AND STRUCTURE

It is impossible not to admire the structure of Bacon's works. Outlines are clear and easily grasped, the argument proceeds firmly through each section, and each topic is covered with thoroughness and precision. There is in all the finished work, and even in some of the fragments, a strong sense of unity—the organic unity of a tree and its branches—which Coleridge perceived, and attributed partly to the unity of the subject and partly to 'the perpetual growth and evolution of the thoughts, one generating, and explaining, and justifying, the place of another...'[1] But, in addition to this intellectual unity, this tough but relaxed control of thought into an essentially positive, onward movement, there is to be felt throughout Bacon's work an effective organisation of the larger units of argument. The method he uses to achieve this tight structure is seen most clearly in the *Advancement of Learning*, and seems to be the deceptively simple one of dividing up the topic into its main heads, subdividing within these, and then following the argument along its respective branches. To find out why Bacon should have used this technique so frequently (and therefore what status it enjoyed in the Renaissance), the most rewarding path seems to be that opened up by Bacon's praise of Plato for having said that 'he is to be held as a god who knows well how to define and to divide' (4. 164; 3. 239), even though the sixteenth-century misunderstanding of this sense of 'divide' may make it a false one.

If we examine this quotation in its context in the *Phaedrus* we find that it comes at a point where Plato first formulates his concept of *diaíresis*, the division of a genus into its species, a division used as a stage towards a greater philosophical goal, for by separating the One from the Many we may ultimately discover the true essence. Socrates outlines the two complementary dialectical principles, first that of 'the comprehension of scattered particulars in one idea', secondly

that of division into species according to the natural formation, where the joint is, not breaking any part as a bad carver might...I am a great lover of these processes of division and generalization; they help me to speak and think. And if I find any man who is able to see a One and Many in nature, him I follow, and walk in his steps as if he were a God. (*Phaedrus,* 265–6.)¹

Those who have this art are worthy to be called dialecticians, which, as R. Hackforth has said, 'is equivalent to saying that the practitioner of Division and Collection is, in Socrates' judgment, the only true philosopher'. Furthermore, 'the verve displayed by Socrates in his account...justifies the belief that here we have Plato's first announcement of a new discovery to which he attaches the highest importance'.² In the *Philebus, diaíresis* is given still more approval, now being described by Socrates as a gift which 'the gods tossed among men by the hands of a new Prometheus', and which is now described in more detail:

all things of which we say 'they are' draw their existence from the one and the many, and have the finite and infinite implanted in them: seeing then, that such is the order of the world, we too ought in every enquiry to begin by laying down one idea of that which is the subject of enquiry; this unity we shall find in everything, and having found, we may next proceed to look for two if there be two, or, if not, then for three or some other number, subdividing each of these units, until at last the unity with which we began is seen not only as one and many and infinite, but also as a definite number. (*Philebus,* 16–17.)

More examples of the technique are given in the *Sophist* (218 ff., 223, 226) and in the *Statesman,* the major part of which (279–90) is taken up with a series of divisions attempting to establish the true nature of the statesman and his relationship with the rest of society.

It is perhaps astonishing to find this method ranked as of equal value to mankind with the discovery of fire, but the comparison is evidence of the crucial part played by *diaíresis* in Plato's later dialectic, and hence of the respect attached to it in the Renaissance. The method as Plato expounds it (and it is an application of

31

division which is unique to him) is one of division in the service of definition: it is a mapping-out of the subject; but that is only incidental, its real function being a progressive sharpening of distinctions, an elimination of inessentials in order to arrive at the irreductible, the essence, the truth. This is indeed an ambitious programme for a dialectical method, and can no doubt be justified at this stage of the development of Plato's thought, but, inasmuch as it depends on the individual's allocation of each part of a topic to the genus or the species, it is open to confusion, and even to abuse when it depends on a pre-formed attitude. Certainly as used by Plato in the *Sophist* it has a formidable argumentative edge, but is just as much at the service of prejudice as techniques with less claim to impartiality or absoluteness. In this dialogue the Eleatic Stranger leads Theaetetus into a discussion to 'enquire into the nature of the Sophist', by first taking a smaller example as a 'pattern of the greater'. The Stranger takes the example of an angler, and by an incontrovertible series of divisions establishes his 'art' to be the acquisitive one of hunting, using violence to trap his prey. Then, however, the Stranger by the mere process of analogy applies the analysis to the art of Sophistry, concluding that it is 'a hunt after the souls of rich young men of good repute' (223). Plato's conclusion may be just, but it is the expression of an opinion which was already formed and not reached by this rigorous dialectical process. So not only is the method complicated and perhaps obscure in its ultimate aim, but it does not seem to establish the truth with any validity.

Aristotle was critical of *diaíresis* on these and other grounds. In the *Analytica Priora* he pointed to the logical flaw:

division is, so to speak, a weak syllogism; for what it ought to prove it begs, and it always establishes something more general than the attribute in question. First, this very point had escaped all those who used the method of division; and they attempted to persuade men that it was possible to make a demonstration of substance and essence. (46a31; also 46b25.)[1]

But, although he criticises it severely here and in other works, he does concede it some validity in the *Analytica Posteriora*, for, although like induction it is not demonstration, it proves nothing 'yet it does make evident some truth' (91 b 29–32). *Diaíresis* is useful in ensuring that things are taken in the right order; it is 'the only possible method of avoiding the omission of any element of the essential nature'; and it only admits elements in the definable form (96 b 29, 35; 97 a 22). So, while denying Plato's concept of the ultimate purpose of division, and preferring the rigours of the syllogism, Aristotle grants division some methodological value—he removes it from logic and gives it what we might call a rhetorical function. And in this reduced capacity he makes considerable use of it himself as an organising factor in the *Poetica*, *Politica*, *Historia Animalium*, and to a lesser extent in works like the *Categoriae*, the *De Sophisticis Elenchis* and the *Ethica Nicomachea*. Partly as a result of Aristotle's criticism, and partly because of the difficulty of making a satisfactory and intelligible synthesis of Plato's theory and practice of division, the concept of *diaíresis* persisted through classical, medieval and Renaissance thought in a weakened form and confused with much less ambitious methodological systems. But although men had only a vague idea as to what division was meant to do they were aware of the status attached to it by Plato's praise, and they seem to have transferred his approval to the more limited Aristotelian system of arrangement.

The persistence of Greek methodology in various guises well into the seventeenth century has been recently shown in detail by N. W. Gilbert's important study, *Renaissance Concepts of Method* (New York, 1960). Mr Gilbert shows how school doctrine discovered no less than four dialectical methods in Plato (the analytical, the definitive, the divisive and the apodeictic), and although he may be thought to underrate the Aristotelian influence on medieval methodologies he can be excused inasmuch as the whole topic was blurred by too much imprecise repetition. Discussion of these four (or five, or seven) methods persists throughout the Renaissance, made more complex by the theories and influence of Galen, Averroës and Melanchthon, until in the sixteenth century major commentaries and discussions of division appear almost every five years.[1] Mr Gilbert's particular success, apart from demonstrating the enormous influence of division (*inter alia*) on Renaissance logic and methodology, is that for the first time we have the necessary perspective against which to judge the only one of these writers still known to the non-specialist, the *enfant terrible* of Renaissance logic and rhetoric, Peter Ramus, whose concept of division is now seen to be not as unique as he or his commentators thought. Of the many reforms which Ramus advocated (few of which were original), the relevant one here is his advocacy of the 'one and only' method, by which the user moved resolutely from general to particular, at each stage dividing the issue into two. It should have been immediately apparent that this dichotomising method was equivalent to a simple selection of one of the techniques expounded in the *Philebus* ('we may next proceed to look for two, if there be two, or, if not, then for three or some other number') and used in the *Sophist*; and that the statutory movement from general to particular is a crudification of the delicate process of separating genus and species taught by Plato and approved of by Aristotle (*Topica*, 109 b 13)—as Mr Gilbert puts it, 'a tendentious leveling of all to one common denominator' (p. 144). However, this doctrine that seems 'the very acme of banality' to us, was regarded as 'original and indeed revolutionary' by his contemporaries, provoking much controversy.[1]

Perhaps because Ramus remains a celebrated figure for students of the Renaissance, it has often been asserted that Bacon's use of division is directly indebted to him.[2] With the wisdom of hindsight it could be said that there was ample evidence of non-Ramist techniques of division before Gilbert's work appeared—in the arrangement of medieval and Renaissance encyclopedias, in various classifications of knowledge, in sermons, in the law, and in all sorts of gnomic wisdom.[3] If it is expecting too much that the significance of these uses of division might have been perceived, then at least it should have been noticed that Bacon took pains explicitly to reject Ramus's method. In the *Advancement of Learning* he makes a brief criticism of dichotomising, without referring to Ramus personally (3. 406), but in the *De Augmentis* Bacon delivers a crushing dismissal:

34

The kinds of method being various, I will begin by enumerating rather than distributing them. And first, for the 'one and only method' with its distribution of everything into two members, it is needless to speak of it; for it was a kind of cloud that overshadowed knowledge for a while and blew over; a thing no doubt both very weak in itself and very injurious to the sciences. For while these men press matters by the laws of their method, and when a thing does not aptly fall into these dichotomies, either pass it by or force it out of its natural shape, the effect of their proceeding is this,—the kernels and grains of the sciences leap out, and they are left with nothing in their grasp but the dry and barren husks. And therefore this kind of method produces empty abridgments, and destroys the solid substance of knowledge. (4. 448–9.)

After so authoritative a dismissal as this (and one which is given still more force in the *Temporis Partus Masculus*)[1] it is hardly necessary to say that Bacon's own concept of division is far more flexible than the rigid dichotomies, using partition into any number of heads—two, three, ten, twenty-seven—however many are needed to reflect and analyse the topic. Further, although Bacon when classifying the sciences uses the traditional movement from general to particular (which was codified by Ramism, ignoring the other methods available), when he uses methodology for scientific inquiry he stresses the need to start with particulars, and develops his own complementary method, induction, which is just the reverse of Ramist dichotomising.

Bacon could hardly have been unaware of the wider discussion of division in classical and Renaissance writings, and Mr Gilbert has pointed to his probable knowledge of the subject (p. 227). However, while bringing out with great clarity the role of division both in the methodology of science (and logic) and in the formulation of *téchnai*, 'arts' or systems generally, Mr Gilbert does not discuss the teachings on division in a tradition which had perhaps as much influence on methods of arrangement as did logic (and for Bacon certainly more)—that of rhetoric.[2] In the second stage of the rhetorical process, *dispositio*, the arrangement of an oration (and so, of any work), the parts distinguished vary from five to seven, but nearly always include the rhetorical division *partitio* (after *exordium* and *narratio*, but before *confirmatio*, *reprehensio*, and *conclusio*).[3]

The distinction between *partitio* and *divisio* is best stated by Cicero, and repeated by Quintilian: 'Cicero further shows that definition is assisted by *division*, which he distinguishes from *partition*, making the latter the dissection of a whole into its parts and the former the division of a *genus* into its *forms* or *species*'.[1] And, whereas with *divisio* the number of divisions is strictly limited according to the number of species, with *partitio* the speaker is free to distinguish under each topic as many 'heads' as he needs. Cicero's fullest discussion of *partitio* comes in the early *de Inventione*, where its organisational advantages are well set out:

> In an argument a partition correctly made renders the whole speech clear and perspicuous. It takes two forms, both of which greatly contribute to clarifying the case and determining the nature of the controversy. One form shows in what we agree with our opponents and what is left in dispute; as a result of this some definite problem is set for the auditor on which he ought to have his attention fixed. In the second form the matters which we intend to discuss are briefly set forth in a methodical way. This leads the auditor to hold definite points in his mind, and to understand that when these have been discussed the oration will be over. (I. xxii. 31.)[2]

If properly used, the second and most common form of *partitio* (the 'methodical statement of topics to be discussed') should bring 'brevity, completeness, conciseness', provided that the orator does not overelaborate the divisions, nor introduce new arguments once the plan has been established. The 'plan' is announced by a *propositio*, and the speaker is advised to complete the sections in the order given there.

Cicero's exposition of *partitio* strikes us as being clear but rather simple, and the pseudo-Ciceronian *Rhetorica ad Herennium* adds nothing to it. For a full realisation of the potentialities latent in earlier rhetorics we have to turn, as ever, to the great *Institutes of Oratory*, much studied in the Renaissance and particularly by Bacon's father.[3] Quintilian's account of *partitio* is fuller and more satisfying, considering objections that Cicero did not foresee, and expertly relating the whole oratorical process to the events in the courtroom. He begins by making a point which Bacon certainly would have agreed with, that *partitio* is not confined to a particu-

36

lar stage in speaking or writing, but is valuable anywhere (III. ix. 2–3). *Partitio* has great practical advantages: it 'makes the case clearer and the judge more attentive and more ready to be instruct-ed, if he knows what we are speaking about and what we are going subsequently to speak about' (IV. v. 1); nothing could be 'simpler or clearer', and the 'adhesion to a definite method is actually of the greatest assistance to the speaker's memory' (IV. v. 3). However, the caution in its use is to avoid overelaborateness: 'those who carry it to extremes, and split up their argument into a thousand tiny compartments...fall into that very obscurity which partition was designed to eliminate' (IV. v. 25).

The real value of Quintilian's discussion, over and above his stress on the efficacy of *partitio* in avoiding obscurity, is his grasp of the psychological effect on the audience of the speaker's progress through a clearly defined plan: partition

will, if judiciously employed, greatly add to the lucidity and grace of our speech. For it not only makes our arguments clear by isolating the points from the crowd in which they would otherwise be lost and placing them before the eyes of the judge, but relieves his attention by assigning a definite limit to certain parts of our speech, just as our fatigue upon a journey is relieved by reading the distances of the milestones which we pass...For nothing need seem long, when it is definitely known how far it is to the end. (IV. v. 22.)

Although of particular interest to the lawyer, this account of the psychology of a known form would be useful to any writer. In addition to the immediate advantages of 'having the end in sight', it suggests analogies with certain types of musical form, where our knowledge of the conventions of the genre gives us a sharper appreciation of the unfolding structure. Quintilian deserves admiration for the intelligent and humane way in which he brings imagination to the study of rhetoric.

The teaching of the *Institutes* undoubtedly drew attention to the uses of *partitio*, and the appearance of the *editio princeps* at Rome in 1470 would have revived interest in the Renaissance, especially given the predominantly rhetorical nature of English education. However, Quintilian does not appear in as many school curricula in the sixteenth century as might have been expected,[1] and the vernacular rhetoricians do not seem aware of his intelligent advocacy of division. The account in Thomas Wilson's *The Arte of Rhetorique* (1553) is perfunctory, repeating Cicero's advice while apparently ignorant of Quintilian's,[1] while even the normally acute John Hoskins, in his *Directions for Speech and Style* (1599), has nothing fresh to say. But if disappointing on the large-scale use of *partitio* the English theorists in rhetoric seem to have taken Quintilian's point as to the multivalency of division, and apply it in terms of particular rhetorical figures. So Puttenham describes the figures '*Merismus* or Distributor' as being 'very meete for Orators or eloquent perswaders' by which we 'utter a matter...peecemeale and by distributiō of every part for amplification sake'. Henry Peacham distinguishes two forms of *propositio*, the normal announcement of topics which should be 'well divided', and the more exact kind, *eutrepismus*, 'which doth not only number the partes before they be said, but also doth order those partes, and maketh them plaine by a kind of definition, or declaration'. Peacham also gives a correct account of the two processes, *divisio* and *partitio*, but (and it is another example of the misunderstanding of the original concepts) assigns the first to rhetoric: '*Diaeresis* in Latine *Divisio*, is a forme of speech which divideth the generall kind into the special kinds, yet not in a dialecticall forme, but in a rhetoricall maner for amplifications sake', whereas '*Partitio* is a form of speech by which the orator divideth yᵉ whole into parts', the use of both being to 'pithily and elegantly set forth and amplifie'.[2] The crossing of the boundaries between the two figures here may however be not so much a confusion of logic and rhetoric, as another sign of the process which Rosemund Tuve has analysed so well, by which rhetoric 'underlined the instructions of logic'.[3]

So at the end of the sixteenth century there was available to an intelligent well-educated reader, such as Bacon so evidently was, a body of discussion on the techniques of division in both logic and rhetoric which derived from the greatest intellectual authorities and which emphasised its advantages in organising any literary work so as to achieve thoroughness, clarity, and a psychological grasp on the audience. But in addition to these channels there was another source of influence open to Bacon, and one which (considering the amount of time and energy which he devoted to it) has been too much neglected by his critics, that of the Law.[1] Although some of the stages of transmission have yet to be studied in detail it seems clear that the use of *partitio* in legal rhetoric continues (despite intermediary breaks) from Cicero and Quintilian to Bacon and Coke in substantially the same form. The whole question of rhetoric's influence on legal oratory does not seem to have excited the interest of legal historians, so I may perhaps be excused for presenting the evidence (much of it cited for the first time) as concisely as possible.

There are signs of the use of division in the Inns of Court, but we do not find it (or any other teaching method) mentioned in the official records, which—like those of many collegiate societies —are devoted mainly to non-intellectual topics such as entertainment and discipline. Nor do we find any trace of instruction in rhetoric, but it was common for students to be admitted to the Inns only after grammar-school or university education—as we learn from this conversation:

Shallow: I dare say my cousin William is become a good scholar; he is at Oxford still, is he not?
Silence: Indeed, sir, to my cost.
Shallow: 'A must, then, to the Inns o' Court shortly. I was once of Clement's Inn...[2]

It can be assumed that (with the standardised education in England, and the universally high place given to rhetoric) the rhetorical teaching on structure would have been familiar to all law-students. That this is so is confirmed by two sources: the actual teaching method of the Inns of Court (which does assume this), and the writings of some theorists on the Law. Much of the student's time was taken up in learning statutes and cases, and in taking part in the two dialectical exercises, the 'moot' and the 'bolt', which consisted of arguments *pro* and *contra*. But the major teaching method, the Reading, which took place twice a year, added to this dialectical structure a well-defined concept of division.

4-2

The Reading seems to have combined exegetical methods with the more normal techniques of the law-court. The chosen Reader was given six months to prepare his work, which would stem from 'one Act or statute as shall please him to ground his whole reading on', expounding 'certain doubts and questions which he hath devised, that may grow upon the said statute, and declareth his judgment therein'.[1] Again the records do not bother to describe the exact form that this takes, but we have the authoritative account of an early legal historian, Sir William Dugdale. After much pomp and ceremony, the Reader's assistant begins:

the Sub-Lecturer doth first, with an audible voice, read over the statute or at least that branch of it, that he hath chosen to read on. This ended, the *Reader* begins with a grave speech, excusing his own weakness,[2] with desire of their favourable censures; and concluding with the Reasons, wherefore he made choice of that Statute: Then he delivers unto them his divisions made upon the Statute, which are more or fewer, as he pleaseth; and then puts ten or twelve Cases upon his first division; of the which, the puisne Cupboard-man, before spoken of, makes choice of one to argue,[3]

being followed in turn by the senior members of the Society, the Reader having the last word to 'maintain his own conclusion'. The exercise would be repeated after dinner, and the Reader would proceed through his various divisions during the Reading, which usually lasted two weeks, on alternate days. This complex method of instruction (in which division plays the major part) seems to have remained constant from the mid-sixteenth to the mid-eighteenth centuries at least, and we can find further confirmation in the accounts of two later Readers.[4]

The legal theorists also attached much importance to division—inevitably so. Abraham Fraunce wrote his *Lawyers Logike* in 1588, and though he was influenced by Ramus he offers some useful non-Ramist remarks on definition and division, which he finds to be so excellent that 'almost they alone doo suffice for the absolute putting downe of any art' (fo. 57r—once more the modern reader is surprised by the high value accorded these methods in classical and Renaissance thought). Most of Fraunce's points are by now familiar, and include the quotation from the *Phaedrus*, and the idea that having divided we are to make 'orderly discourse of every head, using the places of invention, the helpe of iudgement, &c.' (fo. 118v). More valuable is his illustration of how this technique was used by the great English legal authorities: Stamford, Bracton, Perkins and Lyttleton,[1] so adding yet another source for the influence of *partitio*. If Fraunce is useful mainly as a guide to current attitudes, the last writer on the Law to be considered is refreshingly independent, the little-known William Fulbeck. He is sensibly on the side of rhetoric, attacking the logicians' pedantic strictness in division: 'Some do spend a whole decade of howers in doing nothing else, then seeking out the proper *genus*, and difference of one onely thing, and when they have done, they are scarcely so wise as they were before.'[2] It is enough to divide a thing 'briefely', and those who object to the simple traditional divisions are the sort of petty quibblers who 'will finde a knot in a bulrushe'. His final advocacy of division, which also invokes the greatest classical authority on Law, may serve as a summing-up of the virtues of *partitio*:

There is nothing whiche more beawtifieth a mans speeche, then an apt division or partition of the thynges which bee handled, which doth ease the mynde of the hearer, prepareth the mynde of the understander, and refresheth the memorye, and (as Justinian sayeth) the obscuritie which doth ryse of a confused text is by separation and division dispersed and removed. And as the division of fields doth make the tillage more plentiful and sightly, so doth partition in the handling of causes, adorne and garnish them. (fo. 40r.)

I have gone into the development of *partitio* in some detail— although doubtless only to a fraction of its actual extent—because its significance has not been recognised by historians of law or rhetoric or methodology, and this despite its widespread use in English Renaissance literature. It is an important organising principle in such major works as Hooker's *Laws of Ecclesiastical Polity*, Sidney's *Apology for Poetry*,[3] the sermons of Lancelot Andrewes and Donne, Milton's *Areopagitica*, Hobbes's *Leviathan*, and (to give it its full title) Burton's *The Anatomy of Melancholy, What it is. With all the Kindes, Causes, Symptomes, Prognostickes, and Several Cures of it. In Three Maine Partitions with their several*

Sections, Members and Subsections. *Philosophically, Historically, Opened and Cut up.*

Allusions to *partitio* in some of the great imaginative works of the period also testify to its familiarity. In More's *Utopia* the arrogant lawyer dismisses Raphael's account of English injustices with an ostentatious *propositio* of his division:

'For firste I will reherse in order all that you have sayde: then I will declare wherein you be deceaved, through lacke of knowledge, in all our fashions, maners and customes: and last of all I will aunswere youre argumentes, and confute them every one. Firste therefore I wyll begynne where I promysed. Four thynges you semed to me.'—'Hold your peace, quod the Cardinall: for it appeareth that you will make no shorte aunswere, which make such a beginnynge.'

In the great trial scene at the end of Sidney's *Arcadia* the incensed prosecutor Philanax accuses Pyrocles 'as well of the murdering of *Basilius* as the Ravishing of *Philoclea* (for these twoo partes I establish of my accusation)...', and he achieves a great rhetorical effect by getting so angry that he neglects his division: 'Yett see, so farre had my zeale to my beloved Prince transported mee, that I had allmoste forgotten my second parte and the seconde abhominacyon...' In defending himself Pyrocles correctly follows his opponent's division, but with a good aggressive metaphor: 'so, that as this Duble mynded fellowes accusation was duble, Duble lykewyse myne Answer must needes bee...' Sidney even makes a pun on 'partition', but it is not as apt or as witty as one by Shakespeare: in the play-scene in *Midsummer Night's Dream* one rustic, 'Snout by name, present[s] a wall', and describes his various walllike attributes in a simple divisive structure (like Puttenham's *merismus*), on which the noble spectators comment:

Theseus: Would you desire lime and hair to speak better?
Demetrius: It is the wittiest partition that ever I heard discourse, my lord.
(v, i, 164–5.)[1]

II

Bacon's references to *partitio* can also be witty and subtle, but it is perhaps best to begin with a more serious application of it, and one in which he stands nearest to his contemporaries. Bacon's career as

a lawyer has two phases, determined by his office: at first, owing to
connections with Gray's Inn, he is the expounder of the Law in
various cases where it is in dispute; then theory turns to practice
with his appointment as Solicitor-General, and he becomes the
public prosecutor in several important state trials. If we consider
two examples from each phase we observe that Bacon uses the
traditional techniques, but we shall also see his individual intelligent awareness of the processes. His own Reading, delivered in
1600 on the Statute of Uses, begins with the usual 'grave speech,
excusing his own weakness', but with the modesty given a fresh
twist, both in the reference to the first two stages of rhetoric and in
the final image: 'if my invention or judgment be too barren or too
weak; yet by the benefit of other arts, I did hope to dispose or
digest the authorities or opinions which are in cases of uses in such
order and method, as they should take light one from another,
though they took no light from me'. Of course the 'light' is due
to his arrangement of the *partitio*, starting from his division into
'matter without the statute' and 'matter within':

Having therefore framed six divisions, according to the number of readings
upon the statute itself, I have likewise divided the matter without the statute
into six introductions or discourses, so that for every day's reading I have made a
triple provision.

1. A preface or introduction.
2. A division upon the law itself.
3. A few cases, for exercise and argument. (7. 397.)

If no more, this is an admirably clear pedagogic method, and the
same scrupulous clarity is seen throughout the many branches of
the argument, and in his constant insistence that division should
be organic and not arbitrary: 'Though I have opened the statute
in order of words, yet I will make my division in order of
matter' (7. 435).[1] And in a later work of legal theory his awareness of the process of division extends to a psychological point
which is an advance on Quintilian: having established the
division,

out of all these I will prove most clearly the present case. Which parts before
I deduce, I will give you at the first entrance a form or abstract of them, that

forethinking what you shall hear, the proof may strike upon your minds as prepared. (7. 689.)

Here too we find some of the many incidental references to the value of division—'to give you a better light' (7. 697, 706; 11. 273).

In the State prosecutions Bacon both uses division, and comments more and more on it as a process. In so doing he achieves an effect not unlike that of the sort of prefatory material which announces what will follow (the prologues to some Greek tragedies, the head-rhymes to cantos of *The Faerie Queene*): by this terse prediction of the action, the element of surprise is lost, but a more valuable state of mind is produced, in which we have a curious feeling of recognition as the development conforms to its preordained shape, a sense of inevitability which is all the stronger in this context of the unfolding of justice. This sense of the inexorable fulfilment of a plan is best seen in the great *Charge against the Earl of Somerset* (1616) for the murder of Sir Thomas Overbury, where Bacon begins with a very formal and authoritative division:

My Lords, the course which I shall hold in delivering that which I shall say, (for I love order), is this:

First, I will speak somewhat of the nature and greatness of the offence which is now to be tried...

Secondly, I will use some few words touching the nature of the proofs which in such a case are competent.

Thirdly, I will state the proofs.

And lastly, I will produce the proofs, either out of the examinations and matters in writing, or witnesses *viva voce*. (12. 308.)

The effect of confidence and authority produced by the certainty of that division is confirmed when, having worked through the first two heads in brief but powerful detail, Bacon divides the next into its parts, and then turns directly to the prisoner to urge him to attend:

So that there is nothing that I shall say, but your lordship, my lord of Somerset, shall have three thoughts or cogitations to answer it: First, when I open it, you may take your aim. Secondly, when I distribute it, you may prepare your answers without confusion. And lastly, when I produce the witnesses or examinations themselves, you may again ruminate and re-advise how to make your defence. (12. 312.)

Here is a new application of *partitio*: not only for clarity, but so that the accused knows exactly the case against him: 'And this I do the rather, because your memory or understanding may not be oppressed or overladen with the length of evidence, or with confusion of order' (*ibid.*). This punctilious use of division and subdivision, then, is to ensure justice, and, to anyone familiar with some of the unscrupulous tactics of state prosecutors under both Elizabeth and James (including that of deliberately confusing the prisoner), Bacon's fair-minded application of *partitio* seems quite admirable.

But there are also occasions when Bacon is aware that his hearers may want to note down his divisions, just as a congregation would record the main heads of a sermon. Not only must the modern reader acquire an understanding of the theory and practice of *partitio*, but he must try to reconstruct the situation of an educated audience being conscious—and critically conscious— of the mere framing of a division. So in another state trial Bacon almost directs the audience to its 'tables':

Now, my Lords, I beseech you to give me favour and attention to set forth and observe unto you five points (I will number them, because other men may note them...). (12. 138.)

A still more striking example of this practice of recording a division occurs in a letter to the king in 1614 about 'Peacham's case', in which Bacon describes an encounter with Coke, who was opposing the king's handling of the judges in this affair. Bacon comes 'armed with divers precedents', and proposes his division of the point at issue:

Then I placed Peacham's treason within the last division, agreeable to divers precedents, whereof I had the records ready...he heard me in a grave fashion, more than accustomed, and took a pen and took notes of my divisions; and when he read the precedents and records, would say, this you mean falleth within your first, or your second, &c. division. (12. 110.)

The unusually respectful manner of Bacon's great rival testifies to the crucial nature of the division in relation to the treatment of the whole matter, for Bacon's placing of Peacham's treason within his partition of the forms that treason can take thereby defines his view of the case: division is definition. So in both exposition and prosecution this technique of division is of vital importance— indeed there is not one of Bacon's legal works which does not show its effects on every page.

If we move now to Bacon the state counsellor, the man who subscribed to the dominant Renaissance preference for the active life, and followed Sir Thomas More, Wyatt, Sidney and many other writers who became public figures in order to serve their sovereign, then we see a comparable handling of argumentative structure. There do not seem to be any theoretical discussions of political oratory before Bacon, so for evidence we must consider his own speeches. Bacon's parliamentary career lasted thirty years, a formative influence of equal importance with the Law, and equally neglected by his critics,[1] although the political works, both spoken and written, have considerable literary value. He does not in fact formulate a theory of *partitio* for the speaker until the *De Augmentis*, when his career is over, but when he does it has some aspects which are relevant here. In commenting on the saying of Solomon, 'A fool utters all his mind, but a wise man reserves something for the future' (Prov. xxix. 11) he develops a point which he had made in the early *Colours of Good and Evil* (7. 82) and develops it intelligently, away from division as mere amplification towards a more subtle concept:

a speech that is broken and let fall part by part makes far more impression than a continuous one; because in the latter the matters touched are not distinctly and severally apprehended and weighed; and they have not time enough to settle; but one reason drives out another before it has taken firm hold.

So to Quintilian's concept of the efficacy of division Bacon adds a still more refined observation which is based (as so often) on his awareness of psychological reactions—the probabilities of persuasion, the necessary time-lag to allow comprehension. And he adds to it a shrewd sense of tactics which would have appealed to the Roman rhetorician:

if a man does not use all his arguments at once, but delivers them in parts, throwing in one after the other, he will detect by the countenance and answer of his opponent how each is taken, and what effect it produces, and he may thence take warning what to suppress and what to select in that which is to follow. (5. 45.)

As ever, Bacon's improvement on an extant theory is in the direction of making it more detailed and concrete.

Unfortunately we have no record of Bacon in action in this latter role of tactical variation within *partitio*, nor do we have all the evidence for his practice in the first role, for there were then no official Parliamentary reporters, and accounts of his speeches are often fragmentary. But where they do exist we find him using the familiar techniques of division, such as maintaining the proper sequence: 'Having divided the substance of their arguments, *ut supra*, he did pursue the same division in his reply' (7. 593), and being punctilious about the detail involved: so after an illness in 1607, the *Commons Journal* records him beginning a speech, which 'being very long, consisting of many divisions and particulars, and interlaced with much variety of argument and answer on both parts, the time would not allow him to finish, and so was deferred till Monday morning' (10. 326; also 8. 223, 10. 264–84, 10. 192). Bacon's aptitude in division and construction is in itself evidence of a basic intellectual power in organisation and analysis, and he not only excelled in it himself but was constantly in demand to give reports of other men's speeches—in the Lords, at church conferences, in committees—so much so that he has to complain at being too popular in this role (10. 347). One account of him producing an ordered exposition from a mass of material catches a characteristic Bacon metaphor for the process:

'Light of order' (he said) 'casteth beams upon the matter'; and produced a paper containing all the objections heretofore made in the House against the Union in Name; and was directed by the House to stand at the Board and to read it himself, as being best acquainted with the order of it. (10. 197.)

Bacon's devotion to intellectual honesty comes out in comments such as that 'His duty was to report truly and nakedly *rem gestam* ...wherefore he would add nothing of his own, but the order only' (10. 327). He adds order by using division, and again we see the intellectual scrupulousness in his remarkably detailed report of speeches by Salisbury and Northampton on the Spanish Grievances, which records every branch of their argument.[1]

In the few speeches which Bacon took the trouble to write out —usually those of particular importance—we find as ever the traditional rhetorical processes of announcing a division, marking the transitions within it, and ending once the plan is complete, without a peroration. One of these extant speeches, and one over which Bacon took enormous care, as it was of great political significance, is the *Speech on Naturalization* (1607; 10. 307-25), which ranks in brilliance with the great *Argument in the case of the Post Nati of Scotland* (1604; 7. 641-79). In no other work are the divisions so clearly marked, indeed insisted upon, as here, and in the tone of Bacon's writing we hear that note of calm confidence born of being complete master of the subject:

> And yet, to avoid confusion, which evermore followeth of too much generality, it is necessary for me (before I proceed to persuasion) to use some distribution of the points or parts of Naturalization... (10. 309.)

It is a tone which is heard with some justification throughout this magnificently structured argument, and only by extensive quotation could one bring out its strength and force. Suffice it to say that the rare presence of a peroration which states with eloquent restraint that the contract is complete and sincerely maintained, is quite justified:

> Mr Speaker, I have, I take it, gone through the parts which I propounded to myself: wherein if any man shall think that I have sung 'placebo' for mine own particular, I would have him know that I am not so unseen in the world but that I discern it were much alike for my private fortune to rest a 'tacebo' as to sing a 'placebo' in this business. But I have spoken out of the fountain of my heart. *Credidi propter quod locutus sum:* I believed, therefore I spake. So as my duty is performed. (10. 325.)

The contract is more than adequately fulfilled, by using division, in the other political works: in the many Letters of Advice,[1] and in the miscellaneous tracts produced throughout Bacon's career.[2] In all of these, to a greater or lesser degree, *partitio* is more than the sum of its parts: by advancing on such clearly defined paths it suggests that the argument is proved at each stage, so creating in the reader a predisposition to agree, an effect of cumulative persuasion which it is hard to analyse although it is certainly felt.

Once the traditions of division are known it is only to be expected that Bacon should use them in his own oratory, whether legal or political. But the extent to which he associated *partitio* with any speech of argument or exposition is shown rather surprisingly when he constructs such a speech in a fictional context. In *Henry VII* the literary structure is naturally that of a chronological narration and analysis of events, yet, when Bacon has to invent speeches for the various counsellors and prelates, he writes them as he would have spoken them himself.[3] Morton, the archbishop of Canterbury, propounds 'the cause of Brittaine' with a *partitio*, and goes on to a further division using the familiar metaphor of 'opening':

And the better to open your understandings in this affair, the King hath commanded me to say somewhat to you from him of the persons that do intervene in this business; and somewhat of the consequences thereof, as it hath relation to this kingdom, and somewhat of the example of it in general...First... (6. 77.)

Later in the narrative there is an equally authentic use of division, as the French ambassador makes his partition of the political situation, which the Lord Chancellor accepts and reproduces in his reply (6. 106, 111). A still more unexpected instance of *partitio* comes in the *New Atlantis*, which we tend to place among the 'literary' works of Bacon, although he intended it as a programme for a research institute. It is fitting then to discover that the transition from fictitious travelbook to scientific propaganda is made by means of a formal rhetorical division. The Father of Salomon's House (Bacon in disguise) speaks to the narrator thus:

God bless thee, my son; I will give thee the greatest jewel I have. For I will impart unto thee, for the love of God and men, a relation of the true state of

Salomon's House. Son, to make you know the true state of Salomon's House, I will keep this order. First, I will set forth unto you the end of our foundation. Secondly, the preparations and instruments we have for our works. Thirdly, the several employments and functions whereto our fellows are assigned. And fourthly, the ordinances and rites which we observe. (3. 156.)

The exposition inevitably follows this order. Yet, although Bacon makes considerable use of *partitio* to organise his 'oratorical' work, he does not do so in a mechanical way. For one thing, he does not divide according to any preconceived principle or pattern, nor does he rigidly allot the same amount of space to each head: the number of divisions, their length and nature, all vary according to the demands of the subject-matter. And in addition to this organic flexibility we find an intelligent awareness of the process, and one which naturally expresses itself in imagery. Bacon was incapable of writing on any topic for long without using metaphor, and he characteristically turns the possibly formal technique of division into an occasion for witty analogy. In reporting the negative arguments at a conference, he says that they were nine in number,

but might be contracted judicially into a less distinction of matter of allegiance and matter of jurisdiction: like the ten commandments, which were all comprised under two heads, of love of God and love of our neighbour. (10. 330.)

Given another speech to report, he says that one of the King's counsellors 'did use a speech that contained a world of matter, but how I shall be able to make a globe of that world, therein I fear mine own strength' (10. 347). Having, in the course of praising Queen Elizabeth, come to the heading 'excellencies of her person', he demurs with a piece of courtly wit: 'The view of them wholly and not severally do make so sweet a wonder, as I fear to divide them again' (8. 137–8). For division into two parts he finds two metaphors: 'Now...I must fill the other Balance' (10. 318) and again 'what is to be set on the right hand and what on the left in this business' (12. 45); more ingenious still, the eight subdivisions he makes in 'murder by accessary' are 'the eight several points of the compass' (12. 319).

But the most persistent, and the most illuminating metaphors are those of natural origin. The equating of a division with an anatomy is often found, and, though clearly not original to Bacon, it has important connotations for his view of knowledge, as will appear. So we find him using the traditional image but adding a characteristically witty pun, which comes through even in a report: 'To bring out the whole and entire body he would not undertake; but to make an anatomy of it, and shew the lines and parts, which might serve to give a light, though not delight' (10. 327); and he writes to the king: 'my purpose is only to break this matter of the Union into certain short articles and questions; and to make a certain kind of anatomy or analysis of the parts thereof' (10. 218). The 'parts' later become 'branches, lineaments, and degrees' (10. 220). The other favourite analogy is with trees and we see already how Bacon's organic feeling for imagery allows him to take a traditional image and both revivify it and extend it with greater precision. Consider these 'tree' images for *partitio*: 'The second discourse shall be of the second spring of this tree of uses' (7. 397); 'the axe is put to the root of this tree, which root hath three strings' (7. 699); 'Upon this root also grew divers branches of inconvenience' (12. 180); and, in one of his last works, in 1624: 'For grounds of reason, they are many; I will extract the principal, and open them briefly, and (as it were) in the bud' (14. 498).

III

We can now see that Bacon's frequent and creative use of division is in large part due to the circumstances of his career in parliament and in the Law, with their adaptation for oratory of the rhetorical form *partitio*. But his use of division is not limited to actual speeches whether real or fictitious; it is a method which is given much wider currency.

Although the significance of the structure by division does not seem to have been noticed in any of the numerous discussions of Bacon's scientific method,[1] *partitio* is used as an expository device in many of the minor scientific works, which contain the whole rhetorical process, from the *propositio* announcing the division to the transitions being marked, and to the summing up.[1] *Partitio* is also important in Bacon's major project, the *Instauratio Magna*, for the 'Plan of the Work' divides it into six parts, the first being 'Divisions of the Sciences', which is now represented by the Latin expansion of the *Advancement*, which (as we shall see in chapter 7) now uses the technique with still more clarity. In considering Bacon's use of division in the *Novum Organum* it might seem at first that the structure of the work—unconnected aphorisms—automatically excludes any sort of plan. However, Bacon cannot maintain this unconnectedness for long: whenever he begins a complex subject, he has to use some more coherent form of organisation, and when he does so it has to be division. We see this first in the famous account of the idols which beset the human understanding, where from his initial fourfold division (4. 53) proceed a number of subdivisions, particularly for the Idols of the Market-place and of the Theatre, and which in turn provoke discussion of the process of division. So in defining the former idol's confusion of words and names Bacon makes an acute point on the way the conventions of language determine (and indeed limit) our view of experience:

Now words, being commonly framed and applied according to the capacity of the vulgar, follow those lines of division which are most obvious to the vulgar understanding. And whenever an understanding of greater acuteness or a more diligent observation would alter those lines to suit the true divisions of nature, words stand in the way and resist the change. (4. 61.)

(Although this passage raises the important question of how Bacon establishes the divisions amongst the subject-matter of his argument, it is one which could only be discussed by surveying the whole corpus of scientific knowledge in the Renaissance, a procedure which the reader will not expect here—regrettably, we must consider *partitio* as 'order of words' not 'order of matter'.)

Throughout the *Novum Organum* division is in fact the main method of organisation. At the beginning of Book 2 Bacon compiles four Tables of Instances concerning Heat (4. 127–55), which are perhaps rather 'enumerated than placed', but nevertheless have a clear sequential treatment. Having completed these,

Bacon begins to develop his concept of the 'Interpretation of Nature (by) true and perfect Induction', and does so with a rhetorician's *propositio*:

I propose to treat then in the first place of *Prerogative Instances*; secondly, of the *Supports of Induction*; thirdly, of the *Rectification of Induction*...

and so on through nine partitions (4. 155). He then takes the first head, and distinguishes in order twenty-seven Prerogative Instances, with a considerable amount of subdivision, including other quite formal uses of *propositio* (192, 214) and the traditional summing-up (230, 246–7). In fact Bacon only covers the first head before breaking off, but the major part of his most important scientific work is organised by *partitio*, and it seems likely that the remainder would have been too. (We even find the now familiar organic images for division, of 'growth and nourishment' from 'the roots' of a properly formulated division (79), of the 'branches' and 'stem' of knowledge (88) and even its 'veins' (147).) Thus if *partitio* is so central to Bacon's major scientific work we can perhaps begin to understand the respect accorded to it in the Renaissance and earlier.

But in a sense the term 'scientific' is a misnomer in so far as it suggests a separate category of Bacon's work from the 'literary' productions. The truth is that everything he produced outside his two professional spheres of Law and parliament was dedicated to the progress of science. Bacon may use a literary form as a framework, such as the imaginary voyage for the *New Atlantis*, or classical fables for the *Wisdom of the Ancients*, but in each case he redirects the whole work towards his programme for the rebirth of science: observation, experiment, co-operation. Even that most literary of forms, the essay, is redeveloped towards the serious function of analysing man in society, for, as R. S. Crane showed in 1923 (B23), the expansion of the *Essays* in 1612 and 1625 has a thematic intent, that of filling gaps in the discussion of topics which Bacon had noted as deficient in the *Advancement*. Under 'moral knowledge' he had called for study of the formative influences on men, such as:

those impressions of nature, which are imposed upon the mind by the sex, by the age, by the region, by health and sickness, by beauty and deformity, and the like, which are inherent and not extern; and again those which are caused by extern fortune; as sovereignty, nobility, obscure birth, riches, want; magistracy, privateness, prosperity, adversity, constant fortune, variable fortune, rising per saltum; per gradus, and the like. (3. 436.)

So in adding to his *Essays* Bacon considers some of these very *tópoi*: 'Of Youth and Age', 'Of Deformity', 'Of Nobility', 'Of Riches', and so on. Under 'civil knowledge' he had distinguished three topics: conversation, negotiation, and government, and already in the first version of 1597 he had been considering such subjects as 'Of Discourse', 'Of Negotiating', 'Of Followers and Friends' and others, a fact which suggests that even in this embryonic state Bacon had intended the *Essays* as a serious treatise on man.

From the point of view of division it may indeed be something of a relief to find that there are no essentially literary works by Bacon, for neither *partitio* nor *divisio* would be suitable for the exploration of subtle states of mind or complexities of human relationships, nor indeed for any of the narrative processes of mimetic forms such as the novel or the drama. But, as his purpose is to further the culture of human knowledge, then division can be useful in setting the framework for an analysis of the types of human personality and their behaviour. In the 1597 *Essays* only one, 'Honour and Reputation', has an overall division (6. 532), though, as we shall see, this technique becomes more popular in the revisions. But we do find here as in the later volumes that use of division on a small scale in the various rhetorical figures, Puttenham's '*merismus* or distributor', Peacham's 'diaeresis'. They are used, as so often, with 'definition' to analyse a topic from a variety of positions. So the first essay of all, 'Studies', begins with a division:

Studies serue for pastimes, for ornaments, for abilities: their chief use for pastimes in privatenes, and retiring: for ornaments, in discourse; and for ability in Iudgement. (6. 525.)

The sharpness of the trichotomy is maintained in the correlation of 'function' with 'benefit', and is made still sharper—as ever in

Bacon—by the syntactical parallelism. The essay is very short but includes ten such divisions, the last one being the most elaborate:

Histories make men wise; Poets witty: the Mathematiques subtile; Naturall Philosophie deepe: Morall graue: Logique, and Rethorique able to contende.

Again the punctuation and syntax help to sharpen the balance, but these symmetries only follow from the conceptual division, the anatomy of the subject which has the poise that a tree or leaf has, the parts radiating out symmetrically from a central stem. The technique of division used throughout is seen at its simplest in the listing of types of human behaviour in the form 'some men... others' which recurs[1] as a suggestive, if crude, classification of man.

If the *Essays* analyse man in his moral and civil spheres, the *Advancement of Learning* has as its aim nothing less than the classification of all human knowledge. Here we see again the prophetic nature of so many of Bacon's works, their gradual assumption of a role which was not initially foreseen, in that this work is later to become the essential first stage in his scientific programme. The basic structure of the work is that of division and subdivision, and it serves incidentally as a guide to some techniques of division in the more specialised scientific works, but it surpasses them and everything else he wrote in the range and inventiveness of its awareness of the function of these anatomies. Having reviewed the attacks on learning—and replied to them—in Book 1, he begins the main process of division in Book 2 with a characteristically fluent sequence of images: the 'removing of all the defects formerly enumerate' is work for a king,

towards which the endeavours of a private man may be but as an image in a crossway, that may point at the way but cannot go it. But the inducing part of the latter (which is the survey of learning) may be set forward by private travel. Wherefore I will now attempt to make a general and faithful perambulation of learning, with an inquiry what parts thereof lie fresh and waste, and not improved and converted by the industry of man; to the end that such a plot made and recorded to memory may both minister light to any public designation, and also serve to excite voluntary endeavours. (3. 328.)

But, he says, his purpose is only to note omissions and not to begin wholesale criticism and re-creation, and to close the point he extends one of the images still further—'for it is one thing to set forth what ground lieth unmanured, and another thing to correct ill husbandry in that which is manured'. The image of the 'plot' (or map) becomes three-dimensional as he sums up his work: 'Thus have I made as it were a small Globe of the Intellectual World' (3. 490).

It is in this second Book that division is most in evidence, although it is characteristic of Bacon's flexibility in structure that the reader often does not notice the organisation unless he is looking for it: the structure leads you on clearly through an argument and from one topic to another but without drawing attention to its presence. Here we constantly feel the onward movement peculiar to this kind of structure, the overlapping effect which at the same time that it takes you off on to a new branch remains connected to the stem and thus to everything which has gone before (an interlacing which is to become more extensive in the Latin expansion). In the first Book division is also used,[1] but with a new application. Instead of the usual announcement of a division followed by a sequential treatment, Bacon attacks the opponents of learning by running all their criticisms together, so that in place of the clarity normally given to topics worthy of separate treatment we find a great jumble of accusations, made to look still more incompetent by the expansive syntax, larded with doublets:

And as for the disgraces which learning receiveth from politiques, they be of this nature; that learning doth soften men's minds, and makes them more unapt for the honour and exercise of arms; that it doth mar and pervert men's dispositions for matter of government and policy, in making them too curious and irresolute by variety of reading, or too peremptory or positive by strictness of rules and axioms, or too immoderate and overweening by reason of the greatness of examples, or too incompatible and differing from the times by reason of the dissimilitude of examples; or at least that it doth divert men's travails from action and business, and bringeth them to a love of leisure and privateness; and that it doth bring into states a relaxation of discipline, whilst every man is more ready to argue than to obey and execute. (3. 268.)

That mammoth sentence in its very construction mocks the 'politic' critics, who seem to be rambling on in repetitious verbosity without end, just as earlier the 'zeal and jealousy of divines' was made ridiculous by the neurotic repetition of 'that' (3. 264). But in both cases, and in the third discredit of learning ('from learned men themselves'), to the destructive effect of this uncontrolled language Bacon adds the further tactic of controlled criticism by extracting each point from the pile, as it were, and taking it separately:

Again, for that other conceit that learning should undermine the reverence of laws and government, it is assuredly a mere depravation and calumny without all shadow of truth. (3. 273.)

So, despite initial expectations, division has been applied, flexibly and with surprise, and Bacon can justly sum up his partition with a pungent image: 'Thus have I described and opened, as by a kind of dissection, those peccant humours...' (295).

If division is used to a more orthodox purpose in Book 2, it is certainly not rigid, for although a plan commits Bacon to following it through in a certain order it does not determine his attitude to any one part, nor the amount of time he devotes to it: in diagram form the branches have equal value, but in operation not. He is free to place the emphasis where he wishes, and so some parts are longer than others, some more profound—despite the apparent symmetry of design there is considerable variety of tone. Bacon's main task in the *Advancement* is the classification of the sciences to review deficiencies, and if this discussion cannot possibly deal with content here it can at least record Bacon's constant awareness of the implications of form, for all the advantages of *partitio* are stated by him: it avoids ambiguity— 'hoping well to deliver myself from mistaking by the order and perspicuous expressing of that I do propound' (3. 352); it avoids confusion, the 'dizziness' of those who 'leese themselves in their order' (429); and the parts, although separate, are mutually illuminating—'we have endeavoured in these our partitions to observe a kind of perspective, that one part may cast light upon another' (360). This insistence on the interrelationship of the sciences is expressed in a remarkable metaphor for *partitio* at the point where

Bacon makes one of his most crucial divisions, that within philosophy:

the distributions and partitions of knowledge are not like several lines that meet in one angle, and so touch but in a point; but are like the branches of a tree that meet in a stem, which hath a dimension and quantity of entireness and continuance, before it come to discontinue and break itself into arms and boughs... (3. 346.)

In addition to foreshadowing Bacon's increasing use of natural, organic imagery for knowledge (and being a good description of the structure of the *Advancement*), this statement of the function of *partitio* modifies the implications of an 'anatomy', for instead of a cutting-up of nature we are presented with the idea of division as being a temporary highlighting of a branch within the fundamental unity of the sciences. The idea is so important (though it would take a very skilled historian of science to evaluate it) that Bacon repeats it later with yet another image blending into it:

And generally let this be a rule, that all partitions of knowledges be accepted rather for lines and veins, than for sections and separations; and that the continuance and entireness of knowledge be preserved. For the contrary hereof hath made particular sciences to become barren, shallow, and erroneous; while they have not been nourished and maintained from the common fountain. (366–7.)

In this eloquent plea for the 'Unity of the Sciences' the characteristic interplay between image and idea in Bacon makes it hard to separate the one from the other, but we can at least conclude that what may at first have seemed a quite mechanical way of clarifying an argument has been humanised by intelligence and imagination.

I do not want to close this account of Bacon's major structural method by trying to give it a spurious significance—it is not vitally concerned with the 'spatialisation of knowledge' or with 'the problems of approaching experience', nor is it a paradigm of changes in the Renaissance mind. It is, however, an important element in Bacon's writing (and has never been seen as such), but although its implications in his scientific thought may have a wider relevance it does not seem to me to extend beyond a suggestive analogy. However, for the processes of argument, analysis,

exposition and classification, to which much of his life-work was
devoted, *partitio* was extremely valuable and (no doubt influenced
by his professions) Bacon seems to have selected this method from
the variety of traditional modes of organisation available in
rhetoric and elsewhere, and to have applied it with a particular
relevance for his own writing. He avoided its potential weaknesses
—rigidity, mechanical symmetry—exploited and even improved
on its known virtues both in practice and in theory, constantly
embodying its form and function in organic imagery. Of course
partitio is only the first step in composition, but it was one which
provided a firm but fluid framework for more subtle uses of
language and metaphor, and as a mould for the other stages of
literary expression he consistently demonstrated its value. In his
Essay 'Of Despatch' he once described an analogous form of
division and, inasmuch as he heeded his own cautions, what he
wrote there could be applied to the structure of his works in
general:

Above all things, order, and distribution, and singling out of parts, is the life of
dispatch; so as the distribution be not too subtle: for he that doth not divide will
never enter well into business; and he that divideth too much will never come
out of it clearly. (6. 435.)

CHAPTER 3

THE APHORISM

The quality of tough clarity which characterises the overall structure of Bacon's work is also found at a much more detailed level of style, that of individual sentences. While *partitio* ensures a firm but flexible control over a whole argument, the small-scale localisation of meaning and attitude, the tying-down of the particulars of an argument—this is the prerogative of the aphorism. The extensive use of aphorisms is one of the best-known features of Bacon's style, but it is seldom rightly understood. The accepted idea of his 'style' is, from this aspect, that of a tight, close, crabbed manner, a hardheaded denial of the imaginative life, a semi-scientific reduction of language to pure statement, to that ideal equation of words and things which is so beautifully satirised in Swift's vision of the Balinarbian sages carrying their packs of 'things' about with them (*Gulliver's Travels*, Book 3, chapter 5). Of course this idea is a false one: it assumes that Bacon's reasons for using the aphorism are simply the psychological aspect of style—that he was that way inclined, by nature cold, hard and calculating. Less insulting, but equally pernicious, this view ignores the several traditions of the aphorism which Bacon drew on and modified; it ignores the whole question of meaning within this form, and worst of all (seeing that it is based on purely 'stylistic' considerations) it ignores the very great differences within Bacon's own use of it, and the varying effects that aphorism has on his writing.

In order to correct this crude conception of Bacon's aphorisms it is necessary to take up these omissions in some detail, but it would be easy to do so in too much detail, for of all the aspects of style considered in this book the aphorism had the most extensive scope, covering many areas of human knowledge, sometimes disguised under other names. It is also the genre which provoked

The Aphorism

Bacon's richest theoretical discussion of form (indeed, one might say that this was his only adequate discussion of a literary form), but his discussion needs to be placed against the various traditions before we can see where Bacon's innovations lie; and as his pronouncements occur in connection with several disparate disciplines (medicine, law, politics, natural science, literature) some kind of synthesis has to be made. As the purpose of this study is to evaluate Bacon's practice as well as his theory then the *Essays* must be given adequate attention, but as they (alone amongst his works) have received considerable hostile criticism of both content and intention then it also seems necessary to place them in their Renaissance context. Given this profusion and diversity of material to be contained within one chapter some order at least may be acquired from a discreet use of *partitio*: I make therefore a triple division, in the first section considering general attitudes to the aphorism in the English Renaissance, and the particular application of the genre in its recognised three major fields, medicine, the Law, and politics (under each I briefly review Bacon's attitude to the aphorism in that discipline). The second section is also concerned with content, pulling together Bacon's various theories of the aphorism against the historical background set up in the first section, and then considering the value of the form in the light of modern disapproval (or misunderstanding) of the aphorism as a 'direction for life' in the Renaissance. The last section moves from content to form analysing Bacon's use of the aphorism in his scientific and literary works (mainly the *Essays*). And in accordance with the rules of *partitio* the discussion will end there.

I

Certainly to Bacon's contemporaries the aphorism was a thing to be reckoned with and respected, and its major connotation seems to have been not so much pithiness but intellectual authority. When Marlowe's Dr Faustus reviews his tedious supremacy in human knowledge, the acme of being 'a physition', he finds, is to be 'eternizde for some wondrous cure', and he complains:

Why *Faustus,* hast thou not attaind that end?
Is not thy common talk found Aphorismes?
Are not thy billes hung vp as monuments...?[1]

To have your words taken as aphorisms is clearly a triumph
which many would desire, and in his anatomy of the Seven Deadly
Sins Thomas Lodge attacks the vanity of his allegorical character
'Boasting' in aspiring to the authority of a Faustus: 'Though he
looke with a counterfait eie, none must see further then he, and
whatsoever he saith, must be held an Aphorisme, or he flings
house out of the window with his boastings.'[2] Another Elizabethan who shows the same respect for the aphorism as a reposi-
tory of intellectual authority is Spenser's schoolmaster, Richard
Mulcaster, who sums up his *Positions* with the modesty lacking in
Lodge's boaster:

I have uttered my conceit...in plaine wordes...Vpon the stearnesse of resolute
and reasonable perswasions, I might haue set downe my Positions aphorismelike,
and left both the commenting, and the commending of them to triall and time:
but neither deserve I so much credit, as that my bare word may stand for a
warrant: neither thought I it good with precisenesse to aliene, where I might
winne with discourse.[3]

So, if the speaker is a very great authority, his words become
aphorisms, 'warrants' for his profundity, which by virtue of their
depth may scorn conventional connected discourse.

The concept of the aphorism as an intellectual authority is
furthered, naturally enough, by the dictionaries of the time. But
the lexicographers also reveal the confusion prevalent in the
Renaissance about the nature of this form, and the identification of
it with other short pithy forms. So Rider and Holyoke give the
Latin words for

An *Aphorisme,* or principle in an art.
  I. Theorema. II. Maxima, f. aphorismus, m. axioma, principium, pronunciatum, proloquium, effatum.

thus connecting it with some of the terms of traditional logic. And,
although definitions of the aphorism are rare, if we consult Thomas
Thomas on the axiom we find the same indifferent equation of
this form with synonyms which are also applied to the aphorism:

The Aphorism

Axioma. Authoritie or honour by reason of an office, or any notable acte done, a sentence proved, a proposition, a maxime, a principle, a generall grounde or rule of anie arte.[1]

This equation of forms is carried still further by Sir Edward Coke, commenting on Littleton's phrase 'It is a maxim in law' with bluff impatience:

Maxim i.e., a sure foundation or ground or art, a principle, all one with a rule, a common ground, postulatum or an axiome, which it were too much curiositie to make nice distinctions between them.[2]

Clearly it will be easiest to grant the aphorism a certain flexibility of definition, although I shall not extend it to include such short forms as *sententia* or *apophthegm*: the aphorism is not merely pithy, but is also a 'principle', a 'sure foundation', on which others can build.

But, although there may be disagreement about the exact nature of the aphorism, there is no doubt as to its intellectual status. When Faustus reviews all human knowledge he passes through the main heads Philosophy, Medicine, and Law: under each he invokes and then rejects the authority of the great masters of 'the aphorism' in each field, Aristotle, Galen, and Justinian. Similarly when Lyly's hero Euphues makes his long-delayed but exemplary conversion from prodigality, he exclaims:

Philosophy, Phisick, Diuinitie, shal be my study. O the hidden secrets of Nature, ye expresse Image of morall vertues, the equall ballance of Iustice, the medicines to heale al diseases, how they begin to delight me. The *Axiomaes* of *Aristotle*, the Maximes of *Iustinian*, the *Aphorismes* of *Galen*, haue sodeinely made such a breach into my minde, that I seeme onely to desire them, who did onely earst detest them.[3]

Despite the contrived nature of the prose style (and of the conversion) the aphorism seems to be the highest guarantor of profundity in three of the main fields of human learning. That Bacon is aware of this tradition, and working within it, is seen from his first reference to the aphorism, which comes in an important early work of legal theory, the *Maxims of the Law* (1596), where he revises the traditional hierarchy of aphorists by omitting Aristotle and adding the gnomic wisdom of Solomon and two early Greek poets. The aphorism is important simply because

we see that all the ancient wisdom and science was wont to be delivered in that form, as may be seen by the parables of Solomon, and by the aphorisms of Hippocrates, and the moral verses of Theognis and Phocylides; but chiefly the precedent of the civil law, which hath taken the same course with their rules, did confirm me in my opinion. (7. 321.)

We note again the flexible inter-equation of these forms in the Renaissance, and the intellectual supremacy of the aphorism—'all the ancient wisdom and science' chose this medium.

If we begin to investigate the sources of the aphorism's status in some of the subjects traditionally referred to, we uncover a vast if rather inert body of examples of its use, with little articulate theory as to its function. Some of the traditional references are misleading in that they imply that a particular progenitor actually communicated in aphorisms. Thus the 'Axiomaes' of Aristotle cannot refer to the connected structure of argument and analysis which typifies his work, but rather to the various definitions or principles which are suggested in the course of it, although obviously Aristotle's own account of *tópoi* (*loci*, commonplaces) in the first two books of the *Rhetoric* and his distinction between axioms (self-evident propositions, immediately recognised as true, and common to all sciences) and definitions and hypotheses (e.g. *Analytica Posteriora* 72 a 5–24) were enormously influential on all later discussions of such forms, including Bacon's. But N. W. Gilbert has noted that, because Aristotle's works 'abound in dicta easily cited without regard to context', he was quoted much more frequently in the Renaissance than Plato, who provided very few 'maxims and aphorisms'.[1] So, although undeniably having the attribute of authority, Aristotle's 'aphorisms' do not really come within the category of 'separate brief statements' (which for Bacon seems to be the working definition of aphorism) and are perhaps for this reason not discussed by him. A more valid example of aphoristic communication would be the propositions of Euclidean geometry, and though Bacon sometimes refers to them (e.g. 3. 291) or quotes from them (e.g. 3. 348) he does not normally associate them with the aphorism, possibly because they do not spring from the observation of man or nature. But the last of these classical 'scientist' fathers of the aphorism, Hippocrates, is a source which Bacon often uses,[1] generally with approval. And it is from the field of Greek medicine that we have the best stylistic definition of the genre and its self-contained, pithy, 'rich conciseness': Galen, in his *Medical Definitions*, wrote:

Aphorismus est oratio concisa quae perfectam complet sententiam vel sic. Aphorismus oratio est in voce quidem seu dictione perangusta, sententiis vero locuples.[2]

The *Aphorisms* of Hippocrates, usually published in this period with the commentary by Galen, must be the most famous medical work ever written, with an enormous dissemination in the Middle Ages and the Renaissance.[3] Its high status is not altogether earned, for compared with other medical works by Hippocrates it is not outstanding as regards its scientific content, nor is it certain that it was originally composed in aphorisms. However, even if it only represents selections from his work, or his *obiter dicta*, its popularity seems due partly to the form and partly to the suitability of its contents to this mode of communication. The work consists of separate observations:

A dysentery beginning with a black bile is mortal. (IV. xxiv.)
Autumn is bad for consumptives. (III. x.)
Old men endure fasting most easily, then men of middle age, youths very badly and worst of all children. (I. xiii.)

Obviously the form has a practical advantage for the reader in that these simple statements are easily memorised; but, more than this, such disconnected reports on experience are best expressed as aphorisms. They represent the scattered conclusions of observation and diagnosis and because they are so discrete cannot be organised into a system or 'method' but have to be left as a haphazard collection. This disconnectedness was clearly appropriate for the unsystematic stage of medicine, before it was revolutionised by the study of human anatomy, but even today some doctors regard the application of such 'tips' in diagnosis as forming an 'art' which can only be acquired by experience, based on a non-scientific blend of observation with intuition. Certainly Bacon saw Hippocrates as a non-systematiser, an unfalsifying observer of separate particulars:

He was a man of wisdom as well as learning, much given to experiments and observation, not striving after words or methods, but picking out the very nerves of science and so setting them forth. (5. 254.)

If we cannot ever again take the content of Hippocrates' *Aphorisms* seriously, we can certainly appreciate the possibilities inherent in the form, as did at least one of its innumerable Renaissance readers.

The other traditional source for the aphorism is that of the Law, and here the vast influence of maxims and *regulae* has recently been analysed with admirable clarity by Peter Stein.[1] Roman law, from its earliest formulations such as the *Twelve Tables* to more comprehensive systems such as the *Corpus Iuris Civilis*, was often expressed in the form of disconnected rules within a loose overall plan. Professor Stein shows how the formation of legal principles into propositions was influenced by the techniques of Aristotelian logic (pp. 33–40, 156–9) and he traces the enormous growth of collections of *Regulae Iuris* through the classical period into the Middle Ages and most vigorously in the Renaissance ('The period was manifestly the heyday of rules and maxims', p. 175). These rules are equivalent to aphorisms, and a significant connection can be seen between his account of their development in law and the process I outlined earlier by which aphorisms are 'found', or 'held' or 'may stand':

A jurist who formulated a rule of law would not himself normally describe it as a *regula*. The recognition that it was a proposition worthy of perpetuation as an accurate and succinct account of the law was made by other jurists. When they called it a *regula*, they conferred on it a certain cachet. (P. 92.)

Another fundamental connection between the aphorism and the legal maxim is their position as an authority, one which was recognised as much in the later period as earlier: 'What makes a proposition a maxim for the common lawyers of the late fifteenth

century was not so much its degree of abstraction or its epigrammatic form but the fact that it could not be challenged. Maxims
were regarded as part of the original structure of the law, and to
object to them was tantamount to denying the law itself.' In the
words of a popular sixteenth-century textbook, the maxims *are*
the law and 'it is not lawful for any that is learned in the law to
deny them. For every one of those maxims is sufficient authority
for himself.'¹

Bacon was certainly much influenced by the application of
aphorisms in the civil law, as he himself admitted. In his earliest
legal work, the *Discourse on the Commission of Bridewell* (1587) he
praises the aphorism both as a basis for further development and as
itself a form of intellectual condensation:

The Maxims are the foundations of the Law, and the full and perfect conclusions of reason. (7. 509.)

He was so convinced of the value of the form that, as we have seen,
he produced his own collection some nine years later, and in the
preface both allied himself with the traditional masters of the
aphorism and gave some theoretical consideration to the genre.
He chose the aphorism rather than a '*certain* method or order' (my
italics) because

this delivering of knowledge in distinct and disjointed aphorisms doth leave the
wit of man more free to turn and to toss, and to make use of that which is
delivered to more several purposes and applications... (7. 321.)

So again in this field, as in medicine, Bacon had seized on the
aphorism not so much because it was pithy, but for its status as an
authority, a traditional association, and—a more personal idea—
for its flexibility and freedom from system. His own collection
was to have numbered three hundred, but only twenty-five
maxims are extant, consisting of an English commentary on such
regulae as 'In jure non remota causa sed proxima spectatur', and
'Verba fortius accipiuntur contra proferentem'. But his interest in
the legal maxim continued, and in the *De Augmentis* he finally
published a more complete work in this form, the 'Example of a
Treatise on Universal Justice, or the Fountains of Equity, by

Aphorisms', which an authoritative legal historian has described as 'the first critical and jurisprudential estimate of the English law ever made'.[1] Here Bacon certainly achieves the 'rich conciseness' of the form, as in the thirty-first aphorism (which incidentally could be used to describe his own application of quotations):

Examples are to be used for advice, not for rules and order. Wherefore let them be so employed as to turn the authority of the past to the use of the present. (5. 94.)

Besides science and the law, there existed another field not traditionally referred to in which the aphorism was of some significance in the Renaissance, and particularly for Bacon: that of the observation of man in society, for which the nearest modern term would seem to be politics (in the Renaissance 'policy' or *prudentia*). Here the aphorism continues to be not simply an observation, nor a self-contained artistic genre which can be admired from a distance, but an incentive to action. Just as the aphorisms containing 'the equall ballance of Iustice, the medicines to heale al diseases' were valued because they could be applied for direct practical purposes to legal or medical problems, so the maxims of politics were to be drawn on to answer the question 'How to live', and the whole literature of 'Advice to Princes' set out to answer it.[2] Again Aristotle was influential, for in his *Rhetoric* he had given an important place in techniques of proof to the maxim (*gnóme*), which he restricted to a didactic function: it is a statement, 'but only about questions of practical conduct, courses of conduct to be chosen or avoided', and its use 'amounts to a general declaration of moral principles' (Book 2, chapter 21; 1394a25, 1395b15). Perhaps because the question was such an urgent one to Renaissance man, we find the aphorism as a source of authority being expanded to include still more allied forms, which a strict study of the aphorism as a pure mode of communication would have to exclude, such as the collections of apophthegms, the wise sayings of great men, which were often given a political slant, or the many political *florilegia* (the most famous of these was Sansovino's *Concetti Politici*, 1578—translated in 1590 by Robert Hitchcock as

The Quintessence of Wit—which drew heavily on Guicciardini's *Ricordi*). In fact this field of politics produced the most extensive use and discussion of the aphorism immediately before Bacon, the key figure being Machiavelli, and in addition to the importance of the political aphorism in his own work the 'contre-Machiavel' Gentillet laid stress on the Italian's use of the maxim.[1]

The particular significance of Machiavelli's use of the aphorism in relation to Bacon is that it moves the emphasis from the audience to the writer: over and above the value of the form as a pithy authoritative guide to life it now represents a definite attitude to experience, and a way of organising this attitude. A typical development in the *Prince* is inductive, moving from an opening definition, through the analysis of a number of classical and contemporary examples, and culminating in a maxim or admonition. The force of this final summation is well felt at the end of chapter 3, 'On mixed monarchies':

And by experience we have seen it, that the power hereof in Italy, and that of Spain also, was caused by France, and their own ruine proceeded from themselves. From whence a general rule may be taken, which never, or very seldom fails, *That he that gives the means to another to become powerful, ruines himself.*[2]

Machiavelli is always trying to lay down general rules on life, maxims which never fail,[3] and in so doing he is predicting future human behaviour in a scientific way: from empirical data his method generalises by induction, and is thus a close analogue to Bacon's own scientific theories. It is a method which postpones ethical considerations and insists on accurate observation—as Bacon said, 'we are much beholden to Machiavel and others, that write what men do and not what they ought to do'[4]—and for both the formulation and the communication of these data the aphorism is of central importance.

Even from this very cursory account we can see that on this aspect of the aphorism Bacon was again aware of the tradition, and of Machiavelli's significance within it; for in the *Advancement* he discussed a number of the proverbs or 'sentences politic' of Solomon, in connection with the deficient topic of 'negotiation' or business, and pointed to the Italian's example: writing in aphorisms on this topic was not only in use with the Hebrews,

> but it is generally to be found in the wisdom of the more ancient times, that as men found out any observation that they thought was good for life, they would gather it and express it in parable or aphorism or fable. But for fables, they were viceregents and supplies where examples failed: now that the times abound with history, the aim is better when the mark is alive. And therefore the form of writing which of all others is fittest for this variable argument of negotiation and occasions is that which Machiavel chose wisely and aptly for government; namely, *discourse upon histories or examples*. For knowledge drawn freshly and in our view out of particulars, knoweth the best way to particulars again. (3. 453.)

By the italicised phrase Bacon seems to refer to the *Discourses on the first ten books of Titus Livius*, in which Machiavelli bases many of his chapters on the headings, precepts quoted from Livy, which are often themselves aphoristic (as: 'That men seldom know how to be wholly good or wholly bad', or 'That Men rise from humble to high fortunes rather by Fraud than by Force'). But clearly the observation also applies to the *Prince*, for it is a moot point whether Machiavelli had formed the maxims before he considered the examples, or after: as Bacon says later, all that matters is that the two stages be organically related, and that the examples should not be merely brought in for the discourse's sake, like servants.

II

This section of the *Advancement* is a good place on which to make a pause, as Bacon would say, to consider the variety of traditions we have uncovered, and his relationship to them. We note first the flexibility of his terms: 'Aphorism' is paralleled to, if not equated with, 'sentences politic', 'parable', 'fable', and earlier with 'wise and politic axioms' and (in reference to Solomon's 'aphorisms') with 'profound and excellent cautions, precepts, positions' (3. 448). Here is as much inter-equation as in the definitions of his contemporaries. But, although these terms are equated, it is worth noting that Bacon again follows the tradition in that they are not static 'quotations', say, but all have intellectual authority ('axiom', 'position') or have some hidden meaning to be uncovered ('parable', 'fable') or some positive didactic intent ('politic', 'caution', 'precept'). And the direction of this onward movement is also traditional, though possibly given more force by Bacon: they are all thought 'good for life', and have a validity 'arising out of an universal insight into the affairs of the world' (448). Certainly as regards the detailed rationale of their suitability as a guide to life, Bacon is more articulate than any other source known to me, in his insistence on the particularity of the process: this wisdom 'is used indeed upon particular cases propounded, but is gathered by general observations of causes of like nature' (448), for 'knowledge drawn freshly and in our view out of particulars, knoweth the best way to particulars again': that is to say that we shall be able to apply specific insights in specific situations, for 'as actions in common life are dispersed, and not arranged in order, dispersed directions do best for them' (4. 451). This perception of the importance of the ethical *minutiae* of everyday life is repeated with considerable weight by a later moralist, Dr Johnson,[1] but is summed up with precision and grace in Bacon's phrase, 'the Doctrine concerning Scattered Occasions' (5. 35). Besides its value in this sphere Bacon sees the aphorism as a vehicle for the empirical study of man: it is based on 'observation' of concrete situations, whether real or reported ('now that the times abound with history'), and, though he is in the Machiavellian tradition here, Bacon again adds to it in his very original section in the *De Augmentis* on 'the knowledge of Advancement in Life', by urging the 'true politician' to base his observation on 'particular persons' and 'particular actions':

These informations of particulars touching persons and actions are as the minor propositions in every active syllogism; for no truth or excellence of observations or axioms (whence the major political propositions are drawn) can suffice to ground a conclusion if there be error in the minor propositions. (5. 60.)

Both the image, and the injunction, are a fresh extension of the tradition.

It is becoming more and more evident that Bacon uses

aphorisms not because of some personal intellectual aridity but because he assigns a certain definite role to the aphorism—in fact, more than one role, for we have already seen him thinking of various facets of the genre according to the use proposed for it. In addition to his discussion of its function for man in society, where he is nearest to the tradition, Bacon gives the aphorism extended theoretical consideration as a separate mode of communication, and here he seems most original. Mulcaster's brief distinction between the 'preciseness' of aphoristic delivery which might 'aliene', and the greater persuasive power of 'discourse' is the only reference I have found—and it is a very shadowy one—to an aspect of the genre which increasingly occupies Bacon: the relationship between the bare truth of the aphorism and the more connected but equally more distorting form of systematic communication. This idea, like so many others, is hinted at in an early work before it is fully formulated: in the Preface to the *Maxims of the Law* already quoted, Bacon saw that 'this delivering of knowledge in distinct and disjointed aphorisms doth leave the wit of man more free to turn and to toss, and to make use of that which is delivered to more several purposes and application' (7. 321). But a few years later, in Book I of the *Advancement*, he adds to this simple concept of flexibility new ideas on growth: one error in research is 'the over-early and peremptory reduction of knowledge into arts and methods; from which time commonly sciences receive small or no augmentation'. He develops the image of growth in human terms:

But as young men when they knit and shape perfectly, do seldom grow to a further stature; so knowledge, while it is in aphorisms and observations, it is in growth; but when it once is comprehended in exact methods, it may perchance be further polished and illustrate, and accommodated for use and practice, but it increaseth no more in bulk and substance. (3. 292.)

Bacon is insisting on the potential of knowledge: a system forecloses future development, for 'Aphorisms, representing a knowledge broken, do invite men to enquire farther; whereas Methods, carrying the shew of a total, do secure men, as if they were at furthest' (3. 405) This concept of the attractive power of the aphorism in stimulating further thought seems to be quite original to Bacon, and is a very perceptive explanation of that imaginative effect peculiar to fable, parable and other forms of pregnant wisdom. It is stated again in surprisingly similar terms and with equal authority by Blake, in a famous letter to Dr Trusler:

The wisest of the Ancients consider'd what is not too Explicit as the fittest for Instruction, because it rouzes the faculties to act. I name Moses, Solomon, Esop, Homer, Plato.[1]

The corollary of Bacon's opposition between 'seeds' and 'fully grown systems' is that the aphorism should be a vehicle of pure truth, and in Book 2 he develops this idea, applying it directly to the individual user, and to his intellectual truth or deceit. So far 'it hath been too much taken into custom, out of a few Axioms or observations upon any subject to make a solemn and formal art; filling it with some discourses, and illustrating it with examples, and digesting it into a sensible Method'. However, communication by aphorisms cannot produce this sort of deceit because

it trieth the writer, whether he be superficial or solid: for Aphorisms, except they should be ridiculous, cannot be made but of the pith and heart of sciences; for discourse of illustration is cut off; recitals of example are cut off; discourse of connexion and order is cut off; descriptions of practice are cut off; so there remaineth nothing to fill the Aphorisms but some good quantity of observation: and therefore no man can suffice, nor in reason will attempt, to write aphorisms, but he that is sound and grounded. (3. 405; see also *Filum Labyrinthi*, 3. 498; *Novum Organum*, 4. 85.)

Here is the ultimate value of the aphorism for Bacon: we have seen how he has adopted various elements of the Renaissance concept of the genre—its flexibility, its relevance to human life, its basis in empirical data (here it can only be filled with 'some good quantity of observation'). Now he sees it as the ultimate irreducible condensation of knowledge—'the pith and heart of sciences' (though not necessarily 'pithy' in expression), the form which best encourages growth—development, new research—in all spheres, and finally the very emblem of truth, the mere use of which automatically guarantees a man's willingness to expose what he knows and what he does not know. As with *partitio*, Bacon has taken a traditional form and developed it in an individual and creative way, and again with a remarkably articulate awareness of its structural potential.

Bacon gave the aphorism a central position in his own writing on a suitably wide range of subjects, as we shall see, but the best-known application is in the *Essays*. We have already seen something of the vital connection between the *Essays* and his programme for the observation of human nature formulated in the *Advancement of Learning*, and, given the early development of his interest in the aphorism (as in the 1596 treatise on the *Maxims of the Law*), then it is entirely consistent that in their first form of 1597 the *Essays* should consist essentially of detached aphorisms on particular topics. But as such they are often misunderstood, their critics complaining that 'they are a mere collection of apophthegms from his note-book', as if by contract Bacon should have produced a connected piece of writing in the discursive whimsical vein of the tradition from Montaigne to Charles Lamb. Of course such criticism exists in sublime ignorance of the function of the *Essays*, and of the role of the aphorism within them, but it is worth answering the charge that these are merely odd pages from Bacon's notebook. As so often in his development, an early work can be prophetic of future attitudes, and it is significant that here already Bacon associates the aphorism with the study of man in society: each of the Essays is concerned with one aspect of man as a social and political being: 'Of Ceremonies and respects'; 'Of Faction'; 'Of Honour and reputation'; 'Of Negociating'. More than this, several of them are connected: the first, 'Of Studies', mentions conversation in passing, while the next essay, 'Of Discourse', handles it in detail; again 'Of Followers and Friends' deals with suitors, to which topic the whole of the next essay is devoted, and with 'Expence', which is treated in the one after. It is thus not a collection of isolated *aperçus*, but a miniature treatise on some of the spheres in which a Renaissance man would want to control and cultivate his behaviour: it is the sort of book which might have been read by a Philip Sidney—or an Othello. And the attitudes reflected in it as in the later versions inevitably range from the new Machiavellian observation of 'what men do' to the traditional ethics of 'what men should do'.

But it is precisely this aspect of the *Essays* (the 'literary work' as an observation of life which can be usefully reapplied) which has produced most of the unsympathetic criticism directed against them since the Victorians (this is paradoxical, given the dominant moralistic approach of modern criticism). Though my main wish is to discuss them from a literary viewpoint I can hardly overlook these attacks, especially since they seem part of a general debate over the aphorism. Just as the aphorism recurs as a literary form and as a view of life, so there seems to be a constant opposition between proponents of the full potential of the aphorism and those who take a narrower, exclusive view of it. So on its relation to human experience we find George Eliot in *Daniel Deronda* (1876) describing the Rector with a contemptuous dismissal of its role as a concretion of life: 'And in spite of his practical ability, some of his experience had petrified into maxims and quotations.'[1] Yet from a similar nineteenth-century intellectual ethos F. H. Bradley makes the much shrewder distinction that

Our live experience, fixed in aphorisms, stiffens into cold epigrams.[2]

Two modern American scholars create a similar dialectic: in 1944 T. W. Baldwin begins his monumental study of Renaissance education with this oblique (and debatable) attack on Ben Jonson's phrase 'small Latin and less Greek':

A brilliant aphorism is a dangerous thing. It is always a lie and never the truth.

while in 1947 Northrop Frye, in his book on Blake, gives a much fuller and more sensitive account of the aphorism as Christ used it:

Jesus' teaching avoids generalizations of the sort that translate into platitudes in all languages. Examples, images, parables, and the aphorisms which are concretions rather than abstractions of wisdom, were what he preferred.[3]

And as recently as 1951 a creative writer is attracted to the anti-systematic aspect of the genre: in February of that year Albert Camus writes in his notebook:

After *The Rebel* aggressive, stubborn refusal of systems. Aphorisms from now on.[1]

Much depends, then, on the individual's concept of the aphorism: for Camus it represents 'creation in freedom'.

The facet of the aphorism which has been most called into question is its potential as a vehicle for instruction. We have seen how thoroughly Bacon had developed this point theoretically, and how closely his ideas conformed to those of his age. Yet that great scholar C. S. Lewis, who in his sixteenth-century volume of the *Oxford History of English Literature* gave so many intelligent examples of the critic's task of historical reconstruction, challenges Bacon—and that aspect of the genre which stems from Aristotle—head on:

> Even the completed *Essays* of 1625 is a book whose reputation curiously outweighs any real pleasure or profit that most people have found in it...The truth is, it is a book for adolescents. It is they who underline (as I see from the copy before me) sentences like 'There is little friendshipe in the worlde, and least of all between equals': a man of 40 either disbelieves it or takes it for granted. No one, even if he wished, could really learn 'policie' from Bacon, for cunning, even more than virtue, lives in minute particulars.[2]

In the last sentence Lewis has hit on (unwittingly, it seems) the very principle by which the aphorism exists, as 'the genre which more than any other aims at preserving in literary expression the discrete and contradictory nature of live experience', based on the belief that 'reality remains inaccessible save by way of scattered occasions' (J. P. Stern, p. 275). But the point I want to take up is that the *Essays* 'is a book for adolescents': now one may object, as Harry Levin does, that C. S. Lewis is here speaking from 'so top-lofty a plane of maturity'[3] (Lewis goes on to dismiss the 1597 volume as being 'altogether too jejune, too atomic', so misunderstanding the stylistic aspect too), but this criticism rests on a more radical failure of the historical imagination.

We have already seen the considerable status enjoyed by the aphorism as a universal source of intellectual supremacy: it would be strange if men then doubted the possibility of applying this profundity to life. But of course they did not, for the Renaissance was—to an extent which never ceases to surprise one—a notebook culture. The man who did most to influence European education, Erasmus, taught that you should read for the content, not the style; men dutifully read and noted, and the notebook took on a crucial importance, as R. R. Bolgar has so clearly shown.[1] The notebook was invaluable not only as a source for future composition but as a record of anything potentially useful to an individual's experience. The frame of mind revealed in the urgency of Hamlet's 'My tables! meet it is I set it down...' is a constant in Renaissance life, and the philosophy behind it is beautifully expressed (and parodied) in Pandarus' words, as he gropes after consolatory maxims for the parting lovers:

There was never a truer rhyme. Let us cast away nothing, for we may live to have need of such a verse. (*Troilus and Cressida*, IV, iv, 13–22.)

The task of noting down pithy easily applicable precepts was made easier by Renaissance printers and publishers, who inserted in the margin a sign indicating particularly choice examples: sometimes they used a hand and pointing finger (as, e.g., in Ascham's *Scholemaster*, 1570), the mark which Renaissance readers made themselves, as many happily extant books show; or, being more sophisticated, they put inverted commas in the margin to point out 'a precept or a *sententia* worthy of observation'. This practice, most familiar to us from Shakespearian Quartos, was very common in all sorts of printed books,[2] and led the maxim-hunter unerringly to his target. The revised version of Sidney's *Arcadia* has many (but not all) of its hundreds of maxims located in this way, and when Geoffrey Fenton translated Guicciardini's *History* (itself the source of countless maxims) in 1579, he added several passages himself, mostly of a sententious nature, and the majority of them are given marginal inverted commas.[3] The average reader would note down such maxims, and would be prepared to apply them to the 'scattered occasions' of life: he might 'live to have need of' them.

The guiding assumption behind this universal practice was that you could learn about life from books (*abeunt studia in mores*), and that you could learn more, and more quickly and safely. The modern mind prefers to learn direct from life, and is at this point diametrically opposed to the Renaissance. From such a typical and respected book as Ascham's *Scholemaster* we see which was more valued:

Learning teacheth more in one yeare than experience in twentie: And learning teacheth safelie, when experience maketh mo miserable then wise...*Erasmus* the honor of learning of all our time, saide wiselie that experience is the common scholehouse of foles, and ill men: Men, of witte and honestie, be otherwise instructed.[1]

And they were instructed by the experience of others, digested into a manageable and portable shape, often in unadorned aphoristic precepts. The tradition of conduct-book literature is ancient and vigorous (it is not dead yet), running back through Cato's *Distichs* to Isocrates, whose precepts *Ad Demonicum* may (perhaps) be mocked in the mouth of Polonius.[2] It extended, too, throughout society, for at the lower level the middle-class desire for improvement produced a rash of basic conduct-books which were the bourgeois equivalent of more aristocratic treatises, themselves the less ambitious copies of the innumerable 'Advices to Princes':[3] Bacon's *Essays* span all worlds, moving from common-sensical precepts on getting and spending (often in the imperative) to more sophisticated advice on politics in society, and up to topics in which the *Principe* is the real focal centre.[4] When Bacon wrote, in dedicating the 1625 volume to Buckingham, that the *Essays* 'of all my other works, have been most current; for that, as it seems, they come home to men's business and bosoms' (6. 373) he was not making an idle puff: in both public and private spheres they belong to a well-established and honourable tradition, to which the 'maxim' or civil aphorism was closely allied. Added confirmation of the link is provided by that sensitive Elizabethan critic John Hoskins, discussing the vogue of the *sententia*, by which 'the writers of these days imprison themselves in the straitness of these maxims'. In objecting to its over-use, he distinguishes two valid applications of the maxim, the first being its mnemonic function— 'notes for memory', while the second once more leads us back to

Aristotle's assignation of the maxim to 'questions of practical conduct', but is also an exact description of the *Essays*: 'a matter of short direction for life and action' (*ed. cit.* p. 40).

Much more could be said on the validity of the content of the *Essays* in a historical context, but this is perhaps sufficient to make the point before returning to our literary analysis. Yet on a more absolute scale I should be surprised if the unprejudiced reader did not gain some illumination from the content of the aphorisms to be discussed, as well as from their form.

III

Before finally considering how Bacon used the aphorism in his own writings, and what effect it had on his style, it might sharpen our appreciation of his use of the genre to consider how close he comes to being a true aphorist, and a useful way of doing this is to compare him with another writer for whom it was very important, Georg Christoph Lichtenberg (1742–99). In his profound study of Lichtenberg, Peter Stern has illuminated not only many aspects of German literature and philosophy in the eighteenth century and after, but has also produced by far the best theoretical discussion of the aphorism as a literary genre, and on it I base the following outline of a comparison. Lichtenberg was a scientist and philosopher (for the major part of his career professor of Physics at Göttingen University) who in addition to his scientific work wrote with considerable literary imagination, and showed a keen interest in human nature. This minimum description of his life brings out how much it overlapped with Bacon's interests, and indeed Lichtenberg knew and admired Bacon's work, and seems to have drawn on it.[1] But a very great difference between them is that for Lichtenberg the aphorism was the preferred mode of communication—for twenty-five years and more he kept notebooks in which he composed thousands of aphorisms, on all conceivable topics: by comparison, Bacon's use of the aphorism in particular, clearly defined situations seems highly selective. Furthermore, while Bacon uses the genre for objective normative observation of nature or other men, Lichtenberg's aphoristic work can spring from a 'personal mood and factual experiences' (Stern, p. 60), is indeed the expression of a whole view of life, a vision characterised by a 'lack of single-mindedness, of a purpose accomplished or finally renounced, of a predicament accepted or resolutely challenged' (p. 74). Thus (to put aside for the moment the historical perspective and to consider the question in more modern, psychological terms), one might say that the true aphorist has a fragmented kaleidoscopic vision for which this genre is the perfect form. Lichtenberg's disconnected world-view makes use of induction (pp. 82, 113–15) yet is essentially anti-systematic (p. 257), and though he may seem to resemble Bacon on both points Lichtenberg's 'understanding of reality makes him doubt whether it can be represented inside a system at all' (p. 102). By contrast (and again it is one that separates him from the true aphorists) Bacon was quite sure that systems could ultimately be devised for representing and even dominating reality (and spent most of his life designing them), only insisting that the aphorism be used for the crucial preliminary stages where truth must be allowed to grow.

On the particular effect of the aphorism, Dr Stern's analysis brings Lichtenberg nearer to Bacon, as in his comment on Bacon's point that aphorisms 'invite men, both to ponder that which was invented, and to add and supply further' (3. 498):

> Yet what else is every hypothesis except an invitation to ponder? This heuristic quality of the scientific aphorism issues directly from its brevity and pithiness. We feel that so much more could be said on the subject matter of the aphorism, and yet we also feel that when all is said, the original statement (like the proverbial oxhide that was cut into narrow strips) still covers the whole field. (P. 106.)

This description may well apply to Bacon's use of the genre in science (and, if so, it would help answer the perennial charge that he neglected the hypothesis), but, given the flexibility with which the Renaissance used the concept of the aphorism, then Dr Stern's subtle analysis of the 'literary aphorism', differentiating it from such short forms as the maxim and the precept,[1] would seem inapplicable to Bacon. But it may be said that Bacon's 'literary' aphorisms (such as they are) share such characteristics as the condensation of expression which preserves more than one plane of meaning, so that a 'second look at language' is necessary (pp. 194–6); they too show a condensation of the basic antithesis often verging on the paradoxical, which therefore cannot be summarised without limiting the aphorism to a single meaning; and they too have an essentially imaginative mode of language. Lichtenberg's imaginative perception of life through this form can be seen in such aphorisms as 'God, who winds up our sundials' (p. 126) or 'An excessively careful education cultivates dwarf fruit-trees' (p. 238), or 'Whoever has less than he desires must know that he has more than he is worth' (p. 286). But a last difference between them is that Lichtenberg has a very limited self-consciousness about his art, only mentioning the word 'aphorism' once (pp. 111, 120 n.), while Bacon has a fully formulated theory of its nature and function. Paradoxically, Lichtenberg is the real aphorist—for Bacon it is only one form among several, to be used for special purposes, and does not seem to spring from any tendency in his personality.

But if more limited in quantity, Bacon's aphorisms show a width of application and a power of imagination well in keeping with his high concept of the genre's potential. (However, on the scientific works I face the same difficulty as with division, that a literary approach is unable to consider the scientific or philosophic implications of the content, and thus the following brief discussion of the scientific aphorisms will be limited to the general question of form.) In the scientific works he first plans actually to communicate in aphorisms shortly after his advocacy of them in the *Advancement,* for in the notebook of 1608, the *Commentarius Solutus,* he reminds himself of

The finishing of the Aphorismes, Clavis interpretationis, and then setting foorth yᵉ book. (II. 64.)

Spedding notes that he is probably referring to 'the paper entitled *Aphorismi et consilia de auxiliis mentis et accessione luminis naturalis* (3. 793), which appears to be one of the earliest rudimentary forms of the first book of the *Novum Organum*. The *Clavis Interpretationis* was the name which he first thought of giving to the *Novum Organum* itself' (*ibid.*); later in these notes he proposes a History 'of all Mechanical Arts', which is to have as its main research section 'all observacions, Axiomes, directions' (11. 65–6). The *Aphorismi et consilia* (which consists of about a dozen separate 'thoughts') certainly begins, as does the *Novum Organum*, with some of Bacon's most pregnant and far-reaching aphorisms:

> Man, being the servant and interpreter of Nature, can do and understand so much and so much only as he has observed in fact or in thought of the course of nature: beyond this he neither knows anything nor can do anything. (4. 47; for the Latin texts, cf. 1. 157 and 3. 793.)

Within that sentence lie the seeds of a whole new science, and it is significant that the need for 'observation' is basic to it and to the form of the aphorism.

In Bacon's own scientific method, as he begins to expound it in the *Novum Organum*, the aphorism (which is often equated with 'axiom') plays a central part in the inductive process:

> There are and can be only two ways of searching into and discovering truth. The one flies from the senses and particulars to the most general axioms, and from these principles, the truth of which it takes for settled and immoveable, proceeds to judgment and to the discovery of middle axioms. And this way is now in fashion. The other derives axioms from the senses and particulars, rising by a gradual and unbroken ascent, so that it arrives at the most general axioms last of all. This is the true way, but as yet untried. (4. 50.)

So, despite Bacon's use of the aphorism as an ideal form against which to compare the restrictions of other men's systems, he is now himself constructing a system using an 'anti-systematic' form. The resulting structure is best described as cellular, for very few of the aphorisms are really independent: they tend to go in groups, as one idea or attitude is developed across several of them, and—as we have seen—these little clusters of cells are given a definite place in the overall structure by the use of *partitio*. Besides this paradox of a system being built from non-systems, another shock for modern stylistic expectations of the form is that in

Bacon's scientific works the aphorisms are not actually 'pithy': after the first few general principles the individual structures become longer and longer, without even being self-contained. Of course his theory held simply that they should be made of the 'pith and heart' of sciences, but it may come as a surprise—particularly after the example of Lichtenberg—that Bacon should not be interested in condensation and precision. Here, clearly, content is more important than form, for what Bacon is trying to do could not be achieved in short, paradoxical statements. He seems to value the aphorism because it is 'open-ended', it does not predict nor commit him to a definite, fully worked-out system: yet nevertheless he has a clear idea of the place of these aphorisms within his system (as the 'Distributio Operis' shows), and he has already begun to organise within this section of it.

If we turn to the other main group of extant scientific works, we find an analogous situation. In his last years Bacon began to see that his scientific theory of observation and experiment really demanded in the first place a great range of specific observations as the 'stuff' without which the machine could not work. So he abandoned his 'New Instrument' unfinished, and left unsolved the difficulties of devising a method for evaluating experience in order to compile a comprehensive 'Natural and Experimental History'. In such constituent works as the *Historia Densi et Rari* (5. 355 ff.) and the *Parasceve* or 'Aphorisms on the Composition of the Primary History' (4. 253 ff.) and above all the *Sylva Sylvarum* or *Natural History*, the aphorism is again the key method of observation. In his preface to the *Sylva* William Rawley, Bacon's chaplain, secretary, and editor, explained that the work is 'an indigested heap of particulars, and cannot have that lustre which books cast into methods have'; besides preserving this authentic Baconian antithesis he records the two stages of Bacon's methodology of the aphorism: first the preliminary, fragmented stage of 'true axioms' drawn from 'plain experience' which 'must be broken and grinded, and not whole, or as it groweth'; and then the systematic, inductive stage: these aphorisms are 'the bricks' with which the new science will be built (2. 335–7). Although theory and practice are perfectly consistent, here again the literary student is at a loss, for whatever can be said about such an aphorism as this will not come from him:

Solid bodies, if they be very softly percussed, give no sound; as when a man treadeth very softly upon boards. So chests or doors in fair weather, when they open easily, give no sound. And cart-wheels squeak not when they are liquored. (2. 392; Century II, no. 117.)

Certainly in terms of scientific content, they 'invite men to enquire farther'—in this case to understand the significance of such phenomena as these and the effect of friction or moisture on acoustic quality, but they seem to defeat any literary observation. In terms of Bacon's theory such aphorisms are perfectly sound observations on experience, almost aggressively unconnected, and certainly not falsified into any premature system. But their stylistic or other literary properties (for the moment excluding metaphor) are nil: they can only be criticised in terms of their relationship to the topic observed.

It is necessary to pursue this discussion even though it may seem to be yielding a fruitless result, partly in view of the prevailing concept of Bacon's essentially 'bare, aphoristic' style, and partly because there is hardly an area in all his many interests in which the aphorism is not important. In that subsection of the 'scientific' work headed 'the study of man and society', as early as the *Advancement* he had offered a brief example of the value of the aphorism in discussing the 'sentences politic' of Solomon. This section is considerably enlarged in Book 8 of the *De Augmentis*, and takes the form of a collection of thirty-four proverbs, each 'explained' in a commentary by Bacon. The proverbs themselves are aphoristic in their condensation:

Poverty comes as one that travelleth, and want as an armed man. (Prov. vi. 11; 5. 39.)
As dead flies do cause the best ointment to stink, so does a little folly him that is in reputation for wisdom and honour. (Eccles. x. 1; 5. 42.)
Open rebuke is better than secret love. (Prov. xxvii. 5; 5. 52.)

Bacon's own commentary however—like that on the *Maxims of the Law*—does not consist of detached, pithy observations, but of

84

connected discourse (several times clarified by *partitio*) which makes explicit the value of these 'excellent civil precepts and cautions'. Bacon is here making a collection of aphorisms which have had a special meaning for him, so that it is revealing that he automatically places these proverbs in the milieu of the Renaissance 'political axiom', the world of ruler and ruled. The majority of the explanations discuss how a citizen should behave toward his prince, especially in awkward situations:

If the anger of a prince or a superior be kindled against you, and it is your turn to speak, Solomon gives two directions; first, 'that an answer be made', and secondly, 'that it be soft'; the former contains three precepts. (No. 1; 5. 37.)

The focus is so often 'the prince': 'When the prince is one who lends an easy and credulous ear...' (no. 13; 5. 43); 'This compassion therefore has a certain analogy with that of a prince towards his subject' (no. 14; 5. 44); 'It will be also advantageous for him to engage the assistance and mediation of some friend with the prince' (no. 16; 5. 46). It is an English version of Italian statecraft, but rather at the more humble level of the problems of the 'active life' and the recurrent Renaissance duty of 'serving the prince'. This is the main thread, though other aphorisms are directed towards the problems of authority in other spheres—the judge giving decisions (nos. 17, 23, 25), the relationships within a family and servants (nos. 2, 7, 9, 22) or between friends (nos. 26, 27, 29, 33).

When we consider the form of this 'Example of the Doctrine concerning Scattered Occasions' in relation to the other works, it seems that, out of the many facets of the aphorism available to him, Bacon was content to take one or two according to the occasion. In the scientific works he stressed its disconnected, anti-systematic (or rather presystematic) quality, and its suitability for containing observation; in the civil and political spheres, he valued its easily applicable flexibility (although ultimately here too it was going to help to form a system) and its direct relationship to observed human experience, mainly in the well-defined context of Renaissance politics. So in the second part of the discussion of 'Negotiation' in Book 8, concerning 'the Knowledge of Advancement in Life', Bacon handles it in 'heads or passages', 'precepts, some summary, and some scattered or various': and, though these separate precepts are just as much in the tradition of princes and policy as the first part (they contain even more aphorisms from Tacitus), like them they are not 'pithy': thus we have the paradox that of Bacon's aphorisms—according to the usual modern definition of the word—the majority are not aphoristic.

In my preliminary definition of the aphorism I excluded the *sententia* because such proverbs or quotations, although pithy, do not automatically have the pregnancy or the authority belonging to aphorisms. But it may be necessary to include the *sententia* while discussing Bacon's actual practice, for there is one section of the *De Augmentis* which does conform to our stylistic expectations of the genre, that part of the discussion of Rhetoric in Book 6 which is devoted to providing a '*Promptuary* or Preparatory Store' for the writer or speaker, a collection of commonplaces arranged *pro* and *con*: 'Antitheses of Things' (4. 472 ff.). This section consists of sentences juxtaposed on some forty-odd topics; though ostensibly 'For' and 'Against' they are actually often complementary, and their value for us consists not in their juxtaposition but in the fact that the individual 'sentences' are essentially aphorisms. The description which Bacon gives to the *sententiae* shows their affinity with the aphorism; he thought that

the best way of making such a collection, with a view to use as well as brevity, would be to contract those commonplaces into certain acute and concise sentences; to be as skeins or bottoms of thread which may be unwinded at large when they are wanted. (4. 472.)

So he sums up the collection, rather deprecatingly but quite consistently, as being '*seeds* only, not *flowers*' (4. 492). In these images we have, stated in a fresh way, the quality of pregnant applicability which he has elsewhere assigned to the aphorism: but we find mentioned for the first time, I think, the criterion of stylistic pithiness, and from Bacon's many applications of the form, now only in a rhetorical or literary context.

Many of the *Antitheta rerum* are used in (or are quoted from) his most literary-looking work, the *Essays*, and this is significant when we consider that it is largely in the *Essays* that Bacon's aphorisms have, in addition to their other Renaissance qualities, that pithiness which has been undiscriminatingly assigned to his style as a whole. These Antitheses are the bare bones of argument, and conform to this potential of the genre in that they are condensed to a point beyond which it is impossible to go (comparison with their use in the *Essays* would show how even more condensed they are here). At times this condensation verges on the paradoxical:

Seldom comes nobility from virtue; seldomer virtue from nobility. (473.)

And throughout, besides their density, they depend on a variety of literary methods, as do those of Lichtenberg. The example above depended, for the shape which intensified its meaning, on the rhetorical figure *antimetabole*; this one on a similar hinge-like device of repetition, still more condensed:

Dissimulation invites dissimulation. (485.)

Others are based on imagery, sometimes in the more expanded form of the simile, which postpones its wit:

Constancy is like a surly porter; it drives much useful intelligence from the door. (481.)

Here we perceive the force of the image first, while the actual relationship between it and the meaning arrives only afterwards, and with an added shock ('so inconstancy is really more *useful...*'). The teasing effect of ambiguity present there can be conveyed by the more immediate equation of metaphor:

A jest is the orator's altar. (487.)

—there is considerable condensation there, demanding expansion, but this should be given its translation and applications in the mind of the reader. As with Dr Stern's analysis of similar effects in Lichtenberg, to paraphrase the aphorism would be to limit it to one meaning: 'I hate those men of one thought' (487). Very few of the aphorisms depend on literary references, but one that does has considerable force in describing a perversion of nature:

Some persons have wished for Priam's fortune, who survived all his children. (474.)

Others depend on simple observation, as this in a universal sphere (and with a surprising sequence of actions):

Without a good space of life a man can neither finish, nor learn, nor repent. (477.)

—or this in a more particular one, which the academic reader may still read with some discomfort:

Almost all scholars have this—when anything is presented to them, they will find in it that which they know, not learn from it that which they know not. (483.)

There are many other such impressive 'acute and concise sentences', and if Bacon were to be judged as a 'pure' aphorist on the evidence of this collection alone he would not be disgraced.

But this 'Promptuary' was designed for use, and if we turn lastly to the *Essays* we can see how the aphorism is used in context. Obviously the 1597 volume represents the nearest Bacon comes to communicating his observation of man and society in 'pure' aphorisms: the disparate nature of the structure is emphasised by the presence of paragraph signs (¶) separating off new aspects of each topic. But these are used for new sections, not always for separate aphorisms, and even at this condensed level there is a difference between the most tightly knit aphorisms and more diffuse, explicit sentences. The less condensed sections often begin with 'it is a good precept' or 'It is good', and, though they fulfil the function of being 'seeds' for future behaviour in that they contain valuable advice, stylistically they are not sufficiently 'acute and concise' to create an imaginative spark. Generally speaking, there is not as much serious wit here as in the later versions, and even the most condensed aphorisms lack something:

The honourablest part of talke is to guide the occasion, and againe to moderate and passe to somewhat else. (6. 526.)

To use too many circumstances ere one come to the matter is wearisome, to use none at all is blunt. (*Ibid.*)

Riches are for spending, and spending for honour and good actions. (530.)

Discreete followers helpe much to reputation. (532.)

It is commonly seene that men once placed, take in with the contrarie faction to that by which they enter. (533.)

These are all sound observations, ethically unexceptionable, but rather static—one is tempted to apply to them Bacon's own criticism, that 'Reading good books of morality is a little flat and dead' (6. 441). Only a few have any pregnant discrimination in the thought, such as

If you dissemble sometimes your knowledge of that you are thought to knowe, you shall bee thought another time to know that you know not. (526.)

He that hath a state to repaire may not despise small things; and commonly it is lesse dishonourable to abridge pettie charges than to stoupe to pettie gettings. (530.)

And only one of them uses any imaginative resources:

Some mens behaviour is like a verse wherein every sillable is measured. (527.)

Despite the success of the 1597 *Essays* (they were reprinted in 1598, 1604, and 1606) Bacon was not satisfied with them, and produced new, expanded editions in 1612 and 1625. His main motive was undoubtedly that of increasing the coverage of their appropriate fields (a manuscript version of between 1607 and 1612 is entitled 'The writings of Sir Francis Bacon...in Moralitie, Policie, and Historie'; 6. 535) including those which he had noted as deficient, but a subsidiary motive may have been a dissatisfaction with the overtly disconnected structure, perhaps because he feared making the same error as the Stoics, 'who thought to thrust virtue upon men by sharp disputations and conclusions, which have no sympathy with the will of man' (3. 410; in the *De Augmentis* this is expanded to read 'concisis et argutis sententiis et conclusionibus', 'concise and sharp maxims and conclusions': cf. 1. 672, 4. 456). At all events the two later versions look to be more coherent, and, although Bacon has not systematically tied every sentence together, the style is certainly more fluent, being that of his normal discourse. The aphorism is now in a definite minority amongst other literary aids—in fact, to one looking for admissibly condensed sentences it is hard to see how Bacon's style was ever thought to be 'aphoristic' (I hope I have incidentally scotched that error, as well as providing a more positive account of the status of this genre in the Renaissance). But, if in a minority, the aphorism does have a valuable function in many individual contexts— indeed its role here is often to clinch an argument, either as the summing-up of a particular sequence, or by providing an appeal to general experience, and so its force can only be appreciated by quoting the whole context. An example of the first type is that section in 'Of Truth' where Bacon discusses why 'men should love lies', and presents his answer first in two remarkably sensitive images, which are then summed up in an aphorism:

But I cannot tell: this same truth is a naked and open day-light that doth not shew the masks and mummeries and triumphs of the world, half so stately and daintily as candle-lights. Truth may perhaps come to the price of a pearl, that sheweth best by day; but it will not rise to the price of a diamond or carbuncle, that sheweth best in varied lights. *A mixture of a lie doth ever add pleasure.* (6. 377; my italics.)

Here the whole effect of the aphorism is created by placing this subtle psychological observation in a context where it will exert the maximum argumentative force: partly in terms of the transition from the expansive, elliptical, imaginative plane of the metaphors to the limited dimension of the statement which they are illuminating; and partly by the change from a flowing syntactical movement to the suddenly bare, precise, present-tense statement.

A similar use of stylistic contrast, though not quite so abrupt, is provided by the second way of placing an aphorism in the context of an argument, the appeal to universal experience. So in 'Of Unity in Religion', Bacon distinguishes 'two false peaces or unities', and condenses his rational argument on each point with a highly compressed reference:

There be also two false peaces or unities: the one, when the peace is grounded but upon an implicit ignorance; *for all colours will agree in the dark*: the other, when it is pieced up upon a direct admission of contraries in fundamental points. For truth and falsehood, in such things, are like the iron and clay in the toes of Nebuchadnezzar's image; *they may cleave, but they will not incorporate.* (383; my italics.)

The reader would have doubtless agreed with Bacon that these two 'false peaces' are deplorable even before he produced those two crushing references to physical phenomena: now the argument is buttressed by the immutable, predictable laws of nature, and the critic is left trying to analyse just how the effect of finality is produced—I think that the imaginative and syntactical condensation of the aphorism is the crucial factor. In more instances than can be dealt with here, the force of an aphorism depends to a great degree on its context and on its power to act as a sudden flash of illumination. However, there are sufficient aphorisms which stand alone for us to be able to distinguish some of the recurrent forms.[1] One of the most condensed is that which proposes a '*regola generale*', in the properly dispassionate Machiavellian manner, often built on an antithesis:

A man that hath no virtue in himself, ever envieth virtue in others. (393.)

There is in human nature generally more of the fool than of the wise. (402.)

...for there is rarely any rising but by a commixture of good and evil arts. (406.)

There is nothing makes a man suspect much, more than to know little. (454.)

(Of 'Great persons') For they are the first that find their own griefs, though they be the last that find their own faults. (399.)

These predictions built on the empirical observation of men are indisputable (with the possible exception of the third), and act as cool frictionless fulcrums around which an argument can turn with some certainty. But, though they are very efficient, they have not the imaginative force which makes us want to return to them.

If this most concise group of dispassionate observations lacks force, the same could be said of those aphorisms in which Bacon expresses a more positive ethical attitude (this is an aspect of his work which is commonly ignored, but I think that an unbiased analysis would show a constant and non-ambivalent dependence on traditional ethics). In such ethical principles as 'clear and round dealing is the honour of man's nature' (378), or: 'Of great riches there is no real use, except it be in the distribution; the rest is but conceit' (460), or: 'Therefore, as atheism is in all respects hateful, so in this, that it depriveth human nature of the means to exalt itself above human frailty' (415), although the idea is admirable we miss the illumination or the tension of compression felt elsewhere. But Bacon can produce these qualities in this ethical sphere, and when he does so it is mainly by using imagery. So, after quoting Montaigne, he sums up the gist of the quotation not in the language of statement, but by condensing the image:

For a lie faces God, and shrinks from man. (379.)

—and by this personification of the Janus-faced nature of deceit he achieves a crossing of planes which cannot be paraphrased without distortion. Again he describes human selfishness with great contempt:

It is a poor centre of a man's action, *himself*. It is right earth. (432.)

—and the second sentence forces us to return to the first, to realise that 'centre' has a specific astronomical meaning, and so we come back to the second to see that 'earth' combines both scientific and moral dimensions—'Our dungy earth alike / Feeds beast as man.' It is this ability to embody his vision in concrete imagery that above all else makes Bacon such a stimulating writer, and gives force and edge to many aphorisms:

...for boldness is an ill keeper of promise. (402.)

For envy is a gadding passion, and walketh the streets, and doth not keep home. (393.)

Long and curious speeches are as fit for dispatch, as a robe or mantle with a long train is for race. (435.)

This last example also shows Bacon's tendency to postpone the wit of the aphorism until the very end—like a Ciceronian period the sense (and the penetration) is only completed by the full stop, as in this witty observation on the psychology of the professional soldier:

And generally, all warlike people are a little idle, and love danger better than travail. (448.)

The effect of surprise produced by this postponement may be seen in a slightly different form here:

A single life doth well with churchmen; for charity will hardly water the ground where it must first fill a pool. (392.)

The movement of that aphorism is broken at the semicolon, and in the two interdependent parts the image is as necessary as the pure statement—one explicates the other. This double movement is very characteristic of the aphorisms in the *Essays*, and is seen at its simplest in this example:

It is as natural to die as to be born; and to a little infant, perhaps, the one is as painful as the other. (380.)

There Bacon did not need imagery, but developed his first condensed point by a simple afterthought which at the same time expanded it and added a new idea. But often we find him using a highly condensed image which is then 'opened':

This is certain, that a man that studieth revenge keeps his own wounds green, which otherwise would heal and do well. (385.)

The sense there was complete before the 'which', but Bacon risks the danger of anticlimax for the advantage of an explicitness which will underline the observation. Or again, where the first half needs the second to gloss it:

He that hath wife and children hath given hostages to fortune; for they are impediments to great enterprises either of virtue or mischief. (391.)

Elsewhere the relationship between the two parts is not quite as linear as this, but more tangential:

Revenge is a kind of wild justice; which the more man's nature runs to, the more ought law to weed it out. (384.)

Besides (to say truth) nakedness is uncomely, as well in mind as body; and it addeth no small reverence to men's manners and actions, if they be not altogether open. (388.)

In this group the second point is connected to the first, but moves off in a new direction. The angle between the tangents can widen to become paradoxically opposed, even though the repeated forms look alike:

Children sweeten labours; but they make misfortunes more bitter. They increase the cares of life; but they mitigate the remembrance of death. (390.)

As these examples show, Bacon creates a variety of subtle effects with this 'two-part aphorism', particularly a sort of eddying movement which spreads the thought out from one centre to another: though he misses the force and sting of the epigrammatic aphorism, he produces a much more thought-provoking effect. As ever 'form' is at the service of 'content'.

That last-quoted antithesis leads us to the final aspect of the aphorism in the *Essays* which I want to discuss, though it means some anticipation, and that is the use of syntactical symmetry. In several of the examples cited here Bacon falls into a movement in which the often precise syntactical equality of the parts highlights still further whatever thought or image is being used. A simple example is this definition by division:

Men in great place are thrice servants: servants of the sovereign or state; servants of fame; and servants of business. (398.)

There the exactly parallel structure puts a direct emphasis on the three aspects distinguished: 'state: fame: business'. Less precise, but more complex in its uniting of precept and image through the juxtaposition of active and passive, is this:

Be not penny-wise; riches have wings, and sometimes they fly away of themselves, sometimes they must be set flying to bring in more. (462.)

A similar combination of image and the 'two-part' form is given more sharpness by the symmetry:

One foul sentence doth more hurt than many foul examples. For these do but corrupt the stream, the other corrupteth the fountain. (507.)

Finally an aphorism which in addition to being 'useful for life' combines pithiness and precision, fluent and fully realised imagery, the postponement of sense creating tension and release, all given point by the symmetrical structure, and the whole proceeding from a frame of mind not popularly ascribed to Bacon but which was undoubtedly there, and here superbly expressed:

> For a crowd is not company;
> and faces are but a gallery of pictures;
> and talk   but a tinkling cymbal,
>   where there is no love.
>   (437.)

CHAPTER 4

SYNTACTICAL SYMMETRY

If discussion of the aphorism has been lacking in modern criticism, the reverse is true of syntactical symmetry. Indeed, it could be said that no approach to the study of prose has been more assiduously cultivated than that through the measurement of quantity and stress: rhythm, periodic structure, clause-length. Perhaps because it lends itself easily to a purely factual, statistical, non-imaginative interest, this method has been highly developed (often without any consideration of the relationship between structure and meaning), and at the expense of more valuable literary approaches, such as (most obviously) that through imagery. There are at least a dozen major works of modern scholarship which discuss Greek and Latin prose largely on the basis of rhythm and structure,[1] and in the criticism of English prose the nineteenth-century application of classical techniques to the vernacular (which resulted in the laborious 'pedal-system' scansion of George Saintsbury's *History of English Prose Rhythm* (1912)—a method which, as Patrick Wilkinson has well said, 'can dissect anything but explain nothing')[2] has given way to the influential work of M. W. Croll and George Williamson, which pays less attention to rhythm but more to structure, and especially the question of symmetry. The dominance of such purely structural approaches is not only due to unimaginative scholarship, for although it ignores important aspects of prose as a literary form it does at least consider one facet to which prose-writers themselves drew attention. As the nature of Bacon's relationship to the tradition of symmetrically structured prose will be of some importance, it may be well to outline briefly how this tradition developed.[3]

Syntactical Symmetry

I

The structural possibilities of prose were first seen in fifth-century Greece: Thrasymachus is said to have introduced period and 'colon', as well as rhythm, while Gorgias was given the credit for applying in prose rhetorical figures which had previously been used for, and thought peculiar to, poetry. These figures were not 'tropes' (the figures which involve a change of meaning, such as metaphor) but 'schemes', *schemata verborum*, the arrangement of words into patterns, visual and aural. The main figures were all based on parallelism—either of sense (*antithesis*) or of structure, and are usually found in consecutive clauses or sentences (I mean 'consecutive' in the sense of 'immediately following', not with the connotations of Greek and Latin grammar, the 'so that' construction). The most frequently used figures would seem to be: (i) *parison*, corresponding structure in consecutive clauses (i.e. noun matching noun, verb with verb, or even with the same word occurring in the same place in each); (ii) *isocolon*, where the clauses are of the same length; (iii) *antimetabole*, corresponding structure with inversion (i.e. instead of the *a, b, c; a, b, c,* pattern of *parison*, now *a, b, c; c, b, a*); (iv) *paromoion*, where corresponding parts of consecutive clauses rhyme internally (if the rhyme is at the end of the clauses, it is known as *homoioteleuton*); (v) *anaphora*, the same word at the start of consecutive clauses, and (vi) *epistrophe*, the same word at the end. All these devices of repetition work to produce a simple structure, noticeable to the ear in terms of echo-effects, and to the eye—reading the printed page—in terms of vertical and lateral symmetries. Such devices of parallelism and antithesis sharpened by sound-effects are found in Greek poetry, as Edward Norden has shown in his authoritative study—in Homer, in Empedocles, in the Tragedians (in such formal details as the correspondence of strophe and antistrophe), and in Greek prose before Gorgias, from Heraclitus onwards, and in areas which Gorgias could not have influenced, such as Ionic prose: Herodotus in his *History* uses the figures for the more elevated sections, such as the speeches. But there can be no doubt about the influence of the Gorgianic figures on Attic prose (although Gorgias' own tendency towards extremely short rhythmic clauses was not generally imitated), for Norden has convincingly demonstrated the presence of rhetorical symmetries—though with individual variations of style—in Thucydides (despite his love of brevity), in Xenophon, in the orators (with very careful but over-regular patterning in Isocrates, and with just as much deliberate artistry but more intellectual control and variety in Demosthenes),[1] and even in Epicurus, a writer famous for his 'unrhetorical' simplicity. Finally, in the decline of Greek rhetoric into the florid, emotional, bombastic 'Asiatic' style of the third and second centuries the Gorgianic figures persist, but depraved into excessively repetitious parallelism of short clauses and flabby rhythms—a decline which produced a counter-reaction in the consciously archaic 'Atticist' movement of the first century B.C.

The development of symmetry in Latin prose follows an analogous pattern of growth from crudity to fluency, the period of artistic fulfilment being succeeded by counter-movements directed towards a plainer style, formed either of groups consciously reacting against the dominant mode or of a great writer acting alone, such as Sallust or Tacitus, who seem to have consciously avoided rhythmic or symmetrical effects. Indeed, a very similar movement (up to fluency and down to reactionary plainness) could be traced in English prose from 1500 to 1700, say—and, if we consider the parallel and the form that the reaction took in each period, then we should see the importance of not judging a writer or a movement from the viewpoint of any one phase of it and particularly not from what the enemy say about it, as some critics have done, who view Cicero from the position of a Seneca or a Tacitus, or who see Bacon through the eyes of Glanvill or Dryden (this fault is less common: Bacon's style is usually equated with post-Royal-Society style, on the grounds that he was responsible for their reform of language—a wild judgment, even granted the usual confusions about Bacon the writer). Each writer, like each phase, must be judged in terms of his literary use of the traditions within which he chooses to work—it will not do to dismiss Cicero, particularly after Norden has shown the fragmentation of form and content in his Latin predecessors (Nepos dominated by antithesis, excessively fond of alliteration; Caesar cool, factual, using only the simplest rhetorical figures). Compared with such extreme gaps between style and subject-matter Cicero's union of all the resources of rhetoric with an incisive mind in full control of a great variety of knowledge must be counted a major achievement.

The earlier speeches, naturally enough, display an immature use of the externals of rhetoric, the repetition of certain stylistic tricks in a way which almost justifies the criticism 'Asiatic'; but the mature mode is characteristically one where the symmetries of the syntax re-create the movement of the thought:

> Soleo saepe ante oculos ponere,
> idque libenter crebris usurpare sermonibus,
> omnes nostrorum imperatorum,
> omnes exterarum gentium potentissimorumque populorum,
> omnes regum clarissimorum res gestas
> cum tuis nec contentionum magnitudine
> > nec numero proeliorum
> > nec varietate regionum
> > nec celeritate conficiendi
> > nec dissimilitudine bellorum posse conferri,
> > nec vero disiunctissimas terras citius passibus
> > > cuiusquam potuisse peragrari,
> > > quam tuis non dicam cursibus,
> > > sed victoriis lustratae sunt.[1]

The rhetorical figures used there recur throughout the tradition of symmetrical prose: *anaphora* (like beginnings—'omnes...omnes', 'nec...nec'), *homoioteleuton*, in which Latin is so rich ('-orum'; '-end*i*', 'conferr*i*'; '-ibus'; with *paromoion*, internal rhyme—'varietate...celeritate'), many subtle echo-effects (especially the alliteration on 'c', 'p' and 's' in the last few lines), and running through the sentence the two large sequences of *parison*, corresponding structure, reducing to its pithiest equality (*isocolon*) before swelling out into the final resolution of syntax and sense. Such deliberately artistic prose could hardly be expected to please the Atticists with their call for simplicity and conciseness, and Cicero's great achievements were soon belittled by them.

However, from the point of view of syntactical symmetry this revolution in style was not as significant as its leaders might have us think, for, although the triumph of the 'New Style' in the declamation schools led to an enormous vogue for *sententiae* and all short, pointed forms of speech, Norden has shown only too clearly that the style of one of the most representative documents of this school, the *Controversiae* of Seneca the Elder, is characterised above all by antithesis, sometimes merely an opposition of thought, but mostly made syntactically clear by using *isocolon, parison, paromoion* and *homoioteleuton*:

> lege damnata est: habetis iudicium
> deiecta est: habetis exemplum (1. 3. 6)

or by the favourite symmetrical device of *tricolon*:

> damnata est quia incesta erat,
> deiecta est quia damnata erat,
> repetenda est quia et incesta et damnata et deiecta est.
> (1. 3. 2; Norden, pp. 288–90.)

In fact New 'Attic' is but Old 'Asiatic' writ small (Norden, p. 299)—for although it has abandoned the length, copiousness and expansive movement of a Ciceronian period it still depends for its effects on repetition and parallelism: it is symmetrical, but on a smaller scale—and, indeed, the smallness of the gap between the various syntactical parts only draws more attention to the symmetry.[1] Again, the most contentious leader of the new style, Seneca the Younger, who was constantly attacking other people's styles (sometimes for faults which he displayed himself) yet whose self-consciously tidy brevity has made Norden question his sincerity,[2] is certainly characterised by small, highly pointed clauses and periods (*minutissimae sententiae*, as Quintilian called them) but also by the arrangement of these packed 'points' into sharply antithetical, parallel groups, as in the conclusion to *Epistle* 10, which in addition to the usual symmetries adds a form of

antimetabole (hominibus–deus; deo–homines) and matching verbs
(vive–videat; loquere–audiant):

> vide ergo ne hoc praecipi salubriter possit:
> sic vive cum hominibus, tamquam deus   videat;
> sic loquere cum deo,   tamquam homines audiant.

That mathematically precise balance could not be improved on,
however at variance it is with the tenets of the New Style—but
this is not the first time that a movement's manifesto has been
belied by its produce.

The studies of Norden and Polheim trace an unbroken continuity in symmetrical and rhymed prose from the Roman Empire
through medieval Latin to medieval German, and to the Renaissance vernaculars. Once this is appreciated, there is no need to
summarise the development of the tradition beyond this arche-
typal opposition of styles, 'Senecan' against 'Ciceronian', New
against Old. But it is perhaps enlightening to quote a few
examples of the persistence of the symmetries, which conformed
mainly to the fullness of the Ciceronian norm. The most famous
examples of symmetrical structure outside classical Latin are
perhaps the *Sermons* of St Augustine, as this excerpt with its
intricate cross-rhymes testifies:

> Si consideretur in ista passione humana patientia,
> incipit esse incredibilis;
> si agnoscatur divina potentia,
> desinit esse mirabilis.
> Tanta grassabatur crudelitas in Martyris corpore,
> et tanta tranquillitas proferebatur in voce,
> tantaque poenarum asperitas saeviebat in membris,
> et tanta   securitas sonabat   in verbis.[1]

Almost comparable complexity is shown in England, three
centuries later, in Bede's sermon on the Annunciation:

> Nec se tamen de singularitate meriti excellentioris
>   singulariter   extollit,
>   sed potius suae conditionis
>   ac divinae dignationis in omnibus memor,

famularum se Christi consortio humiliter adjungit,
famulatum   Christo devota quod jubetur inpendit.[1]

In Renaissance Latin, symmetrical structure is handled with great dexterity by John Rainolds, lecturing at Oxford in the 1570s and perhaps provoking Lyly to Euphuism:

Quamobrem
vt videmus herbam Anthemidem, quo magis deprimitur, eo latius diffundi,
vt accepimus arborem Palmam   quo grauius oneratur, eo fortius reniti;
vt ager Narniensis authore *M. Tullio* siccitate sit humidior;
vt ignis in Nymphaeo, quemadmodum tradit *Plinius*, imbribus fit ardentior;
vt Leo si vulneretur instat ferocius;
Antaeus postquam deijcitur, pugnat violentius,
        unguentum cum agitatur olet fragrantius,
        aromata cum atteruntur, spirant odoratius:
ita nobis (*Adolescentes Charissimi*) faciendum est, vt in virtutis cursu
        quo magis retardamur,
        eo   magis incitemur.[2]

In English prose of the sixteenth century the same essentially Ciceronian—or Gorgian—symmetries are found in abundance (Euphuism is merely a highly stylised version of this tradition, with its own conventions). To take a few examples, we find them constantly in the vernacular of Sir Thomas More, as in this passage from *The Four Last Things*, which argues that envy, in addition to all its other evils, is also a futile vice because the human object of envy is just as prone to death or disaster as the envier: 'If it so were that thou knowest a great duke', living in princely splendour admired of all men, then

If thou shouldest suddenly be surely advertised that for secret treason
lately detected to the King, he should undoubtedly
                be taken to-morrow,
                his court all broken up,
                his goods seized,
                his wife put out,
                his children disherited,
                himself cast in prison,
                        brought forth and arraigned,
                        the matter out of question,

> and he should be condemned,
>> his coat armour reversed,
>> his gilt spurs hewen off his heels,
>> himself hanged, drawn and quartered:
> how thinkest thou by thy faith amid thine envy
>> shouldest thou not suddenly change into pity?[1]

There symmetry not only clarified the thought but by its climactic growth acted out a parallel movement to that in the sense. On a smaller scale, sharper, and more pedagogic, are the distinctions drawn by Ascham on precocious intelligences:

> Quicke wittes commonlie, be apte to take,
>> unapte to keepe:
> soone hote and desirous of this and that:
> as cold and sone weary of the same againe:
> more quicke to enter spedelie,
>> than liable to pearse farre...
> [they] either liue obscurelie, men know not how,
>> or dye obscurelie, men marke not whan.[2]

These are two examples from thousands: 'Ciceronian' or 'Gorgian' symmetries are used by all the major prose-writers of the traditional Renaissance school at every literary level: Lyly, Sidney; Lodge, Greene, Nashe; Gabriel Harvey, Raleigh, Hooker; Shakespeare, and many others.

But in fifteenth- and sixteenth-century Europe, forces opposing the traditional style began to develop, in a rather similar way, and with rather similar effects, to the Attic versus Asiatic controversy in Greece and Rome. There is a difference, though: the Atticists were self-conscious purists who were trying to revive a primitive purity and plainness to combat what seemed to them to be the decadence of Greek rhetoric following its diffusion through Asia— Cicero was only a subsidiary target; in the Renaissance the 'Anti-Ciceronian' movement is again not directed against Cicero himself, but rather against his fanatical imitators. However, the two controversies are uncomfortably close in the absolute vagueness of their concepts of style. The 'Atticists' were marching under a slogan which was formulated ostensibly on stylistic grounds, but more on a mixture of patriotism and moral disapproval (like those Victorian philologists who elevated something called 'English' prose of the Middle Ages and Renaissance against foreign or classical influences).[1] Thus they attacked Cicero, and with him Asianism, by describing his prose style in images drawn from the human body and its degree of fitness, and he replied (in the *Brutus* mainly, but also in the *Orator*) in the same terms, as Tacitus records:

Clearly, even Cicero had his detractors who thought him swollen and turgid, not succinct enough, far too exuberant and copious, in fact, not Attic enough. You have surely read the letters Calvus and Brutus sent to Cicero; from these one can gather easily enough that Cicero considered Calvus bloodless and thin (*exsanguem et attritum*) and Brutus tedious and disjointed (*otiosum atque disiunctum*) while Calvus criticized Cicero as loose and flabby (*solutum et enervem*) and Brutus called him—to quote his own words—'feeble and emasculated' (*fractum atque elumbem*).[2]

However the mere exchanging of insults (to which so much stylistic controversy has degenerated) tells us little about style: everyone here is speaking from a partisan base and cannot be taken literally. Although we have a rough idea of what 'Asiatic' style involved (and so can see how little Cicero conforms to it), nobody has yet formed a clear picture of what 'Attic' meant (it would have to be a definition by negatives), and the whole controversy must be regarded as sterile—and, in Norden's view, ultimately destructive.[3]

This whole controversy seems to have turned on loosely defined concepts of stylistic economy: Atticists are close, spare, lean, efficient; Asiatics copious, repetitive, bombastic, redundant —there is no discussion of rhetorical figures or symmetrical structure.[4] Precisely the same seems true of the Ciceronian controversy in the Renaissance—whenever 'style' is mentioned one finds the most extraordinary vagueness and confusion. For example, both Erasmus and Ortensio Landi record that Cicero's style has been criticised by some writers as being 'dry, jejune, sapless, bloodless, disjointed, weak and unmanly'. A more inaccurate account of Cicero's style could hardly be imagined, unless it be that of Étienne Dolet, arguing that he is really 'Attic'—or even 'Senecan':

Syntactical Symmetry

Everyone acknowledges that Cicero excels in *sententiae*. You say that Seneca ranks the Publian Mimes first in this. Seneca is a writer of little reputation. Cicero is certainly a better model for brevity than Brutus or Sallust. What is there in Brutus either of brevity or richness? And Sallust wrote history, where brevity was not essential.[1]

Even Julius Caesar Scaliger defended Cicero for his brevity, so we see that this radical confusion about the nature of style was not limited to minor figures. The only sensible stylistic criticism I have found is that of Erasmus, who made the acute point that anyone who sets out to imitate a style inevitably exaggerates it, and will fall into the vices to which the original is prone, but which, by its own internal economy, it avoids:

Thus those who aim at the Attic style become dry instead of clever and charming; at the Rhodian, diffuse; at the Asiatic, bombastic. Brevity is praised in the work of Sallust. Would there not be danger of becoming unduly concise and abrupt, if one should try to imitate this with painful precision? (Scott, 2, 55–6.)

So anyone imitating Cicero alone will be trapped into the faults basic to that kind of writing, but faults which the original himself escaped. Not only does Erasmus exclude Cicero from these faults but he goes out of his way (both here and in his *Letters*) to praise Cicero's style, as do even the two 'New Men' of the sixteenth century who each wrote a *Ciceronianus* attacking the cult, Ramus and—most fulsomely of all—Gabriel Harvey, who praises his eloquence as 'transcendental'.[2]

It is very important to see that the anti-Ciceronian controversy was little concerned with 'Ciceronian' symmetry or rhetoric (though Erasmus sometimes attacks the blind imitation of 'words, figures, rhythms'), but much more with the question of which Latin models the modern Latinist should imitate. The fanatical disciple, such as the character Nosoponus, whom Erasmus creates and beautifully mocks in his dialogue, the *Ciceronianus* (1528), would compile several notebooks from Cicero's work: one listing all the words Cicero ever used, another his special phrases, and a third would have 'all the metrical feet with which Cicero ever begins or ends his periods and their subdivisions, the rhythms which he uses in between and the cadences which he chooses for

each kind of sentence...' (Scott, 2, 24). He would then compose
something of his own, drawing on his notebook or on some
anthology which only used words or formations authorised by
Cicero (such a collection was in fact published in 1535, the
Observationes of Nizzoli, and had a remarkable popularity).
Erasmus's account is fictitious, but disciples did go to lunatic
extremes: Longueil, 'the Cicero of the North', took a vow to
read nothing but Cicero for five years, lest his style should be con-
taminated. Muret has a charming anecdote of how he noticed that
the 'Nizolian paper book' (as Sidney contemptuously called it)
actually omitted some words used by Cicero; accordingly he took
pains to use them in a piece of writing and showed it to the
Ciceronians, who shook their heads in disapproval; at which he
showed them their existence in the original text and they were
transformed to ecstasy and started using the words themselves. The
main issue, then, was whether such a fanatically narrow concept of
'imitation' was valid, and an increasingly violent body of literature asserted that it was not. There were subsidiary issues equally
close to the practical aspect of writing Latin, such as the inability
of a Ciceronian vocabulary to keep up with changes in social
structure, and particularly religion (the distortions brought in by
using Pagan Latin for Christian purposes are shown in a magnificent parody by Erasmus).[1] Whereas our sympathies may not be
with the Atticists, they are certainly with the anti-Ciceronians,
who led an entirely sensible reaction against the sectarian worship
of one style—and not for its rhetorical structure, but mainly for its
language, especially its vocabulary.

I have set out briefly what I take to be the salient features of this
controversy because in a series of influential articles[2] M. W. Croll
has placed Bacon's style within the anti-Ciceronian movement,
but has interpreted it in a very different light. Croll concentrates
mainly on the later stages of the movement (from 1575 to 1700)
and virtually ignores the whole controversy over the imitation of
Ciceronian Latinity, though it is obvious that several of the
writers he quotes are concerned with this problem.[3] Croll's major
interest is to link the anti-Ciceronian movement to the history of

ideas in the period, and he does this by forming the hypothesis that the movement is primarily a philosophical one. The anti-Ciceronians, led—we are told many times[1]—by Montaigne, Lipsius and Bacon, aided by Muret, represented the 'modern spirit of progress in revolt', 'l'esprit moderne', which is devoted to opposing the traditional orthodoxies in all fields; it is associated with the crises of doubt and rationalism (so Pascal, Burton and Sir Thomas Browne are involved too), with neo-Stoicism, with Ramus, with Libertine philosophy; its leaders share basically 'scientific interests', with a common dedication to 'realism'; their attack on traditional symmetry in style—in favour of a vivid, nervous asymmetrical movement—is part of the same movement of ideas which produces the energy and strain seen in the visual arts of the Baroque; it is a movement of the 'counter-Renaissance', following the 'progress of positive and sceptical modes of reasoning' which ultimately results in a triumph of 'acrid and virile realism'; and Croll himself is the 'historian of the positivistic movement in prose-style'.[2]

There certainly was such a movement in the history of ideas, as Hiram Haydn has shown so well, although Croll has widened it indiscriminately to include almost every progressive tendency in the period. And, though these reactions did occur, the links between some of the philosophical schools and anti-Ciceronianism (or Senecanism) seem slight—thus Croll himself mentions that three seventeenth-century writers of the 'curt' style are in fact anti-Stoic and anti-Senecan (*Baroque*, 436; *SRR*, 215). The guiding—and questionable—assumption is that a writer will reproduce the style of the philosophers or historians he admires, or that of the 'movement' to which he belongs: but there is no such one-to-one correlation.[3] Sir Walter Raleigh is intellectually in every respect one of the new sceptical rationalists, yet his prose style is as eloquently Ciceronian and symmetrical as any in English. Gabriel Harvey is equally a New Machiavellian and writes a treatise attacking Ciceronianism, but his Latin style is a tissue of Ciceronian tags, arranged into the traditional symmetries, with over half of the sentences ending in Cicero's favourite *clausulae*[4] (and his English style, one might add, is given—even when he is ranting—to an isometric Isocratean symmetry). Ramus is another 'novus homo', and certainly attacked the orthodox worship of Aristotle, Cicero and Quintilian—yet in his rhetoric, and in all those of his disciples, we find the most detailed Renaissance treatment of the *echt* Ciceronian topic of 'prose-numbers', the *clausulae*.[1] Such contradictions between theory and practice—such paradoxes that 'Bacon revered Tacitus' yet 'writes a prose akin to Euphuism'[2]— are a common feature of the Renaissance, as every student knows. It does not come as a surprise to find that in the 'New Style' Latin of the anti-Ciceronians quoted by Croll (although he says that they avoid symmetry and cultivate roughness) there are quite definite examples of rhetorical balance and figures of sound.[3]

But if in this critical hypothesis the connection between 'history of ideas' and prose style is questionable, still more so are the attitudes to prose structure and the theories based on them. Croll is certainly right in noticing deliberate asymmetry in some seventeenth-century writers (he does a good analysis of this effect in Pascal and Browne),[4] and his categories of the asymmetrical types can be usefully applied—quite directly to Ben Jonson, as the brilliant study by J. A. Barish has proved.[5] But his outline of the development of the Attic–Asiatic controversy is too general and removed from the classical sources (as is his account of 'Stoic style'), and on 'Attic' style he moves from being extremely vague (which is not surprising, given the blurred origin of this concept) to equating it with the *genus humile* (for which quite clearly defined and independent criteria exist).[6] Having seen that the classical controversy, in so far as it can be defined, was between 'copious' and 'brief' concepts of style, he shows that the same concepts were revived in the Renaissance (as we have seen) but goes on to argue that the anti-Ciceronians were also opposing Cicero's use of symmetrical syntax; that is to say that having shown that some of them write asymmetrical prose he ascribes to them theoretical reasons for so doing. However, there seems very little evidence for this: Muret calls for a new style based on purity of idiom, terseness, and aptness, yet he does not attack symmetry. Lipsius actually praises Cicero for having transmitted the traditional techniques:

Mais, dans les conditions actuelles, qui nous a enseigné nos périodes, nos constructions et nos rythmes et l'art d'enchaîner le discours, si ce n'est Cicéron?

And, though Croll says that the anti-Ciceronians 'constantly assert' that the legitimate means of attaining persuasion is 'not by the sensuous appeal of oratorical rhythm', the two mid-seventeenth-century French rhetoricians who are quoted to substantiate this crucial point (in itself a paucity of evidence) either refer to the traditional ends of eloquence ('à prouver, à peindre et à toucher') or to the familiar concept of mimetic vividness ('une image vive et lumineuse', 'vive peinture'): the single reference to the process by which eloquence 'ne présente pas seulement les choses toutes nues, mais aussi les mouvements avec lesquels on les conçoit' is not enough to show any criticism of symmetry.[1]

This is the most significant feature of Croll's thesis, the assumption that the anti-Ciceronians were consciously reacting against a 'rhetorical formalism', 'une manière conventionnelle et vide dans le rhétorique',—in itself probably true, but which he then limits to that of symmetry, and which he then proceeds to attack. He believes that the new style by its asymmetry recorded 'exactly those athletic movements of the mind by which it arrives at a sense of reality and the true knowledge of itself and the world', whereas the Ciceronian symmetry has a purely 'sensuous' appeal, designed for a popular audience (and here his prejudices come out most damagingly):

Its 'round composition' and the 'even falling of its clauses' do not always satisfy the inward ear of the solitary reader. Heard solely by the reflective mind, it is an empty, a frigid, or an artificial style. But it is not meant for such a hearing. It is addressed first, like music, to the physical ear; and the figures with which its large and open design are decorated have been devised with a reference to the attentive powers and the aural susceptibilities of large audiences, consisting of people of moderate intelligence...

These symmetries 'offer nothing that is pleasing to an intellect intent upon the discovery of reality', and so the anti-Ciceronian style 'is designed primarily and chiefly to express a dislike of these frivolities'. Indeed the Ciceronian style cannot in fact be 'reproduced in English, or indeed in any modern language', and those who attempt it court disaster: 'The ligatures of its comprehensive period are not found in the syntax of an uninflected tongue, and the artifices necessary to supply their function must produce either fantastic distortion or insufferable bombast.'

Such a sweeping criticism would of course devalue most of the world's greatest prose (or at least, most of that before 1600, say) and it seems clear that Croll has fallen into the trap of judging one phase of a movement from the standpoint of the reaction against it —he is a Senecan, speaking against all Ciceronians, but attacking them from a quite modern position. His objection (I think it is his own, for I find little evidence for it in this period) seems to be based on a quite simple 'representational' concept of style: if a sentence is symmetrical, then the thought is already planned, the end is known, and no further progress can be made; if it is asymmetrical, it can give the effect of spontaneity, of a mind twisting and turning, in the act of thought. Whereas prose of this latter kind certainly can create (or reproduce) such effects, I don't think it would have occurred to a Renaissance reader to object to symmetrical prose on these grounds—after all, as Lipsius says, Cicero 'has taught us' all we know about artistic prose, and it is a form of prose which has been written for two thousand years without this criticism being made. Croll seems to be judging from a nineteenth-or twentieth-century distrust of artifice and preference for the more obviously mimetic verse-movement of Donne or Hopkins, but this is not to say that verse which works within more regular conventions is therefore debarred from any 'exploratory' effects. And in any case the 'spontaneous' asymmetrical movement is just as much a product of conscious artifice, using such tricks as omitting grammatical connectives, deliberately reversing the subject–object order in consecutive sentences, setting up part of a symmetry and hence the reader's expectations that it will be fulfilled only to frustrate both—this is just as 'artificial' as the movement it is said to replace. Both styles are artistic conventions, with the difference that the 'Baroque' method makes a point of declaring its independence of an orthodoxy on which it is dependent for purposes of contrast, although it may ultimately be using comparably well-defined models (just like the professed originality or spontaneity of a Montaigne or a Sir Thomas Browne, which on closer inspection in many places turns out to be derived from Plutarch or Seneca). My objections on this head have been anticipated by Mr Barish:

One wonders, then, whether baroque writers were not misled, partly by abuses of Ciceronian style, partly by its origin in formal oratory, into thinking that it contained some intrinsic barrier to uninhibited thought; whether, tilting against the reader's expectations, they did not find themselves conducting campaigns of sabotage that involved more premeditation than the premeditated style they were warring against; whether, as a result, their own rhetoric is not parasitic in a peculiar way, unthinkable without the background of 'normal' Renaissance practice.[1]

But Bacon has anticipated modern critics on both issues. In the *Advancement* (in a passage to be discussed from the viewpoint of style later) he diagnosed unerringly the stylistic excesses of Ciceronian imitation, and then compiled his own list of offenders, who are made to seem more mechanical by the sentence structure linking them in identical fashion:

Then grew the flowing and watery vein of Osorius, the Portugal bishop, to be in price. Then did Sturmius spend such infinite and curious pains upon Cicero the orator and Hermogenes the rhetorician, besides his own books of periods and imitation and the like. Then did Car of Cambridge, and Ascham, with their lectures and writings, almost deify Cicero and Demosthenes, and allure all young men that were studious unto that delicate and polished kind of learning. Then did Erasmus take occasion to make the scoffing echo; *Decem annos consumpsi in legendo Cicerone,* (I have spent ten years in reading Cicero:) and the echo answered in Greek, *one, Asine* (thou ass!). Then grew the learning of the schoolmen to be utterly despised as barbarous. In sum, the whole inclination and bent of those times was rather towards copie than weight. (3. 283-4.)

That magisterial catalogue, with its contempt so concisely expressed in the epithets ('flowing and watery', 'curious pains', 'delicate and polished'), sums up the whole narcissistic process, and certainly entitles Bacon to be called an 'anti-Ciceronian'. His main objection is to the substitution of 'copie'—copiousness, fullness—for solid meaning, for 'weight' of thought, of which the style is the natural embodiment. Yet, when Bacon came to revise and expand the *Advancement* in 1623 for its translation into Latin, he added at this point a new paragraph which shows that he was perfectly aware of the vogue for 'Senecan' style, yet viewed it with the same reservations as he had had about Ciceronianism: 'weight' is lacking.

The paragraph is placed just after the attack on those who 'study words and not matter', which ends by predicting that 'the more industrious and severe inquirers into Truth...will despise those *Delicacies* and *Affectations*', and the addition reads as follows (in the Gilbert Wats translation of 1639):

Little better is that kind of stile (yet neither is that altogether exempt from vanity) which neer about the same time succeeded this *Copy* and *superfluity of speech*. The labour here is altogether, *That words may be aculeate, sentences concise, and the whole contexture of the speech and discourse, rather rounding into it selfe, than spread and dilated*: So that it comes to passe by this Artifice that every passage seemes more witty and waighty than indeed it is. Such a stile as this we finde more excessively in *Seneca*; more moderately in *Tacitus* and *Plinius Secundus*; and of late it hath bin very pleasing unto the eares of our time. And this kind of expression hath found such acceptance with meaner capacities, as to be a dignity and ornament to Learning; neverthelesse, by the more exact judgements, it hath bin deservedly despised, and may be set down as *a distemper of Learning*, seeing it is nothing else but a hunting after words, and fine placing of them.[1]

This is a remarkably accurate description of the Senecan style, both in its classical and Renaissance versions, and in its main criticism—'seemes more witty and waighty than indeed it is'—actually echoes the original descriptions of Senecanism—*plus significas quam loqueris; explicationes plus sensum quam verborum habentes* (Norden, pp. 310, 283). If more proof were needed that to be anti-Ciceronian was not necessarily to be Senecan, then the vigorous force of Bacon's attack would provide it: this style is to him also the product of 'vanity' and 'Artifice' and, even though it has pleased 'meaner capacities', by discerning critics it must be 'despised' as a disease of learning. And in his last criticism, that 'it is nothing else but a hunting after words, and fine placing of them', Bacon hits precisely the 'anti-Ciceronians'' deliberate calculation of stylistic effect which must weaken their claim to spontaneity. Although I do not want to fall into the error of judging Senecan style from a traditionally Ciceronian point of view, the objection to its self-conscious artifice does seem a strong one (in view of the spontaneity which is said to be its whole cause and aim), and to answer it one would have to consider, as Mr Barish suggests, 'whether in fact a process of thought has any verifiable reality apart from the words that incarnate it, and whether, if so, the irregular modes of syntax preferred by most of the anti-Ciceronians are necessarily any truer to thought, any more "natural", than the suspensions of the Ciceronians or the perfected antitheses of Euphism...'[1] But 'there is always an appeal from open criticism to nature'—I think a stronger objection to Croll's thesis would be obtained by confronting it with some examples of symmetrical prose in English. First, however, one confusion must be noticed, that between English and Latin syntax. Barish refers to the 'suspensions' of the Ciceronian style, and Croll to its 'ligatures' not existing in the syntax 'of an uninflected tongue'. Certainly English cannot hope to reproduce some of the complexities of Latin syntax, nor such rhetorical figures as *homoioptoton* (rhyme based on identical case-endings), nor of course the truly Ciceronian 'periodic' effect, by which the verb (and hence the meaning) is postponed to the very end of the sentence, and in which the writer should if possible put the verb into 'the perfect subjunctive and passive forms...for only in those forms of many verbs will he find the long penult required in most variations of the clausulae'.[2] But in actual practice few English Renaissance writers try to achieve these effects. There will be complex rhyming and cross-rhyming of course, and quite symmetrical series, but commonly the verb and subject will be at or near the beginning of the sentence, and the symmetries will be applied largely to the predicate and to the elaborations and distinctions within it.

In the sentence quoted above from Ascham, for example, the essential data for full appreciation of the continuation of the sentence are given by the first four words: 'Quicke wittes commonlie be...' and then the patterns begin to develop in full confidence that the reader is not held in suspense but ready to appreciate every turn and twist of the thought, every expected and unexpected return of sound, structure, and sense: 'apte to take, unapte to keepe;...more quicke to enter spedelie, than liable to pearse farre... [they] either live obscurelie, men know not how, or dye obscurelie, men marke not whan.'—In the first few clauses the balance was expected, to complete the sense, but in the last clause on the contrary the exact return of the symmetry was surely a surprise. In such structures the reader is in complete possession of the framework of argument from the beginning and can thus better appreciate the distinctions in the *thought* which are clearly conveyed by the sharpness of the parallelism and balance in the syntax. The sentence from Sir Thomas More (pp. 102–3) is actually nearer to Latin in its use of suspension, but we do not find it in any of the perverse artificialities which Croll's account would lead us to expect. This is partly due to the sequential progression of the argument within the framing suspension: 'If thou shouldest... how thinkest thou', the clear sequence of cause and effect (treason: punishment) in the first section being matched by the dramatic juxtaposition of human reactions in the second: 'envy: pity', and, although this juxtaposition is given more edge by its parallel terminal placing within the sentence, it cannot be said that the sense is wholly suspended until this point. We can almost guess what is coming, indeed the impressive effect of the sentence is to build up to an emotional climax, a movement which is wholly dependent on the parallel clauses listing the stages of punishment —here symmetry re-creates sense. To write such a sentence demands considerable skill, and I think that in this period the first form of simple predication is the most common, although I realise that without extensive analysis this point must be accepted as a hypothesis only. However, I cannot think of many examples in the Renaissance of a competent—let alone a great—English prose-writer creating ludicrously confused contortions because he wants to mimic a Ciceronian suspension.

The last objection to Croll's thesis must be to his very low estimate of symmetrical prose as an art-form. Setting aside his confusions of non-symmetry with naturalness and of convention with deceit, we are left with his description of this style as appealing only to the sensuous ear at a sub-intellectual level ('the aural susceptibilities of large audiences'), whereas, to 'the reflective mind, it is an empty, frigid, or an artificial style', its conventions of sound and structure are 'frivolities', and if used in English would produce 'either fantastic distortion or insufferable bombast'. This jaundiced estimate could be shown to be mistaken by quoting any number of examples which satisfy the reflective mind and the superior intellect. Is the passage quoted from Sir Thomas More frivolous or bombastic? What would the Senecan say about this sentence from Raleigh?—

> there is nothing more to be admired,
> and more to be lamented,
> than the private contention,
> the passionate dispute,
> the personal hatred,
> and the perpetuall warr, massacres and murthers,
> for Religion among *Christians*;
> the discourse whereof hath so occupied the World,
> as it hath well near driven
> the practice thereof out of the World.[1]

There in fact the main idea was held back, but when it did arrive the group of contemptuous parallel clauses had a still greater effect in retrospect. Surely no sensitive reader would dispute the excellence of that union of sound, structure, and sense, the one reinforcing and extending the other? Many examples could be quoted from English Renaissance prose, but I hope that the following account of Bacon's syntax will confirm both points that I have been trying to establish, that the use of structural symmetry in English is the direct continuity (subject to the language's limitations) of the traditional practices of Greece and Rome, and that such a style is—despite what anti-Ciceronians of all ages may have said—a perfectly valid exploitation of the resources of prose, and itself an art-form.

II

But before discussing Bacon's use of this artistic convention, it may be as well, if only for the sake of completeness, to review what the Senecan school of critics said about Bacon. Croll constantly associated Bacon with the anti-Ciceronian movement but seems to have referred to and quoted from his style only twice;[1] and in both cases the shape of his thesis seems to have blinded him to the presence of symmetry—so confirming Bacon's observation that 'men create oppositions which are not; and put them into new terms so fixed, as whereas the meaning ought to govern the term, the term in effect governs the meaning' (6. 383). In 1916 Croll wrote that Bacon uses antithesis 'without...similarity of sound between the opposed words or members', and 'usually avoids balance in its use', citing one example only, the aphorism 'Revenge is a kind of wild justice': of course, hundreds of exactly balanced antitheses could have been quoted instead (several have been seen here amongst the aphorisms). In 1929 he quoted, as an example of 'Baroque' prose, this sentence from the *Advancement of Learning*, which I set out spatially to make its structure clear:

For as knowledges are now delivered,	
there is a kind of contract of error between the deliverer	*A1*
and the receiver:	*B1*
for he that delivereth knowledge desireth to deliver it	*A2*
in such form as may be best believed,	(*i*)
and not as may be best examined;	
and he that receiveth knowledge desireth	*B2*
rather present satisfaction	(*i*)
than expectant inquiry;	
and so rather not to doubt	(*ii*)
than not to err:	
glory making the author not to lay open his weakness,	*A3*
and sloth making the disciple not to know his strength.	*B3*
	(3. 403–4)

It is remarkable that anyone even transcribing this passage should not have noted its precise patterning, but Croll takes the sentence, together with one by Pascal, as characteristic of the 'Baroque' and of its sub-category, 'the loose style', and his analysis tries to show that there are asymmetrical tendencies in Bacon, the only definite stylistic point being that the 'symmetrical development announced at the beginning' is 'interrupted' by a dependent member 'and cannot be resumed', so that the period is forced to 'find a way out', falling back on spontaneous conjunctions. But the symmetry is never interrupted: the initial antithesis (which I have marked as *A1, B1*) persists through the whole sentence, and at every stage we find almost complete symmetry of length (*isocolon*) and certainly exact correspondence between the respective parts (*parison*), even with a slight rhyme-effect on 'deliver*er*/receiv*er*, believ*ed*/ examin*ed*' (*homoioteleuton*). The only variation from the un-cannily exact pattern comes in the expansion of 'receiveth knowledge' (*B2*), where symmetry is maintained but in an unpredictable form, and with a consequent surprise extension of the thought in the distinctions between 'present satisfaction' and 'expectant inquiry' and the unforeseen possible disadvantages of both extremes—'rather not to doubt than not to err'. It is indeed a progression which, as Croll describes it, 'adapts itself to the movements of a mind discovering truth as it goes, thinking while it writes'—but it is pure English Ciceronian. A similar clash between critical theory and the text to which it is meant to refer comes when George Williamson briefly examines Bacon's style and finds uncomfortably more symmetry than his thesis would suggest.[1]

Whether or not Bacon used symmetrical syntax is a question of fact which is easily resolved: he did, throughout his life, for we find the traditional symmetries—if rather stiffly—in the very first letters of 1580 (8. 10–15) but at their richest ever in the early devices of the 1590s (8. 123–43, 332–42, 376–86), and with considerable density in a seminal scientific work, the *Valerius Terminus* (3. 215–52). The Ciceronian symmetries are found throughout his writing in English up to the end, even in the *New Atlantis* and *Henry VII*, where the demands of narrative and reported speech might seem to militate against such artistic effects.[2] So much is

soon shown—but how Bacon used these symmetries in a meaningful artistic way needs more discussion, which is perhaps most convincingly based on the best-known literary works, the *Advancement* and the *Essays*. We have already seen several examples of
symmetry from these works: the syntactical balancing within
many aphorisms in the *Essays*, the use of symmetry to clarify still
further the effects of *partitio* (as in the 1597 Essay 'Of Studies').
From the *Advancement* perhaps the most illuminating example is
that account of the nakedness of resources involved when using the
aphorism: for then

> discourse of illustration is cut off;
> recitals of examples are cut off;
> discourse of connexion and order is cut off;
> descriptions of practice are cut off;
> so there remaineth nothing to fill the Aphorisms but some good
> quantity of observation. (3. 405.)

This sequence illustrates both the traditional rhetorical techniques
(exact length, *isocolon*; exact structure, *parison*; the same word
ending consecutive clauses, *epistrophe*), and the uses to which they
are put. The main effect is one of clarity, as the repetition highlights the important parts of the thought: the very similar beginnings (in meaning) and endings (in form) of each clause put the
stress on the central words 'illustration', 'example', 'connexion
and order', 'practice'. But at the same time the similarity of
meaning between these develops, as the reader progresses, a feeling
of tautology, of pointless repetition which is heightened by the
equation of sense in the first part of each clause ('discourse',
'recitals', 'discourse', 'descriptions') and made more monotonous
by the return of the alliterated 'd' sounds. So the very form of the
prose is building up an effect which reproduces the thought—the
way in which a not very profound idea can be padded out by
repetitions and evasions—but at the same time it is engaged in
juxtaposing this deceiving bulk with the salutary effect of the
aphorism, as each clause runs down on to the sharp deflation of
being 'cut off'. And the final juxtaposition is achieved by breaking
the rhythm thus set up with the long clause 'so there remaineth . . .'

only to return to the same '*x* of *y*' structure which now embodies the density and honesty of the aphorism: 'quantity of observation'. So repetition and symmetry highlight meaning, re-create it in formal terms, and can achieve effects on this plane which the 'pure sense' alone could not.

There is not a page of the *Advancement of Learning* where syntactical symmetry does not unobtrusively further the meaning. The work begins, appropriately enough, with a rhetorical flourish as Bacon pays the requisite Renaissance compliments to the Prince: on the first page he lists James I's intellectual faculties with some straightforward symmetry—'the largeness of your capacity, the faithfulness of your memory . . .' (3. 261), but produces a much more brilliant effect to praise the King's manner of speech. He begins by evoking all the vices that characterise a servile speaker (a subject, not a ruler), and this point is expressed in appropriately heavy, clogged language, where the pattern merely emphasises the clumsiness: such faults as

> speech that is uttered with labour and difficulty, or
> speech that savoureth of the affection of arts and precepts, or
> speech that is framed after the imitation of some patterns of eloquence,
> though never so excellent.
>
> (262.)

In the last clause the deprecatory comment on unspontaneous, prepared speech is given extra point by the reinforcing balance of 'eloquence' and 'excellent'. Now, and by even sharper contrast to that account of clumsy, unnatural, unspontaneous speech comes Bacon's praise of the King himself, smooth, elegant, reinforcing the complete contrast by subtle alliteration and balance:

> But your Majesty's manner of speech is indeed prince-like,
> flowing as from a fountain, and yet
> streaming and branching itself into nature's order,
> full of facility and felicity,
> imitating none and inimitable by any.

The effect of this contrast is immediately apparent and hardly needs analysing, but it should be stressed how much deliberate artifice is required to achieve the triple balance of alliterated 'f' sounds in lines two and four (each occurring in alternate words), the further refinement in line 4 of 'facility and felicity', where the second word repeats the two outside sounds of the first, but inverts the two inside ones ('facil'–'felic'), and the double anti-thesis in the last line: these effects are a full exploitation of the resources of Ciceronian prose. We might note too how the mimetic reflection of meaning achieved by the juxtaposition of a clogged and a flowing movement in the two main sentences is re-echoed within the second one by following the condensed allitera-tion on 'f' by the smoother flow of 'streaming and branching', 'imitating none and inimitable by any'. As further examples of the use of syntactical symmetry in this section praising the king, one might consider the extremely complex opposition of the king's 'virtue' and 'fortune' through eight clauses (p. 262), the more finely chiselled praise of the King's learning (p. 263, with an appropriate and effective use of *epistrophe* on 'learning'), and the final elevation of James to the divine triplicity of King, Priest, and Philosopher (263).

But structural symmetry is not reserved for polite flattery. Bacon uses it whenever it will clarify or extend communication, as to propose the overall division of the work: here we can also see his fondness of using word-pairs, particularly for any solemn or weighty matter (the pairs of words are not tautologous, there being usually some subtle complementary distinction between them). The work will consist of two parts,

the former concerning the excellency of learning and knowledge,
and the excellency of the merit and true glory
in the augmentation and propagation thereof;
the latter, what the particular acts and works are which
have been embraced and undertaken for the advancement of learning,
and again what defects and undervalues I find in such particular acts...

(263–4.)

Symmetry is used for the same purposes of separating the mem-bers of a *partitio* to allow them each full weight when Bacon takes up his first division and introduces a preliminary stage: to defend

learning 'from the discredits and disgraces which it hath received;
all from ignorance'—and with a further subdivision—

> but ignorance severally disguised; appearing
> sometimes in the zeal and jealousy of divines,
> sometimes in the severity and arrogance of politiques,
> sometimes in the errors and imperfections of learned men themselves.
>
> (264.)

And as we saw in chapter 2, the tactical effect of this *partitio*
derives from abandoning the neatness of the initial distinction—
Bacon is always alive to the possibilities of variation from the
norm. One division which is sharpened by this technique of
variation from the expected depends on the figure *epistrophe*
which Bacon puts to skilful use for the crucial separation of
theology from science, exploiting the effect characteristic to this
figure whereby the repetition of the final word shifts the stress
back to the word immediately preceding it, which is therefore
carefully chosen to be the most important one in meaning also:

> the contemplation of God's creatures and works produceth
> (having regard to the works and creatures themselves) knowledge
> but having regard to God,   no perfect knowledge
> but wonder, which is broken knowledge.
>
> (267.)

There the stress inevitably shifts back to '*perfect* knowledge', and
still more to '*broken* knowledge', and so Bacon's point that
theology is a discipline alien to science comes over with maximum
force.

The traditional symmetries of syntax, as used by Bacon, have
considerable value in underlining meaning, in re-creating on the
visual and aural planes subtle distinctions in thought, but these
functions of clarifying expression may also be shared by *partitio*
and the aphorism. In addition to this expository value the symmetries have expressive capabilities which are not present in those
two devices, and thus they are also wonderfully suited to convey-
ing particular emotional attitudes, whether of praise or blame,
admiration or disgust. The symmetries are equivalent in the
structural resources of Bacon's language to imagery in the imagi-

native plane. Because they are so expressive, they make a wonderfully destructive tool for Bacon in his great attack on vanities in
studies, and especially on the decadence of Ciceronianism. In his
initial division of these vanities, the care with which the parts are
balanced is a sign of what is to come, the isolation and sharpening
of each of the darts he has to throw:

> those things we do esteem vain, which are either false or frivolous,
> those which either have no truth or no use:
> and those persons we   esteem vain, which are either credulous or curious;
> and curiosity is either in matter or words.
> (282.)

We might note in passing how the antithetical structure in the
second line clarifies the distinction in the first, and how we are
reminded of the overall distinction between vanity in 'things' and
persons by the echoing sound of 'curious' to 'frivolous', and how
monotony is avoided by the balancing antithesis in line 4 taking
a different form in thought from its twin in line 2. The precision
of this triple distinction is maintained by a still sharper division
of the 'three distempers' of learning:

> the first,   fantastical   learning;
> the second, contentious learning;
> and the last,   delicate   learning;
> vain imaginations,
> vain altercations,
> and vain affectations;
> and with the last I will begin. (282.)

That division (which is neatly inverted by taking the last branch
first—Bacon is not a prisoner of his scheme) could not be expressed
with more conscious artifice, for Bacon has gone out of his way to
sharpen the parallels, in the first group of clauses using *epistrophe*
on the noun 'learning' to put a still greater stress on the forceful
enough epithets: 'fantastical', 'contentious', 'delicate'; and in the
second using *anaphora* to beat home the key-word 'vain', while
the rhyme '-ations' both jangles contemptuously and serves like
epistrophe to place the stress on the first part of the words: '*imagina*-
tions', '*alter*cations', '*affect*ations'. Throughout the passage all the

contemptuous words have an added explosive force by their very sound, with the predominance of hard consonants—'k', 'f' and 't' sounds. Here is contempt channelled into far greater force by skilful use of the simple traditional devices of parallelism and symmetry.

When Bacon comes to describe the distortions caused by the overprecise imitation of Cicero, both contempt and symmetry rise to a commanding height, as he concludes his analysis of the causes of the movement and its disastrous effects in two crushing sentences. Having analysed the process by which early sixteenth-century interests converged in an admiration of 'style and phrase' he sums up these causes sharply in an exactly symmetrical structure (on 'the *A* of *B*' pattern), reinforced by alliteration:

> So that these four causes concurring,
>   the admiration of ancient authors,
>   the hate   of the schoolmen,
>   the exact study of languages,
> and the efficacy   of preaching,
> did bring in an affectionate study of eloquence and copie
> of speech, which then began to flourish. (283.)

Now he presents the effects of the unnatural interest in 'eloquence and copie of speech', using the traditional division between *Res* and *Verba*, keeping the same the '*A* of *B*' pattern, and a simple 'more...than' structure which can be expanded, developing the negative side first: in this season of decadence men began to hunt

> *more* after words *than* matter; and
> *more* after the choiceness of the phrase, and
>   the round and clean composition of the sentence, and
>   the sweet falling of the clauses, and
>   the varying and illustration of their works with
>   tropes and figures
> *than* after the weight of matter,
>   worth of subject,
>   soundness of argument,
>   life of invention, or
>   depth of judgment. (283; my italics.)

In this remarkable sentence the syntax not only follows the sense but re-creates it—in an abused phrase, it 'enacts the meaning'. In the first part, for the narcissistic eloquence of the Ciceronians, we see an effect which can only be achieved by using symmetry, for by establishing a pattern and thus an expected recurrence the writer can produce variations of expansion and contraction. Here the parallel structure and the word-pairs heighten the effect gained by the clauses increasing in length: they seem to wax eloquent, choice, and flabby before our eyes. In the second part the absolute contrast in sense is reinforced by the spare concentration of structure and sound—and here the equality of clause-length has a different effect, strengthening the effect of toughness, while the identical overall structure (with 'of' as the turning point in every clause) in addition to being dependably consistent acts as a matrix against which the oppositions between cause and effect, false and true, eloquence and plainness, become inescapably clear and convincing. If I had to choose one sentence to show the expressive potential of symmetrical syntax, this would be it. And, although carefully constructed, it is not a mechanical device, but one which Bacon varies according to the particular attitude he wants to express, as we see from the next sequence in which he lists all the Ciceronians in that tired series of sentences linked by *anaphora* and *parison* by which the wearied repetitions ('Then grew...Then did Sturmius...Then did Car...') make the Ciceronian movement seem to have stretched out endlessly and unoriginally—as it did.

In the famous attack on the schoolmen which now follows, imagery is arguably more important than syntax, but some syntactical effects do aid the deflating movement. Bacon begins this account of the second 'distemper of learning'—corruption in matter—by saying that it is worse than the former,

> for as substance of matter is better than beauty of words,
> so contrariwise vain matter is worse than vain words.   (285.)

Those hard-echoing repetitions (especially the flat double rhyme of 'matter') are prophetic of the use of sound patterns here to express contempt. So in dividing up this head Bacon finds two varieties of 'suspected and falsified sciences',

> the one, the novelty and strangeness of terms;
> the other, the strictness of positions,
>   which of necessity doth induce oppositions,
>   and so questions and altercations.

Again the echoing sounds carry a meaning, here expressing the futility and repetitiveness of such controversies. As he now applies this criticism to the watertight intellectual world of scholasticism, where the body of knowledge as represented by Aristotle was stagnant and incapable of growth, Bacon invents the splendidly destructive image of organic matter putrefying into worms, and the metaphor is made more effective by being used together with the structural device of setting up a framework and making significant alterations within it—as can best be seen if the two halves are printed side by side (the *A* clauses are to be read first):

A. Surely, like as many substances in nature which are solid do
B. so it is the property of good and sound knowledge to
A. putrefy and corrupt into
B. putrefy and dissolve into
A. worms
B. a number of subtile, idle, unwholesome, and (as I may term them) vermiculate questions...

Here the pattern, set up and followed exactly in the first two pairs of clauses, creates the expectation that it will be maintained into the third, and so the increased size and force of the terms balancing the simple word 'worms' give a still greater striking power, capped by the long-awaited echo to 'worms', the contemptuous metaphor 'vermiculate'.

If meaning can be thus intensified, made polyphonic, by the significant displacement of an expected pattern, it can also be made to carry separate planes of association by making a pattern complete itself into an exact symmetry of form, but which smuggles in an 'a-symmetrical' and discordant change of meaning. This we see in the next sentence where Bacon mocks the schoolmen's claustrophilic dedication to Aristotle, not by any direct denunciation but by the more subtle use of a sort of bland irony which sets up exactly symmetrical antitheses and within the same balanced norm introduces very damaging distinctions in meaning. This 'vermiculate...degenerate learning'

> did chiefly reign amongst the schoolmen;
> who having sharp and strong wits,
> and abundance of leisure,
> and small variety of reading;...

There the blow falls, coolly: up to the very last words of that clause the tone is even, the terms describing the schoolmen either laudatory ('sharp and strong wits') or neutral ('abundance of leisure'), but then the exact symmetry and formal antithesis ('abundance'/'small variety') finally smuggle in the deflating idea —'of reading'—and the mind perceives an attitude running at a lower (and opposed) level to the tone. The effect is repeated in the next clause, but now inverted, with the damaging part placed first:

> but their wits being shut up in the cells of a few authors
> (chiefly Aristotle their dictator)
> as their persons were shut up in the cells of monasteries
> and colleges;...

Here the exact (and comic) correspondence between their 'wits' and 'persons' seems to suggest that this is an entirely normal and common state of affairs—the structure and tone are saying one thing, while of course the reader's mind is saying something quite different.

This dropping of a discordant acid idea into a smooth creamy context is very similar to that used by the great poets of the neo-classical couplet with their variations on the mock-encomium. It reminds us of Dryden in *Absalom and Achitophel* ostensibly praising

> Shimei, whose Youth did early Promise bring
> Of Zeal to God, and *Hatred* to his King;
> Did wisely from *Expensive* Sins refrain,
> And never broke the Sabbath, *but for Gain.*

Were it not for the words which I have italicised, the tone and movement might convince us that the character is being praised—but their presence curdles the whole vision, and the recurrent pattern of the couplet and of antithesis within it strengthen the juxtaposition. The same effect is used, but more subtly, by Pope for his history of Sir Balaam, whose riches move him up the social scale: growing 'polite' he

> Leaves the dull cits, and joins (to please the fair)
> The well-bred *cuckolds* in St. James's air:...
> His daughter flaunts a viscount's *tawdry* wife;
> She bears a coronet, *and pox*, for life.[1]

And just as Pope, although keeping the blandness of tone and movement, could not prevent contempt from breaking into the penultimate line, so Bacon at the end of this sentence (which is of course much more effective when read as a whole) while maintaining the balanced antithetical structure descends from coolness to more positive criticism, as he finally evolves the great image of the spider:

> and knowing little history, either of nature
> or time;
> did out of no great quantity of matter,
> and infinite agitation of wit,
> spin out unto us those laborious webs of learning
> which are extant in their books. (285.)

It is in fact harder to indicate the discordant words in that passage, the effects are so subtle—the split is not so much between some of its words and the sentence as a whole, but between the tone and movement of the whole and its actual meaning. But we can at least pick out two clever details in the second clause, where the symmetrical structure is sharpened further by the almost exact correspondence of sound especially on the letter 't': 'no great quantity of matter...infinite agitation of wit', and where the antithetical structure leads us to expect a 'but' joining these two very damaging points, only to find them resolved into a placid union with 'and'. The comparison with Dryden and Pope is not fortuitous—Bacon is also a master of meaningful variation within a sharply defined stylistic form.

As this destructive account of the causes and origins of scholasticism gives way to an equally devastating description of its method it becomes harder to separate the syntax from the imagery (which I shall want to discuss later). But there are some purely syntactical effects, as when Bacon takes up a criticism made at the beginning, that 'strictness of positions' induces 'oppositions, and so questions and altercations', and in applying it to the schoolmen revives this contemptuous sound-patterning. Their method of handling a knowledge was this:

> upon every particular position or assertion
> to frame objections, and to those objections
> solutions; which   solutions
> were for the most part not confutations, but   distinctions...

In addition to the repetitions of the sound '-ion', which (while actually suggesting the 'Quaestiones' of Aquinas's *Summa*) create an effect of a sterile self-defeating inward-spiralling progression—and which would have been still more mocking if in seventeenth-century pronunciation the ending was disyllabic, as it sometimes was in verse[1]—the whole description is given an appearance of development in that the terms are arranged by the chain-like figure *gradatio*[2] into a seemingly logical structure: 'position' to 'objection'; 'objection' to 'solution'; 'solution' to 'distinction'. But in fact it gets nowhere, returning to the start like a snake with its tail in its mouth. Now in complete contrast to that eddying, pointless movement Bacon condenses the true scientific method into an image conveyed in non-symmetrical syntax:

whereas indeed the strength of all sciences is, as the strength of the old man's faggot, in the bond.

As with the parody of Ciceronianism, the clinching force of a bare statement has been created largely by its stylistic context, setting confusion against clarity, redundancy against economy. As this distinction between true and false method is elaborated Bacon makes further skilful use of syntactical contrast by again referring back to the terms already created: the 'harmony of a science' ought to be 'the true and brief confutation and suppression of all

the smaller sorts of objections', and having thus used the schoolmen's Latinate abstractions against them he now revives the true
image of the sciences as a bond and shows the ease and futility of
their purely negative method:

> but on the other side, if you take out every axiom,
>> as the sticks of the faggot, one by one,
>>> you may quarrel with them
>>>> and bend them
>>>> and break them
>>> at your pleasure.   (286.)

Here the movement re-creates the meaning to a remarkable degree:
starting from the image of the bundle of sticks, the schoolmen
squabbling over petty distinctions are reduced to the level of
someone taking the sticks out of an old man's faggot, and are made
to look toothless and impotent partly by the image (their anger
being applied to thin and defenceless sticks), partly by the choice
of words (how ridiculous to 'quarrel' with a stick—like a puppy,
perhaps), but especially by the symmetrical structure and the
repetition of 'and' and 'them', so inducing a sort of jumpy
progress, like that of an old man—'quarrel with them, and bend
them, and break them', with a further indignity in that they have
to 'bend' the sticks before they can break them. Of course imagery
and syntax, sound and sense, coalesce here—but the symmetries
play no small part. Bacon disposes of this point with a favourite
device, the quotation of a *sententia* which is then applied to the
matter in hand by being duplicated in sound and structure, so
giving an effect of finality (and in this case it also shows his
opinion of Seneca):

A. so that as it was said of Seneca,
B. so a man may truly say of the schoolmen,
A. *Verborum minutiis rerum frangit pondera*
B. *Quaestionum minutiis scientiarum frangunt soliditatem.* (286.)[1]

—that is, as he 'broke up the weight and mass of the matter by
verbal points and niceties', so they 'broke up the solidity and
coherency of the sciences by the minuteness and nicety of their

questions'. And Bacon returns to the contemptuous sound-effects at the end of the paragraph with some new variations—'cavillations', 'digladiation'.

The remarkable density and variety of symmetrical techniques in this section is not to be taken as showing their specifically destructive nature, but rather their suitability for embodying intense emotions of any kind. Where Bacon—or any great Renaissance writer—is most involved in his subject the form is likely not to turn asymmetrical but to become more and more insistent, disciplining and channelling the feeling. We might for example consider a section where syntactical balance is used to a completely different end, the great praise of learning which ends Book 1. In finally affirming the dignity of learning, Bacon sets aside the usual arguments in its praise, such as

> that by learning man excelleth man
> in that wherein man excelleth beasts;
> that by learning man ascendeth to the heavens and their motions,
> where in body   he   cannot come;   (3. 318.)

—to concentrate on that benefit from learning and literature to which man most aspires, immortality; and now Bacon writes his version of *exegi monumentum*, a paragraph in which the symmetries give an added resonance to an eloquence of such a controlled flow that for once we should not submit it to the indignity of separate articulation:

> let us conclude with the dignity and excellency of knowledge and learning in that whereunto man's nature doth most aspire; which is immortality or continuance; for to this tendeth generation, and raising of houses and families; to this buildings, foundations, and monuments; to this tendeth the desire of memory, fame, and celebration; and in effect, the strength of all other human desires. We see then how far the monuments of wit and learning are more durable than the monuments of power or of the hands. For have not the verses of Homer continued twenty-five hundred years or more, without the loss of a syllable or letter; during which time infinite palaces, temples, castles, cities, have been decayed and demolished? It is not possible to have the true pictures or statues of Cyrus, Alexander, Caesar, no nor of the kings or great personages of much later years: for the originals cannot last, and the copies cannot but leese of

the life and truth. But the images of men's wits and knowledges remain in books, exempted from the wrong of time and capable of perpetual renovation. (318.)

At this point the imagery takes over the argument, and moves it on to a still higher plane, but the symmetries have been invaluable in underlining similarities and differences within it without becoming so insistent as to disturb the flow. And having reached this height of eloquence Bacon shows yet again his unerring sense of stylistic context by using symmetrical syntax more densely in the last paragraph of all, but now in the service of half-a-dozen laconic examples of people who continued to prefer custom or habit before learning—a piece of *sprezzatura* like the off-hand conclusion of Sidney's *Apology for Poetry*, and like it reinforcing the eloquence which came before.

Any powerful movement of praise or blame, then, is given much greater force by syntactical structure—but the same techniques can communicate a great range of intellectual and emotional aims. Enough passages have been quoted from the *Advancement* to establish Bacon's deliberate and creative use of symmetry, so perhaps some of the major instances can now be referred to more briefly. The distinction between invention and development as applied to the progress of sciences (289–90) is built around a careful antithesis which breaks down at the end to stress the unfavoured term (the same technique was used to attack scholastic theology, p. 287); the opposite tactic, of presenting the good terms first, and at length, while briefly dismissing the unpleasant ones, is seen in Bacon's account of Queen Elizabeth's government (307). A parallel structure is kept up consistently to clarify 'the two ways of contemplation' (293), to list the misapplications of knowledge, and then its correct form (294–5), to distinguish types of commandment (316) and the successful completion of business (322); to sustain a remarkably complete analogy between the preservation of learning and that of water (323); to argue for parity of reward (323–4), and brotherhood in learning (327); to propose categories of possible actions (328), abnormalities in nature (330), church history (341), the speculative and operative parts of science (351), the three stages of knowledge (357), the value of mathematics (360), physiognomy (368), medical history (374), for predictions in astronomy, physics, and politics (380), for the function of reason and the imagination (382–3), for the abuses of communication (403–4), for the interrelation of sciences (408), and—in extremely careful symmetry—the respective roles of Logic, Rhetoric, and Morality (409–10), and so on. The list could be extended, but reference to the text at any of these points will confirm that Bacon uses the traditional devices of symmetry and parallelism throughout the *Advancement of Learning*, sometimes at the beginning of very important and much deliberated sections (e.g. pp. 462, 488), sometimes at the end (476)—anywhere, in fact, where communication will benefit from the clarity and expressiveness achieved by this means.

At the risk of boring the reader (it seems a risk worth taking, given that the presence of 'Ciceronian' structure has never been seen in Bacon's prose, and that the *Essays* especially have suffered from the confusion between his use of aphorisms and an aphoristic or 'Senecan' mode) I shall now briefly consider the application of symmetrical syntax in the *Essays*. Here at first we may be disappointed, for we do not find it used for such a coherent flow and variety of argument, but this is a weakness which is inherent in the form of the *Essays*. As each is an extremely condensed series of variations on one theme, then there is never enough space or continuity for the development of an argument or personal vision which can produce a force of emotion, and hence of stylistic intensity comparable to that often found in the *Advancement*. Besides not being composed from a consistent impelling attitude or plan, the majority of the *Essays* were of course not composed at one time or as a whole: in expanding the collection Bacon, like Montaigne, added new material at any moderately suitable point, without much thought to the overall development. Of course, as we have seen, Bacon's concept of the aphorisms' relevance to the 'scattered occasions' of life was more important to him than writing 'artistic wholes', so that it would not be a valid criticism to complain of disparateness. But these factors do account for the critical difficulty in dealing with the *Essays*, and suggest that we should regard them as we would a contemporary collection of lyrical poems. As Anne Righter has well said, even

> the 1625 edition is not a tidy knitting together of various ideas which interested Bacon; it is an accumulation of disparate pieces as difficult to generalize about, or to connect internally, as Donne's *Songs and Sonets*, and it is to be read in a not dissimilar fashion. (B77, p. 26.)

And I think it is true to say that we find here some of the 'poetic' effects produced in the *Advancement* by the creation and variation of a pattern, but on a much smaller scale. A final point which explains the stylistic difference between the two works is that whereas in the *Advancement* Bacon's attitudes to his subject-matter ranged along a wide scale from praise to ironic criticism to contemptuous dismissal, in the *Essays* his attitude is conditioned by the whole rationale of the work towards dispassionate objective observation and analysis (the most informative essays, such as those on Gardens and Building, contain least art); hence it is only when he touches on the moral extremities of good and evil, or discusses a topic in which he is personally involved (such as 'Judicature') that we find much artistic intensity. But this point does at least underline the organic nature of Bacon's work, the extent to which form and style depend on context, on meaning and on attitude.

The stylistic norm of many of the *Essays*, especially those containing precepts and advice, is that of a simple equality of phrase structure, a form of 'definition by division' which produces a mnemonic clarity. Particularly in the 1597 volume this results in an exact *isocolon*, as in the whole of 'Studies', or in this from 'Discourse':

> A good continued   speech
> without a good   speech of interlocution sheweth slownesse;
>   and a good reply or second speech
> without a good set   speech sheweth shallownesse and weaknes.
>
> (6. 526.)

The symmetries in 1597 are not all as exact as this, though. In the same essay we find this piece of advice expressed in antithetical clauses with some variation in structure which seems to echo the sense, albeit slightly:

It is good to varie and mixe
speech of the present occasion   with argument,
                        tales   with reasons,
asking of questions with telling of opinions,
              and jest   with earnest.   (*Ibid.*)

But the simple mnemonic patterns persist throughout the later Essays, in complete consistency with Bacon's theory, as in this clear balance of form and thought which highlights a perceptive point about human relationships:

A man cannot speak to his son but as a father;
                  to his wife but as a husband;
                  to his enemy but upon terms;
whereas a friend can speak as the case requires;
        and not as it sorteth with the person.   (6. 443.)

There the parallel structure exposes the various distinctions in the thought, detaches them from each other and then puts them side by side so that we see the correspondence in situation through the differing relationships. A similar effect is often sought for the normative political maxims,[1] such as this one, which is more elaborate than most, and with less symmetry in the structure:

He that seeketh to be eminent amongst able men
    hath a great task; but that is ever good for the public;
But he that plots to be the only figure amongst ciphers
              is the decay of a whole age. (6. 467.)

This impulse to symmetry results (despite Croll and Williamson) in a countless number of balances, and of antitheses where in addition to the opposition in the sense an exact correspondence in the words is deliberately maintained; it produces whole essays arranged on a *pro/con* structure, and which reproduce this anti-thetical symmetry in virtually every sentence;[2] and it repeats that habit of arranging or duplicating *sententiae* into symmetrical structures, even to the deploying of a whole passage from Lucretius into an exactly balanced pattern.[3]

Syntactical Symmetry

But, if symmetry is the prevailing norm, there are sufficient artistic variations from it to justify a discussion, although the separate nature of the aphorisms makes any connected analysis difficult. The structures vary, of course, according to the meaning. A simple cumulative movement can convey at one moment all the attendant particulars which make the process of dying so painful:

Groans and convulsions, and a discoloured face, and friends weeping, and blacks, and obsequies, and the like, shew death terrible. (6. 379.)

(where the repetition of 'and' makes a curiously depressing list), while at another time this cumulative effect expresses perfectly the decline and fall of a prodigal:

The illiberality of parents in allowance towards their children is an harmful error; makes them base; acquaints them with shifts; makes them sort with mean company; and makes them surfeit more when they come to plenty. (390.)

There the quick onward movement of the verbs within a parallel frame underlines the sense, and the lesson from both is summed up sharply in the symmetries of the following sentence:

And therefore the proof is best, when men keep their authority towards their children, but not their purse.

A more extended example of effective stylistic contrast is that sequence in 'Of Youth and Age' where Bacon takes the anti-thetical distinction that 'The errors of young men are the ruin of business; but the errors of aged men amount but to this, that more might have been done, or sooner', and expands it into two sentences in which the movement re-creates the sense:

Young men, in the conduct and manage of actions, embrace more than they can hold; stir more than they can quiet; fly to the end, without consideration of the means and degrees; pursue some few principles which they have chanced upon absurdly; care not to innovate, which draws unknown inconveniences; use extreme remedies at first; and that which doubleth all errors, will not acknow-ledge or retract them; like an unready horse, that will neither stop nor turn. Men of age object too much, consult too long, adventure too little, repent too soon, and seldom drive business home to the full period, but content themselves with a mediocrity of success. (6. 477–8.)

(I deliberately did not set that passage out spatially, so that the reader's eye would not be warned in advance of the impending symmetries, and so have lost their surprise effect.) The structure of the two opposed sentences is identical, with the subject ('Young men'; 'Men of age') being followed by a series of verbs in parallel: this similarity clarifies the difference between the meanings. Again the symmetries for youth are used at first to express two belittling points ('embrace more than they can hold; stir more than they can quiet'), but then are abandoned for a series of long, unsymmetrical, fast-moving clauses which express the unpredictable undisciplined vitality of young men; the symmetries for age ('object too much, consult too long', etc.) express only too well the predictable, repetitive nature of their actions (the movement also suggests the short-breathed doddering syntax of a Justice Shallow), and by contrast the concluding long clause ('seldom drive business home. . .') suggests their hesitancy. Finally there is a further contrast in structure as the follies of youth are listed fully, with their effect; the follies of age are given *tout court*.

The expansive nature of that stylistic contrast is not typical of the *Essays* (though clearly only by such a fluid development of the first section could the extravagance of youth be mimicked in the syntax); for we normally find a quite compressed juxtaposition. Sometimes the quickness of the returning balance surprises us:

there be many wise men that have secret hearts and
transparent countenances. (6. 429.)

Another swift return of an unexpected syntactical balance after a more leisurely start is used in this ironic comment on freedom-loving bachelors (such as Bertram in *All's Well*, who describes Helena as his 'clog'): whatever their other more respectable reasons may be,

the most ordinary cause of a single life is liberty, especially in certain self-pleasing and humorous minds, which are so sensible of every restraint as they will go near to think
their girdles and garters
to be bonds and shackles. (6. 391.)

That surprise echo, enlivened by the alliteration, shows how neurotically extreme such fears can be—as to 'think every bush a bear'. Another postponement of a key point to the end of a sentence comes in this comparison:

> Princes are like to heavenly bodies,
>> which cause good or evil times;
> and which have much veneration,
>> but no rest. (6. 423.)

—a witty variation on 'Uneasy lies the head that wears the crown'. Sometimes the unexpected return or amplification of a parallel can create an imaginative spark which deepens the meaning, as in this comment on the cares of office:

> It is a strange desire, to seek power and to lose liberty:
>> or to seek power over others
>> and to lose power over a man's self. (6. 398.)

—the idea was complete in the first clause, but like other examples of the 'two-part aphorism' its extension is more than a duplication. And in the next sentence in this Essay ('Of Great Place') the form remains constant to highlight a change in the sense:

> *A.* The rising unto place is laborious;
> *B.* and it is sometimes base;
> *A.* and by pains men come to greater pains;
> *B.* and by indignities men come to dignities. (398–9.)

There the established pattern led us to expect that after 'pains' resulting in 'pains' we should have a similar duplication in the last line—but instead we had the surprise chain 'base': 'indignities': 'dignities', a wry reversal which expressed concisely a Machiavellian truth about rising in office.

This skill at variation within an artistic pattern is the most creative aspect of Bacon's use of symmetrical structure. It is not a pattern imposed by habit and overriding the particular differences of each context (as Hazlitt observed with some justice of Dr Johnson's prose at its most ponderous),[1] but one which is always at the service of meaning, which it recreates and extends on its own aural and visual planes. Bacon can use subtle variations in structure to make important intellectual distinctions, such as in this sentence from 'Judicature':

> The partes of a Judge are foure:
> to direct the evidence;
> to moderate length, repetition, or impertinency of speech;
> to recapitulate, select, and collate the materiall points
>   of that which hath beene said; and
> to give the rule or sentence. (583–4.)

This is no mere pattern-making, for the parallel structure makes us aware of the distinctions in the thought: the second term was long to echo the verbosity being corrected; the third term was long to suggest the care needed by the judge in summing up; and the two outside ones are as simple and as absolute as the processes concerned. A comparably meaningful variety in structure is used for the very different world of *Realpolitik*, as for this advice that in negotiations with others the best 'composition' is to have

> openness in fame and opinion;
> secrecy in habit;
> dissimulation in seasonable use;
> and a power to feign, if there be no remedy. (6. 389.)

The final term there upset the symmetry so as to speed up the movement and give added stress to the sense, that 'feigning' is the very last resort and only to be used where the other means have failed. Bacon is no supporter of the hole-and-corner Machiavellianism of the Revenge tragedies, and elsewhere in this essay he skilfully varies the syntax to stress the point that dissimulation is in fact a feeble method of action: a man should develop

> that penetration of judgment as he can discern
> what things are to be laid open,
> and what to be secreted,
> and what to be shewed at half lights,
> and to whom
> and when. (387.)

Here the breaking up of the initial rhythms within a parallel structure acts like the focusing of a beam of light to stress the importance of the final terms, which urge the caution and secrecy needed in this sort of business: the shape on the page is the shape of the thought.

At the diametrically opposed moral pole to this one the variation of a pattern can be just as organic to the sense. In discussing 'Goodness' Bacon points to the traditionally destructive effects of ambition:

> The desire of power   in excess caused the angels to fall,
>   the desire of knowledge in excess caused man   to fall:
>   but in charity there is no excess;
>   neither can angel or man come in danger by it. (403.)

By breaking down the exact symmetry of the first two clauses Bacon suggests syntactically what he is already arguing logically, that 'charity' is totally without these dangers, and the syntactical negation is almost as effective as the logical negation. In attacking human malice Bacon uses a less violent contrast, the effective device of widening the syntactical framework, for by postponing an expected balance the material which is inserted at that point receives extra stress:

> Suspicions that the mind of itself gathers are but buzzes;
>   but suspicions that are artificially nourished,
>   and put into men's heads by the tales
>   and whispering of others,
>   have stings. (455.)

In that example the concluding balance, the closing of the gap that had been widened by the forceful amplification of 'artificially nourished', comes with the greater force of surprise as we only realise then that a structure was forming itself—and, as in the 'worms'/'vermiculate' balance, the sustained image 'buzzes'/ 'stings' resolves the suspension on the imaginative plane. Finally, an example of variation and contrast within a pattern, used for an uncompromising moral attack on man's laxity of habit which makes his 'good resolutions' fickle and insincere: it is a cause of wonder,

to heare men professe,
> protest,
> ingage,
> give great words,
and then doe just as they have done before:
as if they were dead Images
and Engins moved only by the wheeles of custom. (573.)

Those symmetries are not 'frivolities', nor are they mere ornament—the traditional syntactical structures are applied by Bacon
as a powerfully expressive aid to meaning, and his ability to create
significant stylistic variations within a self-imposed convention is
witness of an artistic control which may not unfittingly be called
poetic.

CHAPTER 5

IMAGE AND ARGUMENT

To describe some qualities of Bacon's prose as 'poetic' may seem the excessive enthusiasm of the enlightened, but it could be defended both as a fair comment on the deliberate imaginative artistry with which he wrote and as a historically correct observation on the closeness of the two media. Today poetry is thought of as being diametrically opposed to prose (it would be interesting to trace this separation from the eighteenth century onwards), but in the Renaissance as in classical literature they were of equal status— in Dryden's words, 'the other harmony of prose'—with poetry given the added complication of metrics. In the previous chapter we saw how the traditional syntactical symmetries even produced effects which might be thought proper to metrics—equal line- or clause-lengths, recurrent rhythmic patterns, and rhyme, while prose was also allowed such poetic devices as the rhetorical figures, imagery and a specifically literary vocabulary.[1] Of these poetic qualities the most impressive in Bacon's writing continues to be that of imagery, although it is at the same time the hardest to analyse. In addition to the basic critical problem of describing the planes on which an image works and how it functions in context, there is the more fundamental difficulty of temporarily abandoning modern demands on imagery in order to re-create the criteria which existed in the past and which certainly influenced literary creation then: these contemporary criteria will not of course 'explain' everything in that literature, nor should we abandon the increased insights derived from modern critical methods, but I think it is essential to begin by trying to think ourselves into the theoretical positions which then applied. The mere fact that we tend to describe the use of imagery in prose as being a 'poetic' quality shows how far we have moved towards equating poetry with metaphor—indeed, as W. K. Wimsatt has said, 'The theorist of poetry tends more and more today to make metaphor the irreducible element of his definition of poetry.'[1] And the converse, that prose is not an apt form for metaphor, can be frequently found, as for example—expressed with perhaps above-average dogmatism—by T. E. Hulme, arguing that poetry's language is 'visual, concrete':

Visual meanings can only be transferred by the new bowl of metaphor; prose is an old pot that lets them leak out.[2]

—but his own metaphor gives him away. The use of imagery in prose is sanctioned by all pre-Restoration theorists, and it continued long after that theoretical revolution to be a force in imaginative prose (as in the contrasting uses of Dickens and Henry James, say). With the possible exception of this aspect, the whole question of imagery has been discussed in such fullness that I need only raise the essential points very briefly.[3] But, while I for the last time attempt to reconstruct the concept of a stylistic device as it existed in Bacon's day before analysing Bacon's own use of that resource, this preliminary outline will be given more focus if I relate it to a well-known recent attack on Bacon's imagery. L. C. Knights has complained that 'Bacon's figures of speech are forensic, intended to convince or confound. Some are used simply for apt illustrations of particular points; some serve to impose on the reader the required feeling or attitude. In neither kind is there any vivid feeling for *both* sides of the analogy such as we find in more representative Elizabethans.'[4] The second accusation is one which is easily disproved when I come to analyse the application of image to argument below, but already we have seen examples of Bacon's sensitive and lively response to his analogies in those fully formed images for *partitio*, with their fresh extension of natural processes—the tree, its branches, roots, the soil and all the factors affecting growth—indeed it might be said that Bacon has *too* vivid a feeling for the analogy, for he is often fascinated by it and neglects to develop the argument which it ostensibly supports. For the first objection, that the images are directed at his readers (and not, presumably, in an unconscious way, at the object), again Bacon's practice may qualify it, but, more important, a survey of classical and Renaissance teachings on imagery will show it to be a simple misunderstanding of the dominant convention.

I

The most pervasive modern concept of imagery is that it is an automatic, involuntary event, possibly modified by craftsmanship, but in its essence a product of the writer's particular psychological or imaginative make-up: there is little discussion of the process by which he chooses images, nor of his attitude to his audience. Classical and Renaissance theory is almost completely ignorant of the former approach, but totally dedicated to the latter, that is to legislating on the function of imagery within the writer's conscious plan. Aristotle erected several categories which, with variations, persisted into the Renaissance. In the *Poetics* he briefly defines metaphor as 'the attribution of a name belonging to something else: either from the genus to the species, or from the species to the genus, or from species to species, or by analogy' (ch. 21);[1] it is to be used with decorum, for 'nothing but metaphor would be a puzzle'; its use 'demands originality and is a sign of genius; for to make good metaphors is to perceive similarity' (ch. 22). These remarks are brief and not very helpful, but they are expanded in Book 3 of the *Rhetoric*, and at once we see the natural association, in classical theory and practice, of imagery with prose: metaphor

is most important both in poetry and in prose. But the orator must devote the greater attention to them in prose, since the latter has fewer resources than verse. (Ch. 2, §8.)

There are certain cautions, of course, such as that 'Proper and appropriate words and metaphors are alone to be employed in the style of prose' (2. 6) and that 'the simile is also useful in prose, but should be less frequently used, for there is something poetical about it' (4. 2), but there is no doubt as to the close association between prose and imagery.

Given the accepted place of imagery within prose, then Aristotle's criteria for metaphor and those of later theorists can be (and were) taken to apply to prose too. The most important criterion is that of vividness, for those words are to be chosen for metaphor which are best 'suited to putting the matter before the eyes' (2. 13), that is, 'words that signify actuality' (11. 1–2). Though this crucial point is not developed, Aristotle seems to mean that the metaphor should be 'visual, concrete', and this is certainly what later theorists ask for. Also influential, though perhaps irremediably vague, is his demand that metaphors be appropriate, for 'if they are far-fetched they are obscure', and so 'fail to produce persuasion', which is the whole aim of rhetoric, and hence of most literature (2. 9; 3. 4). A last point which can be isolated is of immense practical significance in English Renaissance literature (and indeed in all writing, though modern theory takes little account of it), the application of imagery to a definite evaluative purpose: 'if we wish to ornament our subject, we must derive our metaphor from the better species under the same genus; if to depreciate it, from the worse'. To illustrate the interchangeable function of imagery within the same image-source Aristotle gives the concise example of a sentence where the two halves point in opposed directions: we can say either 'that the man who begs prays, or that the man who prays begs' (2. 10), and in this and the following paragraph he gives more examples of praise and dispraise using metaphor. The significance of this criterion is that it establishes the role of imagery in a persuasive context: in addition to the overall function of rhetoric as moving to persuasion by stimulating the imagination and arousing the emotions, metaphor is now given the specific task of concentrating and revealing the writer's attitude to his subject-matter, and doing so in a way which will stimulate the audience to agreement. In a sense the business of all imaginative literature is to convince the reader of the validity of the writer's vision, but in a more special sense the image is a focus for judgments ranging from praise to blame, which by the power of artistic condensation can rise to the status of 'arguments' or even 'proofs'. So for example within the genus of food and eating Shakespeare derives his metaphor 'from the better species' in order to present Troilus' anticipation of Cressida and pleasure:

> Th' imaginary relish is so sweet
> That it enchants my sense, What will it be
> When that the watery palate tastes indeed
> Love's thrice repured nectar? death, I fear me. (III, ii, 19–22.)

But, the disillusion complete, Shakespeare takes an image 'to depreciate it, from the worse' species, descending to the scorned waste-products:

> The fractions of her faith, orts of her love,
> The fragments, scraps, the bits and greasy relics
> Of her o'ereaten faith are given to Diomed. (v, ii, 158–60.)

That is a useful example of how Aristotle's formulation of the use of imagery for praise and dispraise has been intuitively applied by poets and prose-writers of all countries and ages—Bacon, needless to say, included.

The Roman rhetoricians accept, or develop, Aristotle's criteria. The pseudo-Ciceronian *Ad Herennium* also stresses that a writer uses imagery with a definite purpose: 'Metaphor is used for the sake of creating a vivid mental picture', and in addition to the criteria of similarity and decorum he writes that it may be used for 'magnifying' and 'minifying' (IV. xxxiv. 45; *ed. cit.*). Cicero himself is an innovator in his discussion of imagery, as A. D. Leeman has shown, ignoring the purely ornamental use of metaphor, and laying great stress on its functional value for clarity and added significance. He is original too in discussing why the use of metaphor gives pleasure, and though some of his suggested explanations are traditional—that a metaphor 'suggests the thing and a picture of the whole' and 'has a direct appeal to the senses, especially the sense of sight, which is the keenest' (*De Oratore*, 3. 160)—he adds a new idea in pointing to the psychological pleasure produced, the agility of the intellect:

There will be metaphors of all sorts in great abundance, because these figures by virtue of the comparison involved transport the mind and bring it back, and move it hither and thither; and this rapid stimulation of thought in itself produces pleasure. (*Orator*, 234.)

By contrast Quintilian limits his many references to metaphor to more familiar concepts: metaphor is certainly valid in prose, is indeed 'the supreme ornament of oratory' (8. 2. 6), although it should not be used in prose as sometimes in verse, through metrical necessity (8. 6. 18); it is above all the means of illumination: 'metaphor will frequently throw a flood of light upon a subject' (5. 14. 34), it 'shines forth with a light that is all its own' (8. 6. 4). It is certainly intended to be used 'forensically', as it were: 'metaphor is designed to move the feelings, give special distinction to things, and place them vividly before the eye' (8. 6. 19). The author of *On the Sublime* also stresses the emotive effect of images, and hence their aptness for 'vigorous emotion and noble excellence of style', and repeats the advice of Aristotle and Theophrastus (and Cicero) that 'there can be some softening of bold metaphors by inserting *as if*, and *as it were*...The qualification, they say, atones for the boldness.'[1]

If we now turn to the major English Renaissance theorists, we will find agreement on the illuminating effect of imagery and on its persuasive power. A popular rhetorical form in the sixteenth century was the similitude, which is a more 'open' form of the metaphor. Aristotle's fourth category of metaphor was the analogy: 'By analogy I mean when one thing is in the same relation to another as a third thing is to a fourth, and the speaker uses the fourth for the second or the second for the fourth', as for example 'old age is to life as the evening is to the day; so the evening will be called the dying day, or old age, as Empedocles called it, the evening of life, or the sunset of life' (ch. 21). This four-part analogy was revived in Renaissance literature with great success (it must be the only instance in English literature at least where men wrote or read mere collections of images) and, although it is not strictly metaphorical and thus may seem irrelevant here, its accepted pedagogic or expository value gives it an important connection with Bacon's use of analogy in his theory of knowledge. This literary fashion, like so many others, was inspired by Erasmus, whose *De Parabolis sive Similibus* (1514), besides its own enormous vogue, provoked many vernacular collections.[2]

These similitudes were soon put to specific 'forensic' use, the most frequent being, naturally enough in Renaissance literature, a moral one, as in this popular comparison derived from Erasmus, and retold by Anthony Fletcher:

And as the Chameleon will be changed into any colour, save white: so are we most apt and prone, to all kinde of vice, but to no vertue. (*Op. cit.* no. 45.)

The early collection by William Baldwin sees these 'Parables' or 'Semblables' as having a valuable elucidatory function, 'Wherein by easy and familiar truthes, harder thinges and more out of use are declared' (*op. cit.* Sig. A4r). Baldwin also provides justification for their rhetorical efficacy, compared with other moral *exempla*:

For whereas the other only commaunde or shewe the thynge symply, thys kinde by vehemency of matter contayned in other thynges, perswadeth the thynge effectuallye. (Sig. Q2v.)

That is, they gain in effect by deriving logical and emotional power from the third and fourth terms of the analogy: as the most influential rhetorician of the sixteenth century, Thomas Wilson puts it, 'Similitudes are not only used to amplifie a matter, but also to beautifie the same,...and to show a certain maiestie with the report of such resembled things...' Wilson also follows Quintilian (5. 11. 23) in saying that similitudes can be drawn from dumb animals and inanimate objects, so that 'those that delight *to prove things by similitudes* must learn to know the nature' of such things. The effective force of this form is also remarked on by Sir Edward Coke, defining 'Similitudes' as 'comparisons which do best confirm our understanding and fastest cleave unto the memory', and their appropriateness for prose (i.e. oratory) is confirmed by Francis Meres, rejoicing 'to see the naked Truth... invested in Similes, loved of Oratours'. Puttenham sums up all the virtues of the similitude, and applies it specifically to prose:

As well to a good maker and Poet as to an excellent perswader in prose, the figure of *Similitude* is very necessary, by which we not onely bewtifie our tale, but also very much inforce & inlarge it. I say inforce because no one thing more prevaileth with all ordinary iudgements than perswasion by *similitude*.[1]

Thus this apparently banal rhetorical device became invested with qualities of ornament, clarification, and indeed proof.

Similar qualities were of course ascribed to metaphor, but not the pedagogic (or should one say hermeneutical?) function of the similitude. Thomas Wilson follows Aristotle, Cicero, and Quintilian in explaining the origin of metaphor, the sources from which it can be drawn, and its illuminating power: if there is any difficulty in the thought, Wilson says, a metaphor 'much lighteneth it', and gives the greatest suggestiveness and stimulus to the imagination 'because every translation is commonly, and for the most part referred to the senses of the bodie, and especially to the sense of seeing, which is the sharpest and quickest above all other'. (One recalls how often Sidney evokes the visual force of literary images in his *Apology for Poetry*.) Puttenham places metaphor under a general head of figures which 'affect the minde' and under a more specific head of 'figures *sensible* such as by alteration of intendmentes affect the courage, and geue a good liking to the conceit', and he gives the third and major example of its use as being 'to enforce a sence and make the word more significatiue: as thus, "I burne in loue"...' These basic criteria of illumination and intensification are stated by Henry Peacham with his usual thoroughness, listing the 'manifold frutes' of 'Apt Metaphors':

First, they give pleasant light to darke things, thereby remouing unprofitable and odious obscuritie. Secondly, by the aptnesse of their proportion, and nearnesse of affinitie, they worke in the hearer many effects, they obtaine allowance of his iudgement, they move his affections, and minister a pleasure to his wit. Thirdly, they are forcible to perswade. Fourthly to commend or dispraise. Fiftly, they leave such a firme impression in the memory, as is not lightly forgotten.

And at the turn of the century we find John Hoskins repeating the dual function in defining the use of metaphor as 'the friendly and neighborly borrowing of one word to express a thing with *more light* and *better note*'.[1]

Behind the whole discussion of imagery in the Renaissance there lies the essential concept of literary communication as developed by rhetoric, that of the writer working to persuade and convince his audience, and in this 'affective' theory metaphor is given the leading part. Quintilian says that 'metaphor is designed to move the feelings, give special distinction to things, and place them vividly before the eye', Puttenham that images 'inforce and inlarge' the sense, Peacham that 'they worke in the hearer many effects'; and all are agreed on the intellectual faculties thus affected—imagination, passions, wit, judgment and memory. Literature to a Renaissance mind is a much more direct form of communication between writer and reader than it has been in later theories. But there is more to the function of imagery than this one-to-one transmission, for the writer in addition to the demands of source or plot-form must also take into account the genre in which he works, the appropriate style, the variations in tone according to the structure, and many more such elements. The relationship of imagery to this whole complex of artistic variables in the Renaissance has been excellently analysed by Rosemond Tuve, and I can do no better than to summarise her major findings. She shows how inappropriate modern concepts of imagery are, especially their demand that an image be mimetically accurate 'and convincing in its sensuous detail', and their willingness to accept 'the accurate representation of an author's emotional experience or state of mind' as in itself sufficient basis for a poem (pp. 80, 14). She destroys for ever the idea that the Elizabethans used images as pure patches of ornament, decorative additions with no relation to the work as a whole: 'the nature of the imagery and the intention of a poem are indissolubly connected' (p. 21), and, whereas a modern writer might develop a poem through its images alone, examples of powerful imagery in seventeenth-century poems which seem to be like this are in fact introduced by direct statement, that is, as analogies supporting an argument (p. 176). When Drayton revises his early poems he makes the images still more logical (p. 69); when Marlowe writes *Hero and Leander* he makes the images change according to the tone and argument (pp. 273–8). No Elizabethan writer is ever content to present his argument merely through images nor without taking up an attitude to the subject (pp. 42, 114, 400), for the 'habit' persisted '(in both writer and reader) of seeing the intelligible in the visible' (pp. 53–6), of making the outward beauty represent an inner quality. Hence the basically organic quality of Renaissance poetry is due to an 'interpenetration of object with meaning in obedience to the nature of the evaluation being expressed' (p. 75). It can be said that 'idea before image' is the normal sequence, and although the great imaginative writers transcend this separation, fusing idea and image, it is not possible to show which 'came first', while the norm is not in any case discredited by being exceeded.

On the more detailed stages of communication Miss Tuve shows that the Renaissance writer has two large shaping duties: on the one hand 'Intention determines form' (p. 137), so that the poet is always careful to ask himself 'what is the poem for?' and to 'show where the poem is going' (pp. 110, 179). So strong is this awareness of the audience that we must postulate a 'constant adjustment to some hypothetical reader', for 'no one seems to hit on the solution of thinking of poems independently of readers' (p. 180), and those readers will be left in no doubt as to the poet's opinion—such a comment as this by a modern critic praising a modern poet: 'We are not told what to think; we are told to look at the situation' (p. 394) would be regarded as a total abdication of the poet's controlling vision. On the other hand the poet must meet the demands of such formal considerations as genre: if he is writing a 'demonstrative' work, involving praise and dispraise, then certain types of imagery are appropriate (pp. 82–4); if (like most lyric poets) he writes within the 'deliberative' vein, to persuade or dissuade—then he will use images of another kind (pp. 84–6), so that differences in imagery between poems by different writers are likely to tell us more about the type of poem than about the poet. For these reasons the concept of decorum legislated quite sharply on the appropriate images for the three styles (pp. 192–3, 230–7), for the various 'kinds' (pp. 237–43) and of course for a variety of speakers: as Puttenham says, 'every mans stile is for the most part according to the matter and subiect of the writer, or so ought to be' (p. 244). Although the modern theorist may be reluctant to admit 'the necessity of this degree of rational control' (p. 212) he must not forget the deliberate process of planning, the constant control over writing which the Renaissance writer exercised: always form your metaphor 'from a thing of equal or greater dignity', Hoskins writes (remembering Aristotle), '*unless your purpose be to disgrace*' (p. 211), and even within this specific kind there are obviously many degrees and ways of devaluation by metaphor. Finally, Miss Tuve brings out clearly and rightly the 'forensic' nature of imagery, showing that 'similitudes are generally advanced not as illustrations but as arguments' (p. 371), and that this dialectical use of imagery is widespread and traditional:

That no startlingly new conception of the functioning of images is needed to make men use them to prove and to convince is quite obvious. Men have always used them so. Moreover, the relation of such image-proofs as I have here exemplified to the old rhetorical aim of persuasion was apparent to everyone. Certainly an honest reader has a hard time telling when a writer's images have persuaded him by moving his affections, and when convinced him by well-taken arguments. (P. 377.)

If Miss Tuve's detailed analysis is taken together with the classical and Renaissance discussions of imagery which I have cited, then a coherent composite picture emerges, against which Professor Knights's objections to Bacon's use of metaphor are seen to be ill founded. To complete this theoretical outline Bacon's own references to imagery can be quickly marshalled. Although he makes enormous and varied use of imagery, we look in vain for any full-scale discussion of it as an aspect of style—like Lichtenberg on the aphorism, the form seems so completely a part of the writer that he doesn't think it worth commenting on. Occasionally Bacon consciously refers to the process in passing, with remarks like 'to vary the metaphor', or 'it can be expressed by an easy metaphor', and once seems to recognise its expressive function, commenting on a pertinent quotation: 'These words (*holpen a little with a metaphor*) *may express* two differing abilities in those that deal in estate' (6. 444; my italics). He is certainly aware of the persuasive power of imagery, reproving the rebel Oliver St John at his trial in 1615 for using this weapon: 'And this I would wish you and all to take heed of, how you speak seditious matter in parables, or by tropes and examples' (12. 145), and he states succinctly the theory behind the Renaissance love of the emblem: 'Emblem reduceth conceits intellectual to images sensible, which strike the memory more' (3. 399). Bacon is equally aware of the strength of argument by analogy, and recalls Wilson and other rhetoricians in the way that he criticises the schoolmen for not having relied upon 'evidence of truth *proved by* arguments, authorities, *similitudes*, examples' (3. 286; my italics). And, like Sidney, he criticises the Euphuists' fondness for similitudes drawn from 'unnatural natural history', but on grounds of factual accuracy: 'for as things now are, if an untruth in nature be once on foot, what by reason of the neglect of examination and countenance of antiquity, and what by reason of the use of the opinion in similitudes and ornaments of speech, it is never called down' (3. 331, 4. 295). This negative criticism also testifies to the argumentative power of analogy.

Clearly these few references could not be used to credit him with a stylistic theory of metaphor. But Bacon does discuss the power of analogy in communication on a larger scale, mainly in the scientific works, and here it has an important function. In the Preface to the *Wisdom of the Ancients* he gives the theoretical justification for the high value he attached to parables and fables, which 'clear and throw light upon' meaning:

Nor is there any man of ordinary learning that will object to the reception of it as a thing grave and sober, and free from all vanity; of prime use to the sciences, and sometimes indispensable; I mean the employment of Parables as a method of teaching, whereby inventions that are new and abstruse and remote from vulgar opinions may find an easier passage to the understanding. (6. 698.)

Here Bacon is clearly in line with contemporary teachings on the value of similitude. Because of the clarifying power of such forms, he argues, in ancient times and when men's understanding was limited, 'the world was full of all kinds of fables, and enigmas, and parables, and similitudes', to aid understanding. But this is not a mere relic of primitive societies: the argument from analogy is of immediate relevance to, say, a man in Bacon's position:

And even now if any one wish to let new light on any subject into men's minds, and that without offence or harshness, he must still go the same way and call in the aid of similitudes. (*Ibid.*)

An 'easier passage', 'new light'—these are Bacon's favourite metaphors for communication, as we shall see, but, over and above this traditional clarificatory function of analogy, Bacon seems to regard it as basic to man's whole conceptual progress. In the *Valerius Terminus*, a first sketch for the *Advancement of Learning*, he deters men from trying to penetrate divine mysteries, for '*there is no proceeding in invention of knowledge but by similitude*: and God is only self-like, having nothing in common with any creature, otherwise than as in shadow and trope' (3.218; my italics). In the *Advancement* he draws several of his ideas together, stressing both the need for analogy in communicating 'that knowledge which is new and foreign from opinions received', so that the men involved in such a process must 'have recourse to similitudes and translations to express themselves' (3. 406–7; *translatio* is the usual Latin term for metaphor: cf. 'a metaphor or translation', 3. 310), and also relating analogy to the process of invention: 'So in divine learning we see how frequent Parables and Tropes are: for it is a rule, "That whatsoever science is not consonant to presuppositions, must pray in aid of similitudes"' (3. 407).

This account of the role of analogy in the human cognitive process might be related to some modern philosophical theories of how men invent conceptual models, and it is an acute perception on Bacon's part. But he goes on to claim a still greater function for analogy, and one in which few readers today can follow him. This is found in the last stage of his application of similitudes to his scientific theory, revealing an interest in magic and alchemy.[1] The *De Augmentis* expands and clarifies a passage in the *Advancement* where Bacon urges the cultivation of a *philosophia prima*, a body of facts and techniques common to all the sciences, to be based on parallels between axioms from different sciences. So, he concludes (and with an image which Shelley praised), men should be encouraged

to note the correspondence between the architecture and fabric of things natural and things civil. Neither are all these which I have mentioned, and others of this kind, only similitudes (as men of narrow observation may perhaps conceive them to be), but plainly the same footsteps of nature treading or printing upon different subjects and matters. (3. 349; 4. 339.)

Some of the assumptions implicit in this idea are developed in the *Novum Organum* (Book 2, aphorism 27), where the sixth Prerogative Instance is that of 'Instances Conformable, or of Analogy, which I also call Parallels, or Physical Resemblances', and which can be used to form axioms. All natural resemblances, between plants and animals, plants and men (one is reminded of Baudelaire's 'Correspondances'), between the elements, between even the physical outlines of continents, are significant, therefore man should study 'resemblances and analogies of things, as well in wholes as in parts. For these it is that detect the unity of nature, and lay a foundation for the constitution of sciences.' And he sums up this section in another effective image, praising 'a certain sagacity in investigating and hunting out Physical Conformities and Similitudes' (4. 164–8). Faced with this massive semi-mystical concept of analogy as a creative force in the universe the literary student is forced to retreat, only remarking that again Bacon seems to have taken over a traditional stylistic form (as with the aphorism) and applied it to very special and ultimately unrevealed purposes. But one wishes that he had been as scrupulous in defining his scientific tools as he was in outlining the ends to which they were to be put.

II

Happily no obscurity surrounds Bacon's actual use of the argument from analogy; indeed it is the aspect of his writing which will most attract the modern reader. Recalling the criteria of the rhetoricians and the analysis of Miss Tuve, it can be said in general terms that Bacon's use of imagery corresponds to the traditional pattern in that it is used to express the writer's attitude to his subject in a direct and illuminating way, and is intended to persuade and convince his readers. His attitude may sometimes be neutrally objective, but is more likely to approach the complementary functions of praise and dispraise, and the imagery will always be used for a particular purpose—as Miss Tuve wittily says, 'not a flea dies in Donne but for a cause' (p. 173). It may seem questionable to apply Miss Tuve's analysis, which is mainly based on Renaissance lyric poetry, to Bacon, but, as we have seen, then as earlier, the criteria for imagery were applied specifically to prose, and in fact Bacon's situation as a prose-writer approaches very close to that of the lyric poet: both are involved in demonstrative and deliberative orations (Tuve, pp. 82 ff.); indeed Bacon's whole life's work is geared to persuade and dissuade the world, in several intellectual spheres (law, science, politics), and in these his writing has an added urgency, being much nearer to action than the poet's. Again, like Bacon the lyric writers are extremely fond of using aphorisms and maxims to convey their wise observations on life (pp. 18–21); in both forms the use of imagery may be termed *univocal*. If we were studying a dramatist we should have to take into account many additional factors: the use of imagery to describe a character, either externally or from within his own language; to convey one character's attitude to another; to present the thematic meanings of the play as a whole, or of particular situations, and so on. But for Bacon or for Donne (and as both Mr Leishmann and Mrs Righter have reminded us the two are not dissimilar in imaginative quality) we are perfectly justified in studying images in relation to the topic they illuminate, and to the writer's attitude to that topic. One last aspect of critical method concerns the relation of images to the artistic work as a whole: as the image is organically related to the context of argument and tone it is essential, at least to begin with, to examine the image as it functions in its place, and so I shall concentrate this analysis on a work conceived and executed as a whole, the *Advancement of Learning*, and especially its first book.

Having praised the king, and announced the two parts of his treatise, Bacon begins the first, 'concerning the excellency of learning' by reviewing the criticisms of it, and he introduces this section with a metaphor drawn from the law-courts:

In the entrance to the former of these,—to clear the way, and as it were to make silence to have the true testimonies concerning the dignity of learning to be better heard without the interruption of tacit objections,—I think good to deliver it from the discredits and disgraces which it hath received... (3. 264.)

Although the image was introduced with an 'as it were' such as the classical rhetoricians recommended to 'atone for the boldness', there is no lack of confidence in the way that it progresses, and we notice at once how Bacon characteristically uses a concrete human situation to clarify an abstract conceptual state, making the 'review of criticisms' a more tangible and solid process, and also reducing these criticisms to the level of a noisy crowd of spectators being silenced by some officer of the law. Bacon reverses the image for a more powerfully tangible and also disapproving effect in Book 2, to convey his opinion of those logicians who have used induction superficially:

they hasted to their *theories* and *dogmaticals*, and were imperious and scornful toward particulars; which their manner was to use but as *lictores* and *viatores*, for sergeants and whifflers, *ad summovendam turbam*, to make way and make room for their opinions, rather than in their true use and service. (3. 387.)

Again a definite human localization for an abstract intellectual process (the image being more 'tactile' than 'visual'), and again this is applied to a belittling effect (the figure *meiosis*), reducing these overhasty logicians' use of particulars to the rough and indiscriminate treatment handed out to a mob by burly 'sergeants and whifflers'. Of course one might question Bacon's attitude to his subject on this and other points, but I simply want to analyse the method and imaginative energy with which he expressed it.

In addition to the movement from abstract to concrete we find already at this stage of his work the choice of metaphors from natural phenomena, as in this image, which is to become so important to Bacon: 'God hath framed the mind of man as a mirror or glass capable of the image of the universal world, and joyful to receive the impression thereof, as the eye joyeth to receive light' (265). We see too the way in which Bacon will allow an image to develop itself, to move through all the stages appropriate to its existence as a thing in itself, while reflecting back illumination on the topic it joins with. So he takes up the criticism that 'knowledge hath in it somewhat of the serpent, and therefore where it entereth into a man it makes him swell,—*Scientia inflat*, (knowledge puffeth up)' (264): this is itself an image for intellectual vanity, but Bacon proceeds to take it seriously, almost literally, developing all the attributes of the metaphor in denying that there is anything in knowledge itself which would make a man's mind

swell or out-compass itself; no, but it is merely the quality of knowledge, which be it in quantity more or less, if it be taken without the true corrective thereof, hath in it some nature of venom or malignity, and some effects of that venom, which is ventosity or swelling. This corrective spice, the mixture whereof maketh knowledge so sovereign, is Charity, which the apostle immediately addeth to the former clause; for so he saith, *knowledge bloweth up, but charity buildeth up.* (266; 1 Cor. viii. 1.)

Bacon is here giving more attention to the analogy than the object, thinking from one stage of the image to the next, creating a whole chain of cause and effect from natural phenomena, so that when he finally returns to his topic it is with a much increased pressure 'to inforce and inlarge' it—and at the end of this section he repeats the image and now translates it: 'only let men beware that they apply both to charity, and not to swelling; to use, and not to ostentation' (268). And he uses a similar chain-effect for the image of medicine for the body and manners (271, 274). This consistency of reference within an image is felt even when the consequences are not fully developed, as in his brief reference to 'wonder (which is the seed of knowledge)' (266): this is again a localised natural image, and contains in itself the basis for a further idea (the growth of curiosity determining the growth of knowledge) which is not stated. A similar effect is produced by this brief metaphor from the Icarus myth: 'divers great learned men have been heretical, whilst they have sought to fly up to the secrets of the Deity by the waxen wings of the senses' (267). The image is consistent, though undeveloped: we know what will happen.

The characteristics of Bacon's imagery so far revealed—clarity, concrete localisation, fluid development of both sides of the image —persist in abundance, and are used, quite rightly, to enforce particular attitudes. Looked at in reference to the structure of the work, this use of analogy as argument is seen more at the end of sections than at the beginning. So for example in answering the second criticism, that learning makes men unfit for politics and business, Bacon begins each part of his reply by mustering all the theoretical arguments and historical examples which support his case, reserving for the end images to clinch the argument, which are often witty and allusive. Thus he sums up the positive lessons for life which a man can draw from books, the last two points being:

Let him but read the fable of Ixion, and it will hold him from being vaporous or imaginative. Let him look into the errors of Cato the second, and he will never be one of the Antipodes, to tread opposite to the present world. (272.)

The highly condensed nature of that final image (a form of serious wit), has a delayed illuminating effect which somehow clinches the whole argument—the eye immediately moves on to the next paragraph and the next topic while the mind is still digesting the fruits of that metaphor. This placing of the most imaginative effect last is seen again at the end of a section arguing that criticism of rulers for being learned is unjust, and is especially

not needful for the present, in regard of the love and reverence towards learning which the example and countenance of two so learned princes, Queen Elizabeth and your Majesty, being as Castor and Pollux, *lucida sidera*, stars of excellent light and most benign influence, hath wrought in all men of place and authority in our nation. (274.)

A last example of this delayed-explosion technique might be the conclusion to Bacon's defence of the honourable 'privateness or obscureness' of the lives of scholars, where again he joins a classical allusion to the image:

learned men forgotten in states, and not living in the eyes of men, are like the images of Cassius and Brutus in the funeral of Junia; of which not being represented, as many others were, Tacitus saith, *Eo ipso praefulgebant, quod non visebantur*; (they had the preeminence over all—in being left out). (276.)

These witty concluding analogies (which of course must be read in context) are effective summings-up of positions already formed, but Bacon does not ask them to carry much weight in argument—the point is made almost without them. Yet an important characteristic of his images is that they are often the imaginative centre of his argument, around which other supporting points revolve. So taking the common criticism of the 'meanness of employment' of scholars, in that 'the government of youth is commonly alloted to them', he turns it upside down with this analogy from the cultivation of plants:

But how unjust this traducement is (if you will reduce things from popularity of opinion to measure of reason) may appear in that we see men are more curious what they put into a new vessel than into a vessel seasoned, and what mould they lay about a young plant than about a plant corroborate; so as the weakest terms and times of all things use to have the best applications and helps. (276.)

Again Bacon has moved from an abstract idea to a concrete process, and to that natural source from which so many of his images come,[1] and with still more conviction to those incontrovertible natural phenomena which, when aptly applied to an intellectual idea (men *are* more careful about younger plants, all colours *will* agree in the dark) result in as near an approximation to certainty as analogy can ever produce. Another way in which Bacon successfully bases an argument on an analogy is to present it with considerable emotional power, usually at the extremes of praise and blame. So he argues that learned men are usually more dedicated to 'their countries or masters' than to 'their own fortunes or safeties' and contrasts them in this to 'the corrupter sort of mere politiques, that have not their thoughts established by learning in the love and apprehension of duty', and from this traditional ethical basis (on which he always distinguishes between mere politic prudence and truly moral, responsible behaviour) he attacks the politicians' selfishness: they refer all things to themselves, and thrust themselves into the centre of the world, as if all lines should meet in them and their fortunes; never caring in all tempests what becomes of the ship of estates, so they may save themselves in the cockboat of their own fortune... (279; see also 6. 431–4.)

There both images are remarkably apt for the self-centredness and separateness of such men, and the force of Bacon's anger pushes him on from that Donne-like metaphor from geometry to the time-honoured image for the honest counsellor—at the tiller of the ship of state—without any intermediate non-metaphorical stage.

In this last example we see a quality of Bacon's imagery which is impressively 'poetic', that emotional or imaginative power which fuses the parts of an image together so that the thought or attitude being expressed becomes essentially metaphorical. Of course he normally conforms to Renaissance expectations in first 'having an idea' and then 'finding the appropriate image for it', but the image is generally so fully realised that it exists as a separate entity which is not servilely dependent on the idea, and in moments of extreme imaginative energy the images develop of their own accord, or even run ahead of the idea. This emotional and imaginative pressure is wonderfully revealed in the central attack on Ciceronianism and scholasticism, one of Bacon's most brilliant pieces of writing. As a final stage in the dismissal of the first 'distemper', the Ciceronians' worship of the mere externals of communication is embodied in uncomfortably apt images: such reverence for ornament is bound to 'discredit learning, even with vulgar capacities, when they see learned men's works like the first letter of a patent or limned book; which though it hath large flourishes, yet it is but a letter' (284). And, although we might argue that ornamental capitals have an artistic value, we have to concede the force of the analogy—whole works made out of such 'large flourishes' are indeed useless—and at once Bacon's scorn finds another image for this decadent split between form and content:

It seems to me that Pygmalion's frenzy is a good emblem or portraiture of this vanity: for words are but the images of matter; and except they have life of reason and invention, to fall in love with them is all one as to fall in love with a picture. (*Ibid.*)

Once more the analogy based on a concrete phenomenon has an irrefutable logical truth to it, while also being very damaging. It seems feeble to invoke the constant criteria for imagery to say that this is 'apt', 'appropriate', or 'illuminating'—it is all of these and much more, for like all imaginative writing it makes the criteria of legislative criticism look like mere blanket generalities, and makes analysis, even after the event, difficult.

In the description of scholasticism which follows, the images really begin to take on a life of their own, and we can discern something of the process of association which generates them. (As we have seen, this passage is also remarkable for its syntactical structures, which work so closely with the imagery that any separation of them, however essential for the purpose of analysis, is forced and artificial.) The initial analogy, drawn as ever from concrete natural processes, is the very deflating comparison between the indisputable phenomenon by which 'many substances in nature which are solid do putrefy and corrupt into worms' and the schoolmen's equally inevitable reduction of knowledge to 'vermiculate questions'. That alone is a wonderfully imaginative analogy, and a great example of *meiosis*, a literal 'diminution' of the schoolmen's concept of learning to the level of small nasty animals which is worthy of Nashe's fantastic reductions. Bacon's imagination continues to move on this low level and ultimately formulates the metaphor of the spider: he does this by no logical progression, rather by a deflating intent and an associative process, yielding a complex and a very real image (the spider is so strongly realised that it seems inappropriate to describe it as a 'metaphor'). Within this image Bacon suspends several strands of meaning, which emerge one by one to deflate the schoolmen still more:

their wits being shut up in the cells of a few authors...did out of no great quantity of matter, and infinite agitation of wit, spin out unto us those laborious webs of learning which are extant in their books. For the wit and mind of man, if it work upon matter, which is the contemplation of the creatures of God, worketh according to the stuff, and is limited thereby; but if it work upon itself, as the spider worketh his web, then it is endless, and brings forth indeed cobwebs of learning, admirable for the fineness of thread and work, but of no substance or profit. (285–6.)

So from the cellular image Bacon developed quite fluently the repellent idea of the schoolman feeding on himself and producing his 'cobweb of learning' which could go on 'endlessly', and uselessly. There is throughout an extraordinary extension of the idea, Bacon's characteristic fully coherent development of the image and all its properties, which at each stage can reapply to the topic the attributes of the image in their appropriate form—as in the final mock-praise of the end-product: 'admirable for the fineness of thread and work...'

Bacon now develops his criticism of the scholastics' futile controversies partly through the squabbling disyllabic suffixes ('objections, solutions') but also with that image for the hypothetical and abstract 'unity of the sciences' which could not be surpassed for concrete natural universality of reference: 'whereas indeed the strength of all sciences is, as the strength of the old man's faggot, in the bond'. There is something rather humiliating about the social connotations of associating the schoolmen with poor old men and their faggots, and further deflation follows in the syntax and in the wonderfully concrete image of the squabbling schoolmen breaking these sticks one by one. But these images, destructive in themselves, are made more so by their imaginative association: Bacon has moved from the spider's cobweb to the old man's sticks by taking up the idea of fragility common to each, which seems to have been a supra-logical extension of the idea, or at any rate one attained by pure analogy. And by the same process, after that ironic reduplication of the Seneca quotation, he carries the argument and the image a stage further, by developing the idea of 'single' sticks as opposed to the whole faggot, but now in terms of light:

For were it not better for a man in a fair room to set up one great light, or branching candlestick of lights, than to go about with a small watch candle into every corner? (286.)

Again the comparison implicit in the analogy is undeniable, for we would avoid the futile hunting with one tiny candle at all costs —and, like the single sticks and the spider's web, the image is so fully realised that we almost forget that throughout the images are directed against the futilities of scholastic controversy. As if realising that his imagination might be leading us away from the target Bacon recapitulates: 'And such is their method...'

But his emotional contempt is not yet exhausted, nor therefore is the imagery. While repeating the comic effect of the Latinate suffixes a new image occurs to Bacon, and he develops it with such speed and imaginative energy that the sequence must be quoted whole, not pre-echoed by analysis:

> their method, that rests...upon particular confutations and solutions of every scruple, cavillation, and objection; breeding for the most part one question as fast it solveth another; even as in the former resemblance, when you carry the light into one corner, you darken the rest: so that the fable and fiction of Scylla seemeth to be a lively image of this kind of philosophy or knowledge; which was transformed into a comely virgin for the upper parts; but then *Candida succinctam latrantibus inguina monstris*, (there were barking monsters all about her loins:) so the generalities of the schoolmen are for a while good and proportionable; but then when you descend into their distinctions and decisions, instead of a fruitful womb for the use and benefit of man's life, they end in monstrous altercations and barking questions. (286–7.)

There is an inexhaustible well of imagery being drawn on here, starting with the word 'breeding'. Bacon seems to have used it at first in its dead metaphorical sense of 'producing', but then to have seen its potential, revived its power as a metaphor and then extended it, possibly rejecting the image of the Hydra head which seems to lie behind 'breeding...one question as fast it solveth another', in order to end with the horrible image of Scylla. But while moving into this analogy he unifies the passage as a whole by reviving and making still more detailed the candle image ('when you carry the light into one corner, you darken the rest') and by continuing the Latinate suffixes down to their appropriately cacophonous close 'in monstrous altercations and barking questions'. Similarly he crosses the gap between tenor and vehicle

with the pun on 'descend' (i.e. logically: 'have a closer look';
literally, in terms of the image: 'go down'—by translating it we
see that the two parts are one), and having brought us back to the
schoolmen he returns to the image and to the quotation to juxtapose 'a fruitful womb' with these 'barking monsters all about her
loins' (one recalls Chaucer's fable of what was found under the
devil's tail). The process of juxtaposition has been operative
throughout at great imaginative speed, flashing back and forth
between image and object, with the metaphors sprouting in
advance of the idea—'these images that yet / Fresh images beget'.

The union of sound, syntax and imagery in the whole passage is
masterly, but the images affect the reader most: in Peacham's
words, 'they obtaine allowance of his judgement, they move his
affections, and minister a pleasure to his wit'—appealing jointly to
our logical, imaginative and emotional faculties—but they do all
this with a force that no rhetorician seems to have foreseen.
Bacon's images certainly correspond to Renaissance requirements,
but they also exceed them, in ways not accounted for by the
theorists. Miss Tuve's argument that Renaissance writers progress
not from image to image but from one prior stage of thought to
another, which is then illustrated and extended by imagery,
sound though it is, would have to be revised to include at least this
passage by Bacon, as it obviously would for much by Shakespeare.
In terms of total effect, the images in the rest of the *Advancement*
may seem an anticlimax, and in a sense it is right that they should,
for Bacon has gathered all his resources here to destroy an obstacle
to future development such as would have inspired any progressive
Renaissance mind to contempt, if not to this degree of eloquence.

But, if the images remaining seem disappointing, that is only
because we can look down on them from a new height: they have
many excellent qualities, and express a great variety of moods. In
sharp contrast to this impassioned denunciation of the distortions
of the past, on the next page Bacon deals with a similar issue in a
very different way, describing how credulity and superstition long
prevailed in ecclesiastical history, so that many false miracles were
accepted: 'yet after a period of time, when the mist began to clear

up, they grew to be esteemed but as old wives' fables...' (288). That image of 'the mist' is again concrete, drawn from natural phenomena, but the tone is now so relaxed, almost throw-away, that it is impossible to regard it as a serious problem any more. These metaphors drawn from nature do not fulfil a major classical and Renaissance criterion for imagery, in that they are not actually 'visual', for, although they may appeal to what Cicero calls 'the eyes of the mind', we are seldom referred to what the vehicle looks like but rather to what it has or does, that is, to its attributes. This focus on the significance of the natural object rather than on its shape, size or colour, is of course quite typical of the Renaissance mind, with its propensity for seeing 'the intelligible in the visible', but Bacon goes further than this, referring not only to known but to predictable behaviour, to processes which are immutable and so form an absolute fixed point around which the analogy turns. So, arguing that in mechanical arts the first inventions are crude and are improved by time, whereas 'in sciences the first author goeth furthest, and time leeseth and corrupteth', he constructs a long complicated balancing of the two ideas, with much syntactical parallelism between them, and many examples, and then suddenly produces this analogy:

For as water will not ascend higher than the level of the first spring-head from whence it descendeth, so knowledge derived from Aristotle, and exempted from liberty of examination, will not rise again higher than the knowledge of Aristotle. (290.)

Nothing could be more absolute than the natural phenomenon, strengthened as it is by the future tense 'will', and nothing could have been better chosen to fit the stagnant nature of passive discipleship—in fact it fits so well that it seems a truism, and we tend to say 'but of course you couldn't improve on Aristotle like this'. But this is just what we should say, for the very successful nature of Bacon's 'deliberative orations' (to persuade and dissuade) is such that we are quite deterred from following that which is mocked: like his aphorisms, the images point to action.

As Bacon goes on analysing the errors which have crept into the discovery and transmission of knowledge, the images illuminate and confirm his argument at every stage, often by their appeal to the laws of nature, or to specifically human experience (e.g. pp. 292–3). But as he comes to 'the greatest error of all the rest' we find a penetrating analysis of human vanity expressed in an unusually long image sequence, where tenor and vehicle are separated in order to accumulate a variety of correspondences, in a remarkably fluent period which also makes use of some syntactical techniques which have been analysed: this 'greatest error' is

the mistaking or misplacing of the last or furthest end of knowledge. For men have entered into a desire of learning and knowledge, sometimes upon a natural curiosity and inquisitive appetite; sometimes to entertain their minds with variety and delight; sometimes for ornament and reputation; and sometimes to enable them to victory of wit and contradiction; and most times for lucre and profession; and seldom sincerely to give a true account of their gift of reason, to the benefit and use of men: as if there were sought in knowledge a couch whereupon to rest a searching and restless spirit; or a terrace, for a wandering and variable mind to walk up and down with a fair prospect; or a tower of state, for a proud mind to raise itself upon; or a fort or commanding ground, for strife and contention; or a shop, for profit or sale; and not a rich storehouse, for the glory of the Creator and the relief of man's estate. (294.)

Syntactically that sentence depends on an overall equality of structure (there are six matching clauses in each part) which is sharpened by the use of such figures as *parison* and *anaphora*, but with sufficient variation in the pattern for it not to become monotonous, and with the whole movement being built up to the climactic last term in each part. The two-part structure is made still clearer by Bacon's separating the various attitudes to learning in the first part from the images in the second part which not only localise the frame of mind which produces each attitude but also present a brief judgment on them. The remarkable aspect of the 'vehicles' is their apt and concrete nature: the desire for 'ornament and reputation' is for 'a tower of state'; that for 'victory of wit' is for 'a fort'; and that for 'lucre' is for 'a shop, for profit, or sale'—such motives could surely not be more definitely localised. And the final and only admirable image is caught up again at the end of the paragraph, and varied slightly in the injunction that 'knowledge may not be as a curtesan, for pleasure and vanity only, or as a bond-woman, to acquire and gain to her master's use; but as a spouse, for generation, fruit, and comfort' (295). Images in Bacon are not just the fruits of a moment, but carry on with the current of his thought, sometimes to a great distance, as we shall see.

This ability to focus an image into clearly localised human terms is a persistent source of delight to the reader of Bacon, not least in the closing pages of Book 1 of the *Advancement*, as in the fluid series of metaphors in the sentence in which he moves from dispraise to praise (295), or in the explanation of these words of Solomon concerning man's enquiry into nature:

'The glory of God is to conceal a thing, but the glory of the King is to find it out'; as if, according to the innocent play of children, the Divine Majesty took delight to hide his works, to the end to have them found out; and as if Kings could not obtain a greater honour than to be God's playfellows in that game. (299.)

The extraordinary ease of reference with which Bacon develops the vehicle there, presenting science as a child's game of hide-and-seek, and the kings as 'God's playfellows', is seen again in his comparison of the folly of those who judge God's works only in their superficiality to the men who value a jeweller according to what he puts in his window (300)—and both these images 'work' on the reader, now persuading us to join in the enjoyable search for what lies behind appearances. But that playfulness gives way on the next page to this equally concrete but more serious image for an ethical point, that genuine innate moral strength persists even when external supports fail: philosopher-kings are the best, for, whatever

their imperfections in their passions and customs, yet if they be illuminate by learning, they have those notions of religion, policy, and morality, which do preserve them and refrain them from all ruinous and peremptory errors and excesses; whispering evermore in their ears, when counsellors and servants stand mute and silent. (302.)

The ideally persistent working of moral principles could not be given more substantial human form than this, nor one more acutely related to the relevant context. And we find the same imaginative power to be able to present abstract ideas in fully realised human terms in this wonderfully illuminating simile for the uneducated man's weakness in self-criticism:

the faults he hath he will learn how to hide and colour them, but not much to amend them; like an ill mower, that mows on still and never whets his scythe. (315.)

Criticism breaks down before such brilliant, but simple and universal analogies: the use of metaphor 'demands originality and is a sign of genius; for to make good metaphors is to perceive similarity in dissimilars'.

As a last example of the variety of imagery in Book 1 of the *Advancement* we can consider two images which correspond to the extremes of praise and dispraise proper to the demonstrative genre. First the latter intent: here is a sombre reminder of man's littleness, a reflection on the 'mortality and corruptible nature of things' which should reconcile us to death:

Certainly if a man meditate much upon the universal frame of nature, the earth with men upon it (the divineness of souls except) will not seem much other than an ant-hill, whereas some ants carry corn, and some carry their young, and some go empty, and all to and fro a little heap of dust. (314.)

That image is a great moral diminution of man, a *meiosis* of humanity, within the same *contemptu mundi* tradition and with the same plangency, as Raleigh or Browne. At the other extreme, that of the enlargement of man's nature and hopes, Bacon can also create strongly localised images, and with that sign of increased imaginative power whereby the images fuse one into another. The following sequence (the quotation of which was broken off at this point in the last chapter) comes as one of the last and most eloquent praises of learning and letters:

But the images of men's wits and knowledge remain in books, exempted from the wrong of time and capable of perpetual renovation. Neither are they fitly to be called images, because they generate still, and cast their seeds in the minds of others, provoking and causing infinite actions and opinions in succeeding ages.

So that if the invention of the ship was thought so noble, which carrieth riches and commodities from place to place, and consociateth the most remote regions in participation of their fruits, how much more are letters to be magnified, which as ships pass through the vast seas of time, and make ages so distant to participate of the wisdom, illuminations, and inventions, the one of the other? (318.)

The onward movement and transformation of those images stem from a creative imagination of supreme power and energy.

If enough space were available, a detailed analysis of the imagery in Book 2 of the *Advancement* would show as much variety, if possibly less intensity, in the imaginative function of the images. The essential qualities of Bacon's imagery have already been outlined, but if we could pick out one aspect from this second Book it would be his continued and possibly increasing tendency to allow vehicle to precede and even displace tenor, that is to think in images. So Bacon argues that there will be no advance in the natural sciences 'except there be some allowance for expenses about experiments; whether they be experiments appertaining to Vulcanus or Daedalus, furnace or engine' (325): he prefers the concrete image, the human (albeit personified) realisation, adding the literal meaning almost as a concession for less imaginative readers. So earlier in this paragraph he stressed the need for practical, not theoretical work, calling upon men to 'sell their books and to build furnaces; quitting and forsaking Minerva and the Muses as barren virgins, and relying upon Vulcan'. The concrete personification again precedes the idea when he complains that no man has yet written a general history of learning, 'without which the history of the world seemeth to me to be as the statua of Polyphemus with his eye out; that part being wanting which doth most shew the spirit and life of the person' (329–30). More and more we find the image presented directly, with the reader being expected to perceive the idea by the means of analogy alone: 'Antiquities are history defaced, or some remnants of history which have casually escaped the shipwrack of time' (333); or the extension of an image proceeds without coming back to ths idea: 'As for the corruptions and moths of history which are Epitomes', they have 'fretted and corroded the sound bodies of many excellent histories, and wrought them into base and un-profitable dregs' (334). Far from being a 'scientific' thinker ruth-lessly intent on pressing his ideas on us Bacon seems sometimes more attracted by the analogy than by the idea,[1] as in his loving exposition of a fable used by Ariosto in *Orlando Furioso* (337), or the way that he develops a comparison between divine and human knowledge as between rain and dew (346), or in this speculation on the fluctuating nature of human health:

This variable composition of man's body hath made it as an instrument easy to distemper; and therefore the poets did well to conjoin Music and Medicine in Apollo: because the office of medicine is but to tune this curious harp of man's body and to reduce it to harmony. (371.)

There Bacon's feeling for the other side of the analogy is so strong, so vivid ('this curious harp of man's body') that the literal-minded reader might complain that he has been told very little about the idea. In fact Bacon shows in such passages precisely the imaginative faculty which L. C. Knights would deny him, by which 'similes and metaphors have a life of their own—sometimes too abundant and vigorous a life for the purpose of logical or "scientific" argument'.

Bacon tends more and more to develop the associations implicit in the image rather than relying on any logical extensions of the original idea: as in a remarkable sequence on the average man's reaction to the 'dry light' of pure philosophy:

The part of Human Philosophy which is rational, is of all knowledges, to the most wits, the least delightful; and seemeth but a net of subtilty and spinosity. For as it was truly said, that knowledge is *pabulum animi* (the food of the mind;) so in the nature of men's appetite to this food, most men are of the taste and stomach of the Israelites in the desert, that would fain have returned *ad ollas carnium*, (to the flesh-pots,) and were weary of manna; which, though it were celestial, yet seemed less nutritive and comfortable. So generally men taste well knowledges that are drenched in flesh and blood. (383.)

Not many readers of the accepted accounts of Bacon would sus-pect him of ever writing 'sensuous' imagery,[2] but in this example his constant drive towards the concrete fully realised image is of that order—or, in general terms, he exploits with ingenuity the full range of associations within the image, even beyond the bounds of what an Elizabethan theorist would regard as decorum. His ingenuity is seen on a much smaller scale too, as at the end of a paragraph discussing Aristotle's argument that 'common-places' (that is, quotations, arguments, images, and so on) are not a necessary part of a speaker's preparation, and to have them in readiness would be as silly 'as if one that professed the art of shoe-making should not teach how to make up a shoe, but only exhibit in readiness a number of shoes of all fashions and sizes'. Bacon answers this directly by inverting Aristotle's image—'But yet a man might reply, that if a shoe-maker should have no shoes in his shop, but only work as he is bespoken, he should be weakly customed'—and then quotes other authorities for the opposite view, ending the paragraph thus: 'All which authorities and precedents may overweigh Aristotle's opinion, that would have us change a rich wardrobe for a pair of shears' (390). It would be a pity to bring this metaphor down from the imaginative plane, but I think that the reader's mind perceives the analogy, and the variation on Aristotle's image, long before he begins to precipitate a logical translation of it—as, say, 'the ready-made rather than the mere tools to make'. Although it may be subordinate to Bacon's actual intent, I am sure that Cicero's suggestion that 'intellectual agility' in itself produces pleasure in the image is well confirmed here, for (as so often) the thought is in the image.

Bacon's freedom in analogy is such that he can freely fuse images, move from one metaphorical plane to another. At the moment of germination of his concept of the four Idols, the 'fallacies in the mind of man', he describes the danger of this inherent tendency to error:

the force whereof is such, as it doth not dazzle or snare the understanding in some particulars, but doth more generally and inwardly infect and corrupt the state thereof. For the mind of man is far from the nature of a clear and equal glass, wherein the beams of things should reflect according to their true incidence; nay it is rather like an enchanted glass, full of superstition and imposture, if it be not delivered and reduced. (395.)

Here we have images within images, moving from the plane of 'dazzle or snare' to that of 'infect and corrupt' and then suddenly to the image of the glass, which by a remarkable fusion of ideas then takes over the dangers inherent in the first group: 'an enchanted glass', and extends these before finally producing the positive antidotes. Faced with this fluid transition from a visual to a medical to a magical tenor, the non-imaginative reader might complain that Bacon has 'mixed his metaphors' here, and ask how it is possible to have a 'glass', 'full of superstition and imposture'. We could perhaps spell it out for him and break down the various stages by which the images were transformed—but it would achieve little, and it would be like those paraphrases of Shakespeare's *Sonnets*, which may trap something of the meaning, but let the poetry escape, such critical reductions being, as Bacon would say, 'like cobwebs; where the small flies were caught, and the great brake through' (7. 150). Let us rather take a last example of this ingenious and illuminating crossing of the planes of imagery, another comment on that respected and sometimes portentously handled modern topic, the difficulties inherent in human communication:

certain it is that words, as a Tartar's bow, do shoot back upon the understanding of the wisest, and mightily entangle and pervert the judgment. (396.)

That concrete witty image sums up pages of more serious discussion, and imprisons it memorably within the sphere of a single imaginative globule.

'Lord Bacon was a poet', said Shelley, and though this is to mistake a quality of imaginative reference open to all Renaissance prose-writers for the more special control of poetic forms and modes, one cannot but agree to the essential truth. Although I have discussed only a tiny proportion of Bacon's contextual use of imagery, reference to virtually any work across his whole range of interests would confirm the qualities of his fundamentally analogical thinking here revealed. D. G. James has pointed to the imaginative qualities which Bacon shares with Shakespeare, and

Image and Argument

C. W. Lemmi has rightly said that '*The Wisdom of the Ancients* is not *The Faerie Queene*, but we shall not understand it if we think of it as something very different' (B 61, p. 213). Even though he heralded a new age, in almost every respect Bacon is not really a 'new man', but an old-fashioned Renaissance mind. He may point out new directions, but he remains very close to tradition, not least in being a 'thinker in images'.

CHAPTER 6

PHILOSOPHY
AND IMAGE-PATTERNS

That Bacon gave great importance to analogy as a method of scientific discovery may be an embarrassment to the non-philosopher, but it takes on peculiar importance when viewed in relation to the language in which he communicated his ideas about science. We have seen how his characteristic development of an image often gave it almost an independent existence, and how his imaginative energy would extend the attributes of that image in advance of the idea which it expressed; so it will not seem unlikely that these images might develop and expand over the years in which he formulated his theories for the new age of science. And if we read through his complete works this is what we actually find: certain images recur throughout, and quite definite patterns emerge, especially those used in connection with his major intellectual preoccupation, the discovery and transmission of knowledge. The image-patterns are at their most coherent when applied to this lifelong endeavour, but there is inevitably some overlapping between the scientific works and those on political and legal topics. In the civil sphere 'star' or 'sun' may be an image for the sovereign, while in the scientific world it may represent a source of light or ordered movement; images from medicine are often used for a favourite and traditional comparison of the body natural to the body politic, but equally well for the diseases which pester the healthy growth of learning. Images drawn from the theatre (which, despite a popular misconception about Bacon, are many and vigorous) are expressive for general human vicissitudes as for particular plot purposes—such as the conspiracies of Perkin Warbeck in *Henry VII*. Some image-groups, on the other hand, appear mainly in the philosophical works: the image of a voyage of discovery is seldom used for anything but the extension of knowledge, and, although the civil works abound in images drawn from the parts of a building, the idea of establishing a sound foundation on which to build a solid structure is almost invariably used as an image for the erection of a philosophical system.

Given Bacon's tendency to think in images, it seems to be a valid critical approach to group and analyse the development of the vehicles of his images when consistently applied to the same tenor —here the advancement of learning, the development of knowledge in all human spheres. Such an approach can be extremely valuable in building up a writer's view of the world, and if by the very nature of the material to be considered here I avoid the distorting effect which it can give when applied to the drama or the novel (for by grouping his chosen sets of images into a neat or evolving pattern the critic often destroys the whole structure of cause and effect on which the work was built) then it is a deliberate, not accidental choice by which I avoid the other main pitfall of this method, its use for biographical reconstruction, as in the pioneer but naïve work on Shakespeare by Caroline Spurgeon.[1] Thus I do not intend to work back from the images to speculation about Bacon's psychological make-up, but rather to keep moving from vehicle to tenor, to try and chart Bacon's attitude to intellectual progress and the terms on which he presents his plan for the future. By this means I shall also keep to my own injunction to study images in their context, for the context remains the same although Bacon is constantly opening new avenues to it. These main image-groups do not exhaust either the range or the depth of Bacon's imagery, but they do amount to more than a third of the total images, and this although there are only five major groups. These are, besides those of building and voyaging, images of natural growth, images involving water, and images of light; and within each group there is usually a related set of images which stand as negatives opposed to the positive trend of the group as a whole. The groups are large, with great variety of reference, and it is necessary to simplify to show the main structures; therefore I shall arrange the groups in increasing order of magnitude so as to discover which images for learning take on most importance for Bacon. Needless to say, the qualities of his imagery already analysed—clarity, vividness of concrete reference, imaginative fluency—are still evident here, even though I have to curtail comment on them in order to bring out the patterns which they form, those constantly expanding horizons of knowledge.

I

The smallest group numerically is that of 'building', though its importance for Bacon seems to grow with time. We find it first, albeit faintly, in the *Valerius Terminus* (accepting Spedding's early date for this work), where the Pyrrhonists are criticised: 'they ought when they had overthrown and purged the floor of the ruins to have sought to build better in place' (3. 244). In the *Advancement of Learning*, although we have such metaphors as 'the judicial place or palace of the mind' (3. 346), and a comparison of 'exact methods' with buildings that look neat but are 'more subject to ruin than those which are built more strongly in their several parts, though less compact' (3. 484), the only images drawn from the process which was to become a dominant concern for him are those used to compare human and divine knowledge: 'And although the human foundation hath somewhat of the sand ...yet the divine foundation is upon the rock' (3. 473—earlier, God is described as the 'arch-type or first platform...', 3. 295) and the advice to 'build upon that foundation which is as a corner-stone of divinity and philosophy' (3. 473). (Obviously that image is Biblical in origin, and I should perhaps say here that I do not intend to investigate the sources of the images—they are traditional, but they are re-energised by Bacon.) By the time of the *Great Instauration*, however, the image of building becomes one of the most significant emblems for him of his attempt to begin the study of nature afresh on the basis of observation and experiment. In the *Prooemium* to the work he describes the errors of the present way of proceeding and its consequences:

whence it follows that the entire fabric of human reason which we employ in the inquisition of nature is badly put together and built up, and like some magnificent structure without any foundation. (4. 7.)[1]

To combat man's tendency to prefer the false powers of the mind to the true ones, there 'was but one course left, therefore,—to try the whole thing anew upon a better plan, and to commence a total reconstruction of sciences, arts, and all human knowledge, raised upon the proper foundations' (4. 8). This image now sums up the whole direction of his life-work.

What he considers to be the 'proper foundation' is explained in the 'Epistle Dedicatory' to James I, who is urged to follow the example of Solomon

in taking order for the collecting and perfecting of a Natural and Experimental history true and severe...such as philosophy may be built upon...that so at length, after the lapse of so many ages, philosophy and the sciences may no longer float in air, but rest on the solid foundations of experience of every kind, and the same well examined and weighed. (4. 12.)

Bacon outlines his own position within this reconstruction programme by simply extending the metaphor:

I have provided the machine, but the stuff must be gathered from the facts of nature.

In the *Preface* he repeats the image (4. 16, 21) and in the 'Plan of the Work' he makes it still more precise:

For I also sink the foundations of the sciences deeper and firmer; and I begin the inquiry nearer the source then men have done heretofore. (4. 25.)

This idea is linked up with two other recurrent images of Bacon's, first that of digging into nature, as into a mine, to discover truth:[2] he describes his own method in the preceding paragraph as being 'extracted not merely out of the depths of the mind but out of the very bowels of nature'. Secondly, he connects it in his fluent way with the mirror of human knowledge, which is to reflect accurately the image of nature: 'Of this reconstruction the foundation must be laid in natural history, and that of a new kind and gathered on a new principle. For it is in vain that you polish the mirror if there are no images to be reflected' (4. 28).

This image of laying the foundation of the sciences is repeated time and again in the scientific works: in the *Parasceve* (4. 252), in the *Novum Orbis Scientiarum* (5. 121), in the *Descriptio Globi Intellectualis* (5. 507–9) and, most of all, in the *Novum Organum* (4. 49, 63, 105–6, 107, 110, etc.), where in constant repetition it becomes a focal point of his work. So in two consecutive aphorisms we find the following cluster of images: he marks the end of the first part of the *Instauration*, 'which is devoted to pulling down', and describes his intentions with a typically concrete and human application of the metaphor:

For whereas in this first book of aphorisms I propose to prepare men's minds as well for understanding as for receiving what is to follow; now that I have purged and swept and levelled the floor of the mind, it remains that I place the mind in a good position and as it were in a favourable aspect towards what I have to lay before it.

The image reaches completion as he declares his intention not to bother with mere speculation:

My purpose, on the contrary, is to try whether I cannot in fact lay more firmly the foundations, and extend more widely the limits, of the power and greatness of man. (4. 103–4.)

This dominant 'building' image suggests other related images— the 'Door' of the senses (4. 192; repeated in the *De Augmentis*, 4. 292–3), the 'outer courts' of Nature, where philosophy rests, unable to penetrate to 'her inner chambers'[1] (4. 124), and, most ingenious, the argument for not presenting footnotes and acknowledgments:

the ancients...thought it superfluous and inconvenient to publish their notes and minutes and digests or particulars; and therefore did as builders do—after the house was built they removed the scaffolding and ladders out of sight. (4. 111.)

But the optimism with which Bacon had propounded this image in the *Instauratio Magna* was not, as we know, supported by any movement, public or private, to help him in his work. So it was that he feverishly tried to compile his own 'foundations', in the fragmentary *Historia Naturalis et Experimentalis* and in the completed, but disappointing, *Sylva Sylvarum*. His images suffer a parallel disillusionment, and the confident announcement to the king that 'I have provided the machine, but the stuff must be gathered from the facts of nature', becomes a sad but remarkably articulated extension of this image of construction which perfectly conveys the humiliating reversal of his plans. It is presented in a brief form in the *De Augmentis*, where Bacon comments on the irony that 'being one that should properly perhaps be an architect in philosophy and the sciences, I turn common labourer, hodman, anything that is wanted' (5. 4). The aptness of the metaphor in relation to his whole plan is exact, for, as Rawley records in the Preface to the *Sylva*:

the scope which his lordship intendeth, is to write such a Natural History as may be fundamental to the erecting and building of a true philosophy...For, having in this present work collected the materials for the building, and in his *Novum Organum*, of which his lordship is yet to publish a second part, set down the instruments and directions for the work; men shall now be wanting to themselves if they raise not knowledge to that perfection whereof the nature of mortal man is capable.

And now Bacon focuses the image on himself as Rawley seems to catch him in conversation:

And in his behalf, I have heard his lordship speak complainingly, that his lordship, who thinketh he deserveth to be an architect in this building, should be forced to be a workman, and a labourer, and to dig the clay, and burn the brick; and, more than that (according to the hard condition of the Israelites at the latter end), to gather the straw and stubble, over all the fields, to burn the bricks withal... (2. 335–6.)

The aptness of the Biblical analogy is impressive, and the extraordinary completeness of Bacon's identification of himself with his metaphor shows once more his innate preference for the concrete, fully realised image, here carried to the ultimate.

Identification of actor and image is seen again in the next group of images, that drawn from a journey, on land and sea, which is for Bacon a metaphor for the search for knowledge, the pilgrimage for truth. This idea is always present in the philosophical works,[1] and he elaborates it in great detail: we can appreciate this best, perhaps, by considering it stage by stage, first on land. In the *Advancement* physicians are urged to use 'the true approaches and avenues of nature' (3. 373), the image of an 'entrance' often occurs (3. 264, 268, 363, 390) and in the *Abecedarium Naturae* Bacon describes himself as one 'just entering on the path' (5. 210). The nature of the path is important: already in the *Advancement* we have in embryo the sense of obstruction caused by its being oblique: 'For Physic carrieth men in narrow and restrained ways, subject to many accidents of impediments, imitating the ordinary flexuous courses of nature' (3. 357). By the time of the *Novum Organum* the importance of this image of the pathway, as of the other major groups, has increased enormously and we can trace its complete development there. It is vital to choose the right path to knowledge, because 'as the saying is, the lame man who keeps the right road outstrips the runner who takes a wrong one. Nay it is obvious that when a man runs the wrong way, the more active and swift he is, the further he will go astray' (4. 62).[1] The present way men have of conducting experiments is 'blind and stupid', for 'wandering and straying as they do with no settled course and taking counsel only from things as they fall out, they fetch a wide circuit and meet with many matters, but make little progress' (4. 70). Whereas Bacon's method, the Interpretation of Nature,

commences with the senses, and leads from the perceptions of the senses by a straight, regular, and guarded path to the perceptions of the understanding. (4. 192.)

As the work develops the image is used for a surprising range of reference: the road of Bacon's method 'does not lie on a level, but ascends and descends; first ascending to axioms, then descending to works' (4. 96), and 'opens broad roads to human power' (4. 122); 'the roads to human power and to human knowledge lie close together' (4. 120); curious unions can occur in 'the beaten and ordinary paths of nature' (4. 122; repeated in the *De Augmentis*, 4. 420); Metaphysics should be called Magic, 'on account of the broadness of the ways it moves in, and its greater command over nature' (4. 126); the 'parting of the roads' even provides another metaphor for *partitio* (4. 180, 182). The persistence of this image shows how relevant Bacon finds it to his own situation, and there are many references to 'paving' or 'opening' a way—'an astonishing thing it is...that no mortal should have seriously applied himself to the opening and laying out of a road for the human understanding direct from the sense, by a course of experiment orderly conducted and well built up' (4. 80; also 4. 124, 173; *Thema Coeli*, 5. 555, 557; *De Augmentis*, 4. 437). As ever, the attributes of the image are quite consistent as Bacon's imagination moves fluently between tenor and vehicle, finding illuminating analogies even to the smallest details. Thus (to give a simple example), on any journey one needs to know the direction, so the fourteenth of the Prerogative Instances consists of 'Instances of the Fingerpost; borrowing the term from the fingerposts which are set up where roads part, to indicate the several directions' (4. 180; the image is also found in the *Advancement*, 3. 328); the eighteenth instance is the 'Instance of the Road' which 'points out' the direction for nature to follow (4. 201). Bacon sums up the process of striking a path towards knowledge with another remarkable instance of the identification of himself with his image:

If there be any that despond, let them look at me, that being of all men of my time the most busied in affairs of state, and a man of health not very strong (whereby much time is lost) and in this course altogether a pioneer, following in no man's track nor sharing these counsels with any one, have nevertheless by resolutely entering on the true road, and submitting my mind to Things, advanced these matters, as I suppose, some little way. (4. 102.)

The idea of cutting a path seems in fact to have become identified with the *Novum Organum* in Bacon's mind, judging from the criticism in the *Historia Naturalis et Experimentalis* of those who have not listened to his warnings: 'they prefer to walk on in the old path, and not by the way of my Organum, which in my estimation, if not the only, is at least the best course' (5. 133).

The other philosophical works are less firmly connected to one image, and also take a less sanguine view of the chance of success.

The obstacles to the progress of knowledge are several: the path may be blocked (4. 81), or no exit may be visible (4. 8); the footing may be unsure (4. 149; 5. 524), the traveller may grope in the dark, as does the haphazard experimenter (4. 413), or he may lose his way (4. 412). Bacon's favourite word for this predicament is 'to wander'; in the *Sylva Sylvarum* he prophesies: 'knowledge will be ever a wandering and indigested thing, if it be but a commixture of a few notions that are at hand and occur' (2. 614; also 6. 133; 3. 331; 4. 371; 5. 503). Of all the negatives which oppose positive progress in this group, the most potent for Bacon is that of the place in which man gets lost, be it a wood, a maze, or a labyrinth. The idea occurs in all the main philosophical works—the *Valerius Terminus* (3. 250); the *De Augmentis* (4. 288, 370); the *Sylva Sylvarum* (2. 337), even the *Novum Organum* (4. 81). It takes on its most important meaning in the Preface to the *Instauratio Magna*, where it becomes an emblem of man's difficulty in understanding the universe, expressed in a characteristically fluid imaginative extension of metaphor:

But the universe to the eye of the human understanding is like a labyrinth; presenting as it does on every side so many ambiguities of way, such deceitful resemblances of objects and signs, natures so irregular in their lines, and so knotted and entangled. And then the way is still to be made by the uncertain light of the sense, sometimes shining out, sometimes clouded over, through the wood of experience and particulars; while those who offer themselves for guides are (as was said) themselves also puzzled, and increase the number of errors and wanderers. (4. 18.)

The only hope is for steps to be 'guided by a clue' (*ibid.*), and in his interpretation of the fable of Daedalus in the *Wisdom of the Ancients* Bacon sees the labyrinth as an allegory for mechanical inventions, which are both created and understood by the man who knows 'the clue of experiment' (6. 735). So the proper cure of diseases is called 'the Physician's Clue' (4. 390), and a work which attempts to solve one specific problem is called, by an entirely coherent extension of the image (whether conscious or not), the *Filum Labyrinthi*.

But the labyrinth is only an intermediate difficulty—man can solve it, and can win through to open country, an image which is often[1] used by Bacon to convey the success of a traveller who has persisted through darkness and confusion till he at last achieves freedom and light. So, in the *Novum Organum*, he describes how scientists without a plan wander round and round in nature, 'as in a labyrinth; whereas a method rightly ordered leads by an un-broken route through the woods of experience to the open grounds of axioms' (4. 81). As an image for triumph, however, it lacks the sense of completion attained by the corresponding image in the parallel group of images, those of voyage by sea, which is, of course, the harbour. In the *Advancement of Learning*, Divinity is reserved 'for the last of all, as the haven and sabbath of all men's contemplations' (3. 351); in the *De Augmentis* this image occurs at the end of Book 8, and Bacon catches it up at the beginning of the next and last Book, to form the basis of a magnificent extended image-sequence: 'Seeing now, most excellent King, that my little bark, such as it is, has sailed round the whole circumference of the old and new world of sciences...' (5. 111.)

The image of a sea-voyage is perhaps capable of less elaboration than that of a journey by land, but it can make an equally strong impression, and Bacon finds it of great value to express the progress of learning, particularly the idea of discovery. To those who think it impossible to discover forms he retorts curtly—'As for the possibility, they are ill discoverers that think there is no land when they can see nothing but the sea' (3. 355). Just after this section of the *Advancement* Bacon uses within two pages a whole sequence of voyage images, as if by free association. So after an image already quoted comparing Physic to the 'ordinary flexuous courses of nature', he maintains the image in a quotation from Solomon and in his comment on it: '"thy steps shall not be strai-tened; thou shalt run and not stumble." The ways of sapience are not much liable either to particularity or change.' In the next paragraph he moves from land to sea, as in attacking those who have discussed final rather than physical causes, 'to the great arrest and prejudice of further discovery', the idea of discovery halted suggests at once the halting of a ship; 'for this I find done not only by Plato, who ever anchoreth upon that shore, but by Aristotle, Galen and others, which do likewise fall upon these flats of *discoursing causes*'. To these two causes of 'arrest', anchoring and shipwreck, Bacon adds an ingenious third, comparing these obstructive methods to the sucking-fish believed by the ancients to have the power of staying the course of any ship to which it attached itself:

Nay, they are indeed but remoras and hinderances to stay and slug the ship from further sailing, and have brought this to pass, that the search of the Physical Causes hath been neglected and passed in silence.

And towards the end of the paragraph the image moves back to land, but with a difference: he objects to their methods 'Not because those final causes are not true, and worthy to be enquired, being kept within their own province; but because their excursions into the limits of physical causes hath bred a vastness and solitude in that track' (3. 357–8). Again we see that the ability to think in images does not involve a rigid development of one vehicle, but a fluid movement which is always responsive to variations in the thought.

Images of discovery always imply, as here, the idea of breaking through hindrances, of sailing out boldly into the ocean, an enterprise which must abandon the cautious and fruitless hugging of the shore.[1] So Bacon sums up the present ways of making inventions in the sciences: 'But these are but coastings along the shore, *premendo littus iniquum*' (3. 361). In the Plan of the *Instauratio Magna* he uses the image to describe the first part of that work, the 'Divisions of the Sciences' now represented by the *De Augmentis*, in exactly the same terms in which he had described that 'summary or general description of the knowledge which the human race at present possesses': 'We will therefore make a coasting voyage along the shore of the arts and sciences received; not without importing into them some useful things by the way' (4. 22), and the second part, the *Novum Organum*, is described with an extension of the metaphor: 'Having thus coasted past the ancient arts, the next step is to equip the intellect for passing beyond' (4. 23). This crucial step is prepared for in the Preface to the *Great Instauration*, and again quite consistently in terms of a voyage penetrating the farther reaches of knowledge (it is as if Bacon has a set of images which are intuitively drawn on in connection with the recurrent principles of his scientific theory). The inventions of the ancients, Bacon writes, are not to be despised:

> But as in former ages, when men sailed only by observation of the stars, they could indeed coast along the shores of the old continent or cross a few small and mediterranean seas; but before the ocean could be traversed and the new world discovered, the use of the mariner's needle, as a more faithful and certain guide, had to be found out. (4. 18.)

Again a remarkably 'complete' image, which can point to further extensions of the idea: so the discoveries hitherto in the arts and sciences, which are shallow and obvious, will only be replaced by something that reaches 'the remoter and more hidden parts of nature' by means of 'a more perfect use and application of the human mind and intellect'.

There are obstructions to be overcome first, of course, and these are embodied for Bacon in the images of storm, tempest, and shipwreck, which are frequent and powerful throughout his work. As so often with the images of obstruction and opposition, they are linked by him with enemy philosophers. So he describes how in the dark ages of learning,

> when on the inundation of Barbarians into the Roman empire human learning had suffered shipwreck, then the systems of Aristotle and Plato, like planks of lighter and less solid material, floated on the waves of time, and were preserved. (4. 76.)

(It is clearly a partisan opinion, but the image is a brilliantly damaging expression of it—and in historical terms, as R. F. Jones has shown, reverence for Aristotle was the greatest obstacle to the development of new thought). Similarly Bacon recalls how Ramus also suffered the appropriate fate, shipwreck, when his 'attempt to amend propositions drove him upon those epitomes and shallows of knowledge' (4. 453).[1] So the ship of knowledge, tossing upon the 'waves of experience'[1] must use ballast[2] if she is to reach the 'New World of the Sciences'. The most famous of these obstructions to learning became a symbol for Bacon, and an intellectual image takes on visual form in the emblem of Hercules' Pillars, the *ne plus ultra* of human progress. Bacon refers to this for the first time in the *Advancement of Learning*:

for why should a few received authors stand up like Hercules' Columns, beyond which there should be no sailing or discovering. (3. 321.)[3]

Later in the work, in the section on Cosmography, he discusses the benefits for learning to be gained from a greater knowledge of the world, and quotes Charles V's motto 'plus ultra' as well as the words of the prophet Daniel, without making the metaphoric connection between either the ideas or the quotations (3. 340). But by 1620 this had taken on infinitely greater importance for him, and he chose the device for the magnificent engraved title-page of the *Novum Organum*, showing the ship of learning in full sail, passing between the two pillars, and heading confidently for the open sea, with the motto from the Vulgate 'Multi pertransibunt & augebitur scientia': 'many shall run to and fro, and knowledge be increased'.[4] This obstruction was one which, metaphorically and literally, he triumphantly overcame, pointing the way for the New Science even if it was left for others to reap its fruits.

If the sea is a vehicle of images for the discovery of knowledge and the enlarging of its boundaries, the other image-group that Bacon uses involving water is concerned mainly with the source of knowledge itself. The dominant metaphor for this process, and one which Bacon uses to a surprising extent, is that of a spring-head or fountain. The *Advancement of Learning* uses both images often, always as vehicles for the tenor, knowledge, and each time with great acuteness, as in this elaborate comparison, which again separates the parts for greater clarity:

For as water, whether it be the dew of heaven or the springs of the earth, doth scatter and leese itself in the ground, except it be collected into some receptacle, where it may by union comfort and sustain itself; and for that cause the industry of man hath made and framed spring-heads, conduits, cisterns, and pools, which men have accustomed likewise to beautify and adorn with accomplishments of magnificence and state, as well as of use and necessity; so this excellent liquor of knowledge, whether it descend from divine inspiration or spring from human sense, would soon perish and vanish to oblivion, if it were not preserved in books, traditions, conferences, and places appointed, as universities, colleges, and schools, for the receipt and comforting of the same. (3. 322.)

The correspondence is exact and illuminating, of course; but, more than this, Bacon has created with this image a great sense of the fragility of learning—like water cupped in your hands—and the vital need to *preserve* it (again a dead metaphor is brought to life). Elsewhere he develops the premise of this image: the knowledge of man is 'as the waters, some descending from above, and some springing from beneath', the latter, coming from the light of nature, being 'cumulative and not original; as in a water that besides his own spring-heads is fed with other springs and streams' (3. 346).[1] This section is called 'Philosophia Prima, sive de Fontibus Scientiarum', and Bacon continues the metaphor in reporting it deficient, for 'the profounder sort of wits...will now and then draw a bucket of water out of this well for their present use; but the spring-head thereof seemeth to me not to have been visited'.[2] Again the critic can only point to a degree of concrete realisation present in the image which surpasses all expectations.

Images of fountains are peculiarly attractive to Bacon and, unlike some of the other images, were already formulated in the early works, being especially frequent in the *Advancement of Learning* and proportionally less so in the later scientific works,[3] which may suggest a line of intellectual development. A difference is noticeable, too, in the way he elaborates the image: in the later works as in the earlier, he will use it quite briefly as a metaphor for the origin, or physical source, of learning, but it is only in the *Advancement* that he permits himself long and extended comparisons, such as the one cited above, or the even more precise analogy for the 'true and sound interpretation of the scriptures, which are the fountains of the water of life'. This 'divine water' is 'drawn forth much in the same kind as natural water useth to be out of wells and fountains', and Bacon develops this idea with total consistency:

either it is first forced up into a cistern, and from thence fetched and derived for us; or else it is drawn and received in buckets and vessels immediately where it springeth. The former sort whereof, though it seem to be the more ready, yet in my judgment is more subject to corrupt. This is that method which hath exhibited unto us the scholastical divinity; whereby divinity hath been reduced into an art, as into a cistern, and the stream of doctrine or positions fetched and derived from thence. (3. 483.)

We may remember some of the images that Lancelot Andrewes draws from 'cisterns' and 'conduits', which are similarly improbable at first sight but which successfully extend and localise the meaning.

The fountain is obviously an inspiring image for the rich sources of knowledge waiting to be tapped, and Bacon rarely introduces his negative term at this stage: it is only when water, like knowledge, is in motion, that obstructions can occur. The famous comparison which occurs in all the major works,[1] of Time with a river which brings down to us the ephemera of antiquity, is used always to derogate received philosophies; the worship of Aristotle in particular is devalued by that image of water descending from its first spring-head (3. 290, 227; 4. 16). But, although Bacon is consistent in using these negative terms to attack the delusions of enemy philosophers, they are quite rare: stemming perhaps from one attribute of his image, the ability of flowing water to overcome obstacles, the sense of obstruction connected with it is slight, and the dominant tone of this image-group (as of the others, but with less opposition here) is one of optimism. This can be summed up in a metaphor which also shows how the dual process of the invention and cultivation of knowledge is absolutely fundamental to Bacon's thought:

Let there be therefore (and may it be for the benefit of both) two streams and two dispensations of knowledge; and in like manner two tribes or kindreds of students in philosophy—tribes not hostile or alien to each other, but bound together by mutual services;—let there in short be one method for the cultivation, another for the invention of knowledge. (Preface to the *Novum Organum*, 4. 42.)

The imagery of light, which is of even greater importance to Bacon, can express this dual process with more power and more precision, and raise it to an altogether higher level of significance. The immediate connection, of course, is with divine illumination, and this is made constantly by Bacon, starting from the direct equation of the two in the *Advancement*: the second degree of angels, he says, is traditionally those of 'light': 'the angels of knowledge and illumination', and he goes on:

To descend from spirits and intellectual forms to sensible and material forms; we read the first form that was created was light, which hath a relation and correspondence in nature and corporal things, to knowledge in spirits and incorporal things. (3. 296.)

The *locus classicus* for this image of divine light is the important Essay 'Of Truth':

The first creature of God, in the works of the days, was the light of the sense; the last was the light of reason; and his sabbath work ever since is the illumination of his Spirit. First he breathed light upon the face of the matter or chaos; then he breathed light into the face of man; and still he breatheth and inspireth light into the face of his chosen. (6. 378.)

This identification of light and knowledge runs throughout his work, nowhere more eloquently than in the prayer which ends the Plan of the *Instauratio Magna*:

Therefore do thou, O Father, who gavest the visible light as the first fruits of creation, and didst breathe into the face of man the intellectual light as the crown and consummation thereof, guard and protect this work, which coming from thy goodness returneth to thy glory. (4. 33; see also 4. 298; 5. 462; 3. 147; 6. 378.)

The connection is naturally not original to Bacon, though it is of serious importance to him; what he makes of it, however, *is* original, for it becomes linked to one of his most meaningful ideas, that of the mirror, which, although simply reflecting light, transmits it in the process. The idea which this suggests at once is that of the accuracy of the medium for reflection and transmission, which itself suggests a larger and overruling concept in Bacon's scientific method, that of the need for an exact approach to nature, reflecting and reproducing one's findings without distortion—a sort of scientific *mimesis*. References to this concept in the *Advancement of Learning* are legion—the basic idea is seen in his criticism of one of the 'diseases' of learning, that it destroys

the essential form of knowledge, which is nothing but a representation of truth: for the truth of being and the truth of knowing are one, differing no more than the direct beam and the beam reflected. (3. 287.)

It is, then, a metaphor for the process of sense-perception, and has an important role in Bacon's theory of knowledge—'God hath framed the mind of man as a mirror or glass capable of the image of the universal world' (3. 625; again 3. 380, 452, 220). The image is localised even more precisely within the organ of perception itself:

Are not the organs of the senses of one kind with the organs of reflection, the eye with a glass... (3. 349.)

However, the truth of the image depends on the accuracy of the glass, and Bacon's perception of this factor gives rise to that great image for the inherent weakness of man's perception, the 'enchanted glass'. The image seems to occur to him first when he begins the section on 'knowledge of ourselves', as the idea of knowledge as a ray of light suggests how the nature of the ray is altered by the medium through which it passes:

Thus have we now dealt with two of the three beams of man's knowledge; that is *Radius Directus*, which is referred to nature, *Radius Refractus*, which is referred to God and cannot report truly because of the inequality of the medium. There resteth *Radius Reflexus* whereby Man beholdeth and contemplateth himself. (3. 366; 4. 337.)

But man's mind is a far from accurate mirror, being so 'full of superstition and imposture' that 'the beams of things' are not reflected 'according to their true incidence' (3. 394-5; 4. 27, 54); this is a distortion inherent to man, as he explains in the *De Augmentis*, the human mind being 'dimmed and clouded as it is by the covering of the body' (4. 431). The image has so far been developed with complete consistency to an unexpected length, and is taken still further on a plane parallel to the developing ideas. The remedy for this inaccuracy is given by Bacon in the whole of his theory of scientific method, his positive proposals for the reconstruction of philosophy, which involve, first, removing these subjective distortions of the human mind, and, having cleaned the glass, to begin with new material for observation and experiment based on an accurate study of nature: 'Of this reconstruction the foundation must be laid in natural history, and that of a new kind and gathered on a new principle. For it is in vain that you polish the mirror if there are no images to be reflected' (4. 28). This plea for an accuracy of observation which will remove the subjective distortions of human theory is most powerfully stated at the end of the 'Plan' of the *Instauratio Magna*:

And all depends on keeping the eye steadily fixed upon the facts of nature and so receiving their images simply as they are. For God forbid that we should give out a dream of our own imagination for a pattern of the world. (4. 32–3.)

So Bacon's estimate of the *Sylva Sylvarum* as a work which, based on this new principle, 'is the world as God made it, and not as men have made it; for that it hath nothing of the imagination' (2. 337) is not to be interpreted in the sinister way that some critics have proposed (ignorant, perhaps, of that delusory power commonly attributed to the imagination in the Renaissance): it is simply an announcement of Bacon's belief that his work would purge this 'enchanted glass' and allow once more the clear reflection of truth.

This image of the mirror lies at the very heart of Bacon's philosophical theory, but his other images of light are hardly less important. Light is knowledge; darkness is ignorance: this is the most fundamental of all the many antitheses that Bacon uses. It is always intellectual darkness that he describes, as the sight of the mind is obscured or overcast. An ingenious and damaging analogy links Telesius and the Peripatetics: both 'are very owls in looking at experiments; and that not so much from weakness of vision, as because it is clouded by opinions, as by cataracts, and from impatience of full and fixed consideration' (5. 497). Not all the images of darkness are as ingenious as this, however, though all are concrete and fully localised: images of gloom or shadow, of the vaults and caves of the human understanding, of sight being 'veiled' or covered by 'clouds' and 'vapours', of 'groping in the dark', or of blindness.[1] One cause of error is that men have stood too far away from their object, instead of viewing it at close range (3. 372–3; 4. 382), but on the other hand knowledge has the advantage of intellectual height, and looks out on the world as from a hill. This idea is present in the *Advancement*, but in a rather confused form: 'no perfect discovery can be made upon a flat or a level: neither is it possible to discover the more remote and deeper parts of any science, if you stand but upon the level of the same science, and ascend not to a higher science' (3. 292). The connection between physical and intellectual domination is more clearly implied in the often quoted passage from Lucretius (*Suave mari magno*) but only receives explicit statement in the *Wisdom of the Ancients*:

all knowledge may be regarded as having its station on the heights of mountains; for it is deservedly esteemed a thing sublime and lofty, which looks down on ignorance as from an eminence, and has moreover a spacious prospect on every side, such as we find on hilltops. (6. 756; also 3. 235, 355; 4. 171, 335, 378.)

To aid this clearness of perception the eye is obviously the most important single agent, and Bacon shows the coherence of his imagery of knowledge and sight by insisting that the eye of the understanding must have all the qualities of the physical eye. In the *Advancement of Learning* he declares: 'he that cannot contract the sight of his mind as well as disperse and dilate it, wanteth a great faculty' (3. 279) and in the *Sylva Sylvarum* he develops the analogy ingeniously for his theory of observation: 'The eye of the understanding is like the eye of the sense; for as you may see great objects through small crannies or levels, so you may see great axioms of nature through small and contemptible instances.'[2]

From the image of sight as the perception, we pass to that of light as the transmission of learning. This is implicit in Bacon's criticism of disputatious philosophers in the *Advancement* as having only a 'small watch candle' with which to illuminate knowledge.

A fuller statement of the image comes when, in interpreting the fable of *Sphinx* as 'Science' in the *De Sapientia Veterum*, Bacon explains that wings were added to the creature 'because the sciences and the discovery of science spread and fly abroad in an instant; the communication of knowledge being like that of one candle with another, which lights up at once' (6. 756). By the time of the *Novum Organum* this image has developed, and he uses it to show the difference between his method of experiment, and the present unplanned accidental way, which is

a mere groping, as of men in the dark, that feel all around them for the chance of finding their way; when they had much better wait for daylight, or light a candle, and then go. But the true method of experience on the contrary first lights the candle, and then by means of the candle shows the way... (4. 81.)

And in the *De Augmentis* the image is used to describe the essential process of the communication of knowledge, the 'Handing of the Lamp, or Method of Delivery to Posterity' (4. 450), with its inspiring reminiscence of the runners in a Greek torch-race, each one passing on the flame of knowledge to the runner of the next stage. This *Traditio Lampadis* represents for Bacon the ideal communication of learning, with each worker sacrificing himself so that the race may continue: again there is a continuity between image and action in the history of Bacon's last years, with his desperate attempt to light all kinds of torches for the future.

Bacon divided successful experiments into 'experiments of light' and 'experiments of fruit' (4. 95), and his division of the progress of the sciences into the intellectual advance of pure knowledge, and the bringing of this knowledge to fruition in the practical affairs of man, may serve as a fitting transition to the last, and greatest, of these image-groups in Bacon's writing, that of natural growth. He uses this image in relation to knowledge in every possible way, directly reflecting the cyclic processes of nature, and seems to do so consciously:

So supposing that in the revolution of time and of the ages of the world the sciences have their ebbs and flows; that at one season they grow and flourish, at another wither and decay. (4. 90.)

This is another image-group which was well developed in the early work, and we have already seen in other contexts some of the natural images from the *Advancement*, as in this quite coherent group related to methodology: aphorisms are made from 'the pith and heart of sciences' and are to be preferred to 'the canker of Epitomes', and especially to the end-products of Ramism: 'certain empty and barren generalities, being but the very husks and shells of sciences, all the kernel being forced out and expulsed with the torture and press of the method'. Here as ever intellectual processes are presented in clearly defined natural form, as in those organic images for *partitio*, most memorably in the insistence that

the distributions and partitions of knowledge are not like several lines that meet in one angle, and so touch but in a point; but are like the branches of a tree that meet in a stem, which hath a dimension and quantity of entireness and continuance, before it comes to discontinue and break itself into arms and boughs...
(3. 346.)

(The fact that, in order to do justice to this aspect of Bacon's imagery, we ought to be doubling back to recall more material already discussed is another proof of the coherence of attitude and expression in his work.)

But a tree and its cultivation is also an image for intellectual growth in general terms:

And this I take to be a great cause that hath hindered the progression of learning, because these fundamental knowledges have been studied but in passage. For if you will have a tree bear more fruits than it hath used to do, it is not any thing you can do to the boughs, but it is the stirring of the earth and putting new mould about the roots that must work it. (3. 324.)

That image might have seemed as detailed and coherent and as fully in touch with natural processes as could be imagined, but Bacon has greater reserves of all these qualities, as he shows later in the *Advancement*, and again in order to convey intellectual concepts in tangible form. He is arguing that in the communication of knowledge as practised now 'there is a kind of contract of error between the deliverer and the receiver', instead of that useful mode of communication whereby knowledge 'is delivered as a thread to be spun upon', and he develops the distinction in natural terms:

a man may revisit and descend unto the foundations of his knowledge and consent; and so transplant it into another as it grew in his own mind. For it is in knowledges as it is in plants: if you mean to remove it to grow, then it is more assured to rest upon roots than slips. So the delivery of knowledges (as it is now used) is as of fair bodies of trees without the roots; good for the carpenter, but not for the planter; but if you will have sciences grow, it is less matter for the shaft or body of the tree, so you look well to the taking up of the roots. (3. 404.)

Here, as so often, the thought is in the metaphor rather than in the argument, and, even when the reader of Bacon gets used to his imaginative skill in extending and modulating images, such fully sustained analogies still come as a surprise. As we read on it seems as if Bacon has deliberately brought in the whole range of natural processes: so he advises historians to record in detail all particular events, as by this means

the compiling of a complete History of Times might be the better expected, when a writer should arise that were fit for it: for the collection of such relations might be as a nursery garden, whereby to plant a fair and stately garden when time should serve. (338.)

If not elsewhere as brilliantly placed as that, images of seeds and sowing recur,[1] as in the great peroration to Book 1: 'the images of men's wits and knowledges remain in books...and cast their seeds in the minds of others'. Again image results in identification, for in the *Novum Organum*, as at the end of the *De Augmentis*, Bacon sees himself as the sower: although he may not complete the work, he holds it enough 'if in the intermediate business I bear myself soberly and profitably, sowing in the meantime for future ages the seeds of a purer truth' (4. 104).

For the plant to flourish, there are certain necessities, and in the *Valerius Terminus*, that brilliant but little-known work, the ill fortunes of learning are diagnosed entirely in even more precise natural terms:

The encounters of the times have been nothing favourable and prosperous for the invention of knowledge; so as it is not only the daintiness of the seed to take, and the ill mixture and unliking of the ground to nourish or raise this plant, but the ill season of the weather by which it hath been checked and blasted. Especially in that the seasons have been proper to bring up and set forward other more hasty and indifferent plants, whereby this of knowledge hath been starved and overgrown. (3. 224–5.)

That remarkable example of thought in imagery is supported by many other full and rich analogies drawn from agricultural processes.[1] The prime injunction is not to sever knowledge from its roots in nature, which is yet another metaphor for Bacon's ever present scientific programme of observation and experiment. In the *Novum Organum* he writes that much can be learned from the analysis of the progress of 'systems and sciences':

For what is founded on nature grows and increases; while what is founded on opinion varies but increases not. If therefore those doctrines had not plainly been like a plant torn up from its roots, but had remained attached to the womb of nature and continued to draw nourishment from her,

then the sciences would not have been barren, as they have been since Aristotle. Both natural and human processes are again combined in pointing out the contrasting advantages of the 'mechanical arts', which, 'founded on nature and the light of experience... are continually thriving and growing, as having in them a breath of life' (4. 74; see also 3. 228; 4. 78, 79).

Images of roots and growth can also be used to describe the unwelcome appearance of pernicious elements in the sciences, as in the *Sylva Sylvarum*:

The philosophy of Pythagoras, which was full of superstition, did first plant a monstrous imagination, which afterwards was, by the school of Plato and others, watered and nourished. (2. 640; also 4. 48, 53.)

Other by now familiar natural images for intellectual blight can be applied to unwanted phenomena—'moths', 'canker', 'distempers', 'ventosity or swelling'. But as an antidote to these we are presented with the image of knowledge itself as a medicine which 'ministers to all the diseases of the mind; sometimes purging the ill humours, sometimes opening the obstructions, sometimes helping digestions, sometimes increasing appetite, sometimes healing the wounds and exulcerations thereof' (3. 315; also 3. 271; 4. 89)—again we note the thought-process by metaphor. But the imagery of disease, like that of weeds and tares, is relatively infrequent in the philosophical as compared with the civil works, and this whole image-group of natural growth is by far the most positive of the major patterns in Bacon's thought. Early works, such as the *Valerius Terminus*, may present a rather pessimistic view of the state of knowledge, but the later ones are far more confident, and, although this may seem to contradict the despair revealed in his report of being both architect and hodman, that referred to the present: these metaphors point to the future. In addition his own work has now produced more positive results and proposals, and we find one recurrent image growing in pressure, that of bearing fruit, both in natural and in human terms.

The image of fruition in mankind is found of course in the *Advancement of Learning* when Bacon insists that the 'last end' of learning should be to make knowledge 'as a spouse for generation, fruit, and comfort'.[1] The positive side of this image of marriage and birth is developed in the *Instauratio Magna*, first in the Preface, where he writes that by his method 'I suppose that I have established for ever a true and lawful marriage between the empirical and the rational faculty, the unkind and ill-starred divorce and separation of which has thrown into confusion all the affairs of the human family' (4. 19). In the 'Plan of the Work' he carries the image a stage further in concluding his account of the refutation of the Idols in the *Novum Organum*, and making a sort of hymeneal celebration for the New Science:

> The explanation of which things, and of the true relation between the nature of things and the nature of the mind, is as the strewing and decoration of the bridal chamber of the Mind and the Universe, the Divine Goodness assisting; out of which marriage let us hope (and be this the prayer of the bridal song) there may spring helps to man, and a line and race of inventions that may in some degree subdue and overcome the necessities and miseries of humanity. (4. 27.)

Further proof of the complete assurance with which Bacon handles metaphor is given by his witty logical extension of this

image: the next part of the Instauration is designed to 'supply a
suckling philosophy with its first food' (4. 29).

The other fruit-imagery in the scientific works may be noted
more briefly. The *Descriptio Globi Intellectualis* proposes 'the pro-
curing of such fruits and benefits to the human race' as are possible
(5. 513, 523), and the *Wisdom of the Ancients* attacks 'anything that
yields no fruit' (6. 706) while the *Parasceve* is 'only a granary and
storehouse of matters' (4. 255). The *Novum Organum* has many of
these metaphors: 'Of all signs there is none more certain or more
noble than that taken from fruits. For fruits and works are as it
were sponsors and sureties for the truth of philosophies' (4. 73);
axioms rightly discovered and established supply practice with its
instruments, not one by one, but in clusters (4. 71); intellectual
barrenness is to be despised (4. 74, 83), practice yields fruit (4. 41,
71), and the harvest is patiently expected: 'Nor do I make haste to
mow down the moss or the corn in blade, but wait for the harvest
in due season' (4. 105). The *Instauratio Magna* repeats the attack on
barrenness (4. 24) together with the image of harvest and 'clusters'
of axioms (4. 29), and attacks 'preposterous subtlety and winnow-
ing of argument' (4. 28). The *Historia Naturalis et Experimentalis* is
the 'first fruits' of Bacon's Natural History (it is itself 'like a grain
of mustard-seed') and in it he warns us to expect no fruit from
extant philosophy (5. 127, 131). He admits the inadequacy of the
title of the *Historia Densi et Rari*: it 'only gleans the ears, and does
not reap the crop' (5. 395); similarly the section on education in the
De Augmentis is not complete, 'Nevertheless, I will as usual give a
few hints, gleaning an ear here and there' (4. 494–5). Finally, of the
great many fruit-images in his other work, it is perhaps fitting to
quote from one of the last letters he wrote, where he described his
scientific writings sadly but accurately: 'to say the truth, they are
the best fruits I now yield' (14. 536).

II

The *De Augmentis* itself was but 'a seed', but, like the rest of his work, it bore fruit in the seventeenth century and that well, 'not in knots, but in clusters'. Despite the limitations of Bacon's theories, and despite his own lack of understanding of some major developments in science, the call for observation, experiment, and co-operation was essentially right for that stage of scientific development, and was responded to with great eagerness, the most immediate result being the foundation of the Royal Society. And, if one reads the pronouncements of any of those followers of Bacon up to the time of Boyle and Newton, such as for example that representative cross-section quoted and discussed by R. F. Jones in *Ancients and Moderns*, it becomes obvious that what they took over from Bacon was not the precise details of his scientific method but the recurrent images in which he analysed deficiencies and prophesied new growth.[1] For with Bacon an idea invariably became an image, and in his hands its striking power was thereby increased infinitely. All the major images have this quality, that they appeal to human experience at a level which is both universal and immediate—as he said, 'ordinary and common matters' are paramount, 'for life consisteth not in novelties or subtilities...' (3. 418). The 'Advancement of Learning' can be a dull enough subject, of interest to few except those professionally engaged in it, but, when it is embodied in such imaginative conceptions as these, few who approach it with an open mind can resist being both moved and persuaded.

For the progress of knowledge is not conceived by him in abstract, intellectual terms, but always in the most concrete terms possible, and those involving man or nature in action, in some positive process which overcomes negative and restrictive forces. It is seen as the clearing of old ground, and the establishing of a strong and sure foundation for the construction of a new science, with Bacon, unaided, having to 'dig the clay and burn the brick' himself. Knowledge is a journey, if on land, then an arduous search for the right path, with the hazards of a wood or labyrinth of misguided notions, and the need to make new roads which will lead from confusion to clarity; if on sea, then the bark of learning is subject to the waves and tempests of rival philosophies before it can discover new countries, or reach harbour. Learning is a spring-head or fountain, the source of all good things, or a stream flowing into a wider sea. It is equally a source of light, of divine origin, and the search for a new science will enable the mirror of man's mind to reflect this light, and the light of nature, accurately. As a means of perception, the eye of knowledge, like the physical eye, is subject to the hindrances of darkness and cloud, but it is as flexible as the eye of the body, and has a permanent vantage point overlooking ignorance; as a means of transmission, knowledge is handed on as a man uses one candle to light others, and scientists pass on the torch like runners at the Olympic games. Most important, knowledge is a seed, which will produce a plant that, if carefully looked after and preserved from disease, will in time give fruit richly, and permanently nourish man.

These images are all rooted in the simple but eternal needs or experiences of man—light, water, food, a dwelling; going a journey, cultivating nature; this gives them their universality. Within each group they are applied with an imaginative eye for particulars which gives them their characteristic acuteness—the Peripatetics as owls, the human mind as a distorting mirror, knowledge misapplied as a harlot or slave. In addition to these basic qualities of universality and acuteness, the images take on another dimension, as there is always the sense of difficulty overcome, of limitations transcended: Bacon *dramatises* intellectual enquiry, in those metaphors of being faced with an uncharted country, the roads either blocked, non-existent, or misleading; a ship avoiding rocks and weathering storms; light piercing darkness, growth and fruition conquering barrenness and blight. Bacon's images are so exciting, now as then, because there is always this feeling of triumph, the successful outcome of a struggle on which the fortunes of both the individual in the dramatised situation, and the human race looking on, depend. The contest is presented in strongly conceived human terms, and Bacon not only sets the scene with great particularity but produces himself as the chief actor, urging others to imitate him—he is not only the architect, but the labourer in the fields, and the pioneer in the new path of learning—there is a sense of heroic endeavour here, which, when we consider the magnitude of the attempt, is not misplaced. It has succeeded, too, at least the most important part of it, and that success can be summed up by one of those powerfully imaginative images which are fundamental to his way of thinking, and which have accounted both for his influence as a philosopher, and his greatness as a writer, that prophetic emblem of knowledge passing beyond the known limits into the open sea of the future, moving like a ship through the Pillars of Hercules:

Multi pertransibunt, et augebitur scientia.

CHAPTER 7

LITERARY REVISIONS

A final and comprehensive check on the validity of my analysis of the main qualities of Bacon's writing can be had by inspecting the revisions which he made in his two major English works, the *Advancement of Learning* and the *Essays*. The motive behind Bacon's revisions was not primarily a stylistic one: he was not intent on revising the style of an earlier version so as to conform either with a generally accepted new style, as did Joseph Glanvill for his *Vanity of Dogmatizing*, or with a writer's own very changed attitude to the appropriate decorum of style, as did Henry James for *Roderick Hudson*.[1] Bacon was concerned in both works to expand the treatment of topics which had been inadequately handled, and to add new ones. But in so doing he inevitably reflected his developing attitudes to style, for under the categories so far defined we can see distinct alterations. And (to anticipate a little), unlike James, Bacon does not become dissatisfied with an earlier style, but rather develops still further the techniques which he has gradually built up.

I

The analysis of Bacon's revisions and expansions is not a mere exercise in stylistics: any student of Bacon, whatever his interests, must give considerable thought to such changes, for they are a key to the understanding of his whole approach to work, in all fields. The impulse to revision was constant, as his chaplain, secretary and editor, William Rawley, testifies:

His book of *Instauratio Magna* [the *Novum Organum*] (which in his own account was the chiefest of his works) was no slight imagination or fancy of his brain, but a settled and concocted notion, the production of many years' labour and travel. I myself have seen at the least twelve copies of the *Instauration*, revised

year by year one after another, and every year altered and amended in the frame
thereof, till at last it came to that model in which it was committed to the press;
as many living creatures do lick their young ones, till they bring them to their
strength of limbs. (I. 11.)

But the constant drive to revise and improve was not a fussy
expression of indecisiveness, rather the sign of an intellectual
horizon which was always expanding, of a reach which invariably
exceeded the grasp and left not over-written works but unfinished
ones.

On the outer sheet of a bundle of papers which includes the
Filum Labyrinthi and is now in the British Museum, there is a note
in Bacon's hand: 'Several fragments of discourses.' The *Colours of
Good and Evil* is described as a 'fragment', the *Valerius Terminus*
has just 'A few fragments of the first book', the *New Atlantis* is
unfinished; many of the 'particular topics' which were to make up
the *Natural and Experimental History* exist as prefaces only, and the
Novum Organum itself breaks off after having announced the next
stage of inquiry. Bacon was constantly beginning new works
which he could not, and did not, complete, and though he can
hardly be blamed for leaving them unfinished—on the contrary,
the scope and nervous intensity of his interests show an admirably
Faustian urge for knowledge—this unceasing onward movement
does explain the peculiar nature of much of his extant work. The
reader is continually finding ideas, images, quotations, and even
long sections in one work which remind him of some other work,
or even another still: there is an intricate web of cross-reference,
as Bacon adds parts of uncompleted works to others which will
also remain uncompleted, and takes from these for yet another
purpose. He comments on the process himself in a letter to Sir
Toby Matthew in 1610: 'My great work goeth forward; and after
my manner I alter ever when I add, so that nothing is finished till
all is finished' (11. 145). Indeed, after the *Advancement of Learning*,
which itself sums up much of his thought to that date, it can be
said that there is no single work of Bacon's which does not incorporate parts of earlier works. Given this piecemeal revision, it is
surely remarkable that the works themselves are not seriously faulty

in construction—but in fact the reader has to inspect the various stages of development very carefully before he can discover the joins, and with the possible exception of the *Sylva Sylvarum* there can be little dissatisfaction with the overall structure of the works, and certainly not with their invariably clear and far-sighted grasp of the issues involved. As D. D. Heath, one of Spedding's co-editors, put it: 'In any known treatise of Bacon's, whatever else may be unfinished, the preface and introduction, the laying out of the plan and conception of the work, are perfect: it is obviously the first step he took, and he often went no farther; and if such a preface was lost or was in fact never written, the body of the treatise might be aphoristic, but never ill planned' (7. 455).

Both the tendency towards constant incorporation and the excellence of planning can be seen in the *De Augmentis Scientiarum* (1623), the expansion of the *Advancement of Learning* (1605), which Bacon wrote in English and had handed to the translators by 30 June 1622 (1. 415). The *Advancement* had consisted of two Books, the first attacking both the vices of learning and its critics, the second surveying the whole field of knowledge, noting deficiencies, and proposing improvements. The *De Augmentis* retains the first Book almost exactly, Bacon making only the first of several cuts in discussions of religion, so that the work would be acceptable in the rest of Europe:

I have been also mine own *Index Expurgatorius.*

he wrote wryly, adding a characteristic pun—

For since my end of putting it into Latin was to have it read everywhere, it had been an absurd contradiction to free it in the language and to pen it up in the matter. (14. 436; see the notes at 3. 277, 477.)

The second Book is now divided into eight parts, which, with additions, become eight separate Books, the size of this part being doubled in the process. The new work takes on impressive proportions but, if we examine it closely, we find that the additions are mainly made up of existing work, with slight revisions.

In Book 2 the three examples of 'Parabolical Poesy' now given are taken from *The Wisdom of the Ancients* (the fables of Pan,

Perseus, and Dionysus), which are here made the vehicle for Bacon's criticism of enemy philosophers (the Greeks, 4. 320, and Donius, 4. 325). In Book 3 the new section on Physics and Astronomy is taken from the *Descriptio Globi Intellectualis*; in Book 4 the smaller revisions are taken from various sources, and in Book 5 the *Novum Organum* is used for the sections on Experiment, the 'Inquiry concerning Heavy and Light', and the treatment of the 'Four Idols'; Book 6 adds two main 'Appendices' on Rhetoric: the first consists simply of a reprint of the *Colours of Good and Evil* of 1597, with minute additions; the second, the *Antitheta Rerum*, is a collection of sentences *pro* and *contra* arranged under various heads: as we have seen, over half of these *tópoi* are the same as titles of the *Essays*, and many of the sentences are quotations from the *Essays* and other of his works. Book 7 has only minute changes, but Book 8 shows the same pattern of reincorporation, the example of the *Proverbs of Solomon* being an expansion of this section of the *Advancement* and including many proverbs to be found elsewhere in Bacon, while the *Example of a Summary Treatise touching the Extension of Empire* is simply the Essay 'Of the True Greatness of Kingdoms' in a new guise. The only new piece in the *De Augmentis* is to be found in this book, the *Treatise on Universal Justice or the Fountains of Equity*, which he had 'begun' for the *Advancement* (3. 475-6). Book 9 has the largest cuts, but these are because the subject is Religion and Philosophy, which is now tempered down considerably.

Not much of the *De Augmentis* is new, then. But we must not accuse Bacon of any sinister leaning towards self-plagiarism in inserting so many of his own works. His avowed aim is to clarify,[1] as he explains in introducing the *Colours of Good and Evil*: 'But as I set this down as deficient, I will according to my custom support it by examples; for precepts would not give sufficient illustration of the thing' (4. 458). By doing so, he is also aiming at greater fullness[2] than in the *Advancement*, and a more adequate coverage. He has read, thought, and experienced a great deal since then,[3] and besides the substantial additions of scientific work, the sections of History, Mathematics, and Medicine are much more satisfactory.

The many small alterations, as a word-by-word comparison of the two texts has revealed, are all in the direction of an increased clarity. This may represent Bacon's constant awareness of the responsibility of the scientist to communicate as accurately as possible—as he wrote in the *Advancement,* discussing 'Proof and Demonstration': 'the great sophism of all sophisms being equivocation or ambiguity of words and phrases' (3. 394).

Clarity was particularly needed for the actual presentation of so much material, and it is here that *partitio* comes into its own. The *De Augmentis* takes over the divisions of the *Advancement of Learning,* and expands within them: it is able to do this so convincingly because the divisions of the earlier work were so clearly established. Whether or not Bacon had reduced his subject to tabular form before writing the earlier work, we are now presented with a complete *Partitio Universalis Doctrinae Humanae,* in all its complexities, which spreads over twelve pages in Wats's 1640 translation. Each chapter is now prefaced with an announcement of the divisions that it contains, as here from Book 5, chapter 4:

Partitio artis judicandi in judicium per inductionem et per syllogismum...
Partitio prima judicii per syllogismum in reductionem rectam et inversam.
Partitio secunda eius in analyticam, et doctrinam de elenchis. Partitio doctrinae de elenchis...Partitio idolorum...

The process can be seen most clearly in Book 3, which begins with a division of Science (inherited from Book 2) into Theology and Philosophy. Theology is reserved for the last book of all, while Philosophy is divided into three doctrines, those of the Deity, Nature, and Man. The first is treated briefly in chapter 2, the third is held over till Book 4, and acts as the joint between them; the second is now divided into Speculative and Operative, chapter 4 dealing with the first, through eight further divisions, and chapter 5 handling the second in less detail. The last chapter deals with an appendix, Mathematics, which is divided into Pure and Mixed. The opening chapter of Book 4 takes up the Section on Man from Book 3, and part of its initial division, the Soul of Man, is left over for Book 5, which leaves part of its division for Book 6, and so on.

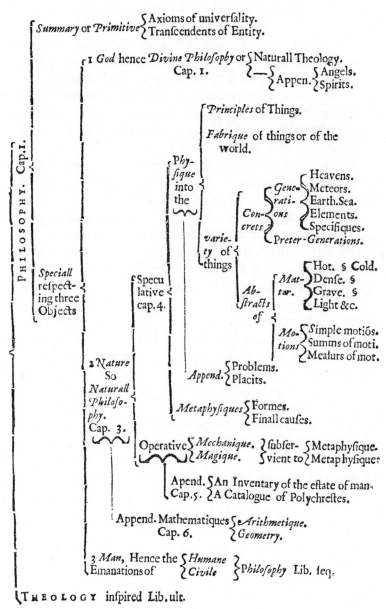

Summary or *Primitive* { Axioms of univerſality.
Tranſcendents of Entity.

PHILOSOPHY. Cap. I.

Speciall reſpect-ing three Objects

1 *God* hence *Divine Philoſophy* or { Naturall Theology.
Cap. 1. —{ Appen. { Angels. Spirits.

Specu lative cap. 4.

Phy-ſique into the

Principles of Things.

Fabrique of things or of the world.

varie-ty of things

Con-crets { *Gene-rati-ons* { Heavens. Meteors. Earth.Sea. Elements. Speciſiques.
Preter-*Generations.*

Ab-ſtracts of { *Mat-ter.* { Hot. § Cold. Denſe. § Grave. § Light &c.

Mo-tions { Simple motiós. Summs of moti. Meaſurs of mot.

Append. { Problems. Placits.

Metaphyſiques { Formes. Finall cauſes.

2 *Nature So Naturall Philoſo-phy.* Cap. 3.

Operative { *Mechanique.* *Magique.* } ſubſer-vient to } { Metaphyſique. Metaphyſique.

Apend. Cap. 5. { An Inventary of the eſtate of man. A Catalogue of Polychreſtes.

Append. Mathematiques { *Arithmetique.* *Geometry.*
Cap. 6.

3 *Man,* Hence the *Emanations of* { *Humane* *Civile* } *Philoſophy* Lib. ſeq.

{ Tʜᴇᴏʟᴏɢʏ inſpired Lib. ult.

The Partition of Book 3, *De Augmentis,* from the translation by
Gilbert Wats (1640).

The structure spreads out like the branches of a tree or, to use one of Bacon's metaphors, rises like the stones in a pyramid, where fittingly the last book, as the highest point, is reserved for God.

Within this strong overall structure, where all the parts dovetail and interlock, division is used to give further strength and clarity in each section. Many new divisions[1] are proposed, in order to give a better disposition of the material than in the *Advancement*. The treatment of the precepts in the *Faber Fortunae, sive de Ambitu vitae* treatise in Book 8 for example is much clearer than in the earlier work, although little has been added; all that Bacon does is to change the rather confused ordering of the *Advancement* into a more logical progression, and to add a *propositio*, the formal announcement of the distribution: 'Knowledge of men may be derived and obtained in six ways: by their countenance and expressions, their words, their actions, their dispositions, their ends, and lastly by the reports of others' (5. 60). By this simple means we are alert to the movement through the division. On several other occasions Bacon tightens up the structure of the early work by replacing its simple listing of points (the rather aimless 'Another precept'…'Another precept') with a numerical progression: 'The first precept'…'The second', which gives a definite (if simple) shape.[2] This desire for absolute clarity resulting in enumeration is now so strong that he uses it not only for such formal listing of points, but even for the separate parts of an analogy. In elaborating his image of 'Behaviour…as a garment of the mind', he writes in the *Advancement of Learning*—'For it ought to be made in fashion: it ought not to be too curious; it ought to be shaped so as to set forth any good making of the mind, and hide any deformity; and above all, it ought not to be too strait or restrained for exercise or motion' (3. 447). In the *De Augmentis* he numbers each stage: 'For first, it ought to be made in fashion; secondly it should not be too curious or costly; thirdly, it ought to be so framed…lastly, and above all…' (5. 34).

The movement towards enumeration suggests what is indeed borne out by the uses of *partitio* here, that Bacon, in his literary development, shows an increasing preference for a clearly articulated structure. And his constant translation of intellectual processes into concrete metaphor results in the by now familiar images for *partitio*: the divisions used by commonplace books, which are described as 'pedantical' in the *Advancement of Learning* (3. 398), are now unsatisfactory because they do not 'pierce to the pith and heart of things' (4. 435); in the earlier work he writes that 'The knowledge of man is as the waters, some descending from above, and some springing from beneath' (3. 346) but now he joins this image to the concept of *partitio* itself, adding 'and in like manner the primary division of sciences is to be drawn from their sources: of which some are above in the heavens, and some here below' (4. 336). To these metaphors from plants and water he adds the most significant, that from the anatomy of a human body or a leaf: 'endeavouring as I do in these divisions to trace out and pursue the true veins of learning, without (in many points) following customs and the divisions which are received' (4. 315). And we find all the usual stages of the partition, the *propositio* or announcement, the marking of transitions, the summing-up, even the repetition of a division for unmistakable clarity.[1] It is significant that the only completely new section of the work, the aphoristic treatise on the *Fountains of Equity*, is also organised by *partitio* with all the characteristics we have come to expect.[2] It is this strong and clear outline which makes the *De Augmentis* so impressive a structure, and which rightly earned Rawley's praise of it:

As for his lordship's love of order, I can refer any man to his lordship's Latin book, *De Augmentis Scientiarum*; which if my judgment be anything is written in the exactest order that I know any writing to be. (2. 337. Preface to the *Sylva Sylvarum*.)

Of the two other structural elements important in Bacon's prose, the aphorism and syntactical symmetry, there seems little significant development beyond the *Advancement*: the aphorism did not play much part in that work, and though (as we have seen) Bacon adds or expands treatises written in aphorisms on law, civil policy, and science, these are quite separate sections, and there is no movement towards an aphoristic manner as such.

Again the techniques of symmetrical syntax were fully developed
in the earlier work, and continue to be used here: the only fresh
question here is whether in revising Bacon has worked with an
eye to specifically Latinate effects. He seems to have written in
English and then passed his text on to a miscellaneous band of
translators (which may have included George Herbert), choosing
the most pleasing combination from their work.[1] If we compare
the two versions (and for the following comparison I have used
Spedding's translation checked with that by Gilbert Wats)[2] we
find that there are innumerable small and insignificant alterations
in phrasing,[3] some of which seem to be conditioned by Latin
constructions.[4] In terms of symmetry, the expansions sometimes
make for a sharper effect in Latin, as in this sentence from the section on 'cosmetic', where the additions made in the *De Augmentis*
are represented within round brackets:

For cleanness (and decency) of body is rightly esteemed to proceed from (a
modesty of manners, and from) reverence, first of all towards God (whose
creatures we are;) then towards society (wherein we live); and then also towards ourselves, (whom we ought to reverence not less, but rather more, than
others.) (4. 394; 3. 377 for *Advancement*.)

This elaboration, though partly affecting the sense, is surely made
for the subtle sound-effects and cross-patterning of the Latin:

> Corporis enim munditia
> et decor   honestus,
> recte existimatur promanare a modestia quaedem morum,
>   et a reverentia;
> inprimis erga Deum   , cujus creaturae sumus;
>   tum erga societatem, in   qua   degimus;
>   tum etiam erga nosmetipsos,
>   quos non minus
>   imo magis quam alios,
>   revereri debemus. (1. 602.)

Similarly complex patterning can be found in the new passages
added in the revision. So in commenting on one of Solomon's
aphorisms Bacon explains that the sort of man who would wreak
most destruction in a state is in fact the 'scorner', and arrives at

this climax by reviewing and dismissing all the apparently more
vicious types:

non hominis	superbi	et insolentis;
non	tyrannici	et crudelis;
non	temerarii	et violenti;
non	impii	et scelerati;
non	injusti	et oppressoris;
non	seditiosi	et turbulenti;
non	libidinosi	et voluptarii;
non denique insipientis		et inhabilis;
sed		derisoris. (1. 756.)

That climactic crescendo is worthy of Cicero (attacking Catiline,
say), and is obviously designed for the resources of Latin. But
elsewhere comparison of passages which are simply translated for
the revision shows that, although the Latin version may add conciseness in some places, it is more often unable to reproduce
specifically English effects of balance.[1]

If the evidence from syntax is ambiguous, in the last aspect of
the revisions to be considered, that of the imagery, there is a clear
line of development, for in elaborating the images of the *Advancement* Bacon always achieves clarity and avoids obscurity or
ambiguity, though it is sometimes at the cost of a dissipation of
poetic energy. Some examples might suggest that he now has a
preference for the simile rather than the metaphor: this is a measure of the amount of clarification the images receive. A clear
instance of this process is the analogy used for the inquiry into final
causes, which is stated in a direct metaphor in the *Advancement*:

Nay, they are indeed but remoras and hinderances to stay and slug the ship from
further sailing. (3. 358.)

In the *De Augmentis* this is expanded to a simile:

Nay, as I was going to say, these discoursing causes (like those fishes they call
remoras, which are said to stick to the sides of the ships) have in fact hindered
the voyage and progress of the sciences, and prevented them from holding on
their course and advancing further. (4. 363; Latin: 1. 569.)

Spedding's version is a little too explanatory (the parenthesis in the
Latin text reads 'instar Remorarum, uti fingunt, navibus adhaeren-

tium') and the change may be partly dictated by the demands of translation into Latin, but it is illustrative of the general tendency to make images more immediately understandable. So, in the *Advancement*, Bacon praises philosophers for 'their balancing of virtue with virtue', and adds in the later work 'as to which outweighs the other' (3. 420; 5. 6). He again makes an idea quite explicit in urging the use of 'Prenotion' as an aid to memory, by which the number of possibilities is limited and we are directed 'to seek in a narrow compass', now adding 'like the hunting of a deer within an enclosure' (3. 399; 4. 436). And in recommending that 'the proofs and persuasions of Rhetoric ought to differ according to the auditors' he explains—'like a musician accommodating his skill to different ears' (3. 411; 4. 457).

As we can see from these examples, the process is one of explanation: Bacon's normal tendency in imagery is towards localization, and he now adds images on to images to ensure that every point is completely understood. So, in discussing the bad effect that doubt has on men's minds, he concludes in both works that 'men bend their wits rather to keep the doubt up than to determine and solve it', but makes a great improvement on the earlier work's rather dry statement of the process by which the doubt takes root in men's minds: 'When a doubt is once *received*' (3. 364, my italics), by working the idea up with great vigour into a completely localised and embodied incident: 'a doubt if once allowed as just, and authorized as it were, immediately raises up champions on either side, by whom this same liberty of doubting is transmitted to posterity' (4. 358). A conceptual statement again becomes a physical one as he exposes the errors made in science by not dealing with the subject in detail. In the *Advancement* he writes

for as the sense afar off is full of mistaking but is exact at hand, so is it of the understanding; the remedy whereof is not to quicken or strengthen the organ, but to go nearer to the object. (3. 372–3.)

The *De Augmentis* retains this exactly, but inserts at the semicolon a further sentence which now makes the image still more localised, and in an even more definite human context:

But men are wont to look down upon nature as from a high tower and from a great distance, and to occupy themselves too much with generalities; whereas if they would come down and draw near to particulars and take a closer and more accurate view of things themselves they would gain a more true and profitable knowledge of them. (4. 382.)

Another way in which Bacon's revisions show him carrying further an already well-developed characteristic of his imagery is the addition of still more images of natural growth. The sceptics are condemned in the *Advancement*, as they supported their doctrine of *acatalepsia* by arguing that the human mind was capable of apprehending appearances only—'and thereby', the revision adds, 'pulled up the sciences by the very roots' (3. 338; 4. 412). The later work retains the long parallel drawn in the earlier one between human knowledge and the cultivation of plants, but improves on its conclusion, which had been that one of the essentials was to 'look well to the taking up of the roots'. Now the caution is much more precise and delicate: 'that the roots be taken up uninjured, and with a little earth adhering to them' (3. 404; 4. 450). So it is fitting that at the very conclusion of the work he should add a metaphor from this source: 'as even the greatest things are owing to their beginnings, it will be enough for me to have sown a seed for posterity and the Immortal God' (5. 119).

Bacon's increasing tendency to think in images is seen not only in the revisions, but in the dozens of new images which appear in the *De Augmentis*, and is perhaps best demonstrated by considering the completely new parts of the work—first, for the use of imagery in the context of argument, the treatise on Justice in Book 8; and then, for more extended movements, the exordiums which now open each book. *The Fountains of Equity* is a serious and penetrating work of legal theory, set out in aphorisms, that most 'scientific' of forms, yet Bacon does not hesitate to use metaphor and simile where it will give more point or meaning to his writing. The essentially concrete, human reference in his imagery is shown again in that the largest group of images in this short tract is that based on the human body. The successful administration of the law, for example, is said to depend on the power of the government and the constitution, so that 'if this part of the constitution be sound and healthy, the laws will be of good effect' (5. 89), but at the opposite extreme, and more concretely, Bacon writes on a completely metaphorical plane to urge that 'above all things a gangrene in our laws is to be avoided' (5. 99). From the health of the body we pass to its power of movement with the recognition that for the happiness of the people, for peace, prosperity, and good government—'for all these objects laws are the sinews and instruments' (5. 89). The analogy is pressed even closer in the forty-third aphorism, resulting in a sort of physically defined 'body' of the Law:

> It is of the greatest importance to the certainty of laws (of which I am now treating), that Praetorian Courts be not allowed to swell and overflow, so as under colour of mitigating the rigour of the law, to break its strength and sinews, by drawing everything to be a matter of discretion. (5. 96.)

Lastly in this group, two images based on bodily actions which show the same move towards concrete, physical embodiment: 'In ordinary laws...everything should be more fully explained, and pointed out, as it were with the finger, to the capacity of the people' (5. 102), and, most subtle, the advice that there should 'be power also to inflict...a light disgrace; punishing the offender as it were with a blush' (5. 95).

Bacon's use of imagery in this treatise also corresponds to the patterns we have traced earlier in that many analogies are based on water and its attributes,[1] and that all the images are used in a concrete, fully realised way.[2] So Bacon advises us not to use obsolete examples to illustrate the law, as those examples 'which have lain as it were buried in desks and archives and have openly passed into oblivion, deserve less (authority). For examples, like waters, are most wholesome in a running stream' (5. 93–4). These images from water seem to suggest the sea to convey the idea of stability: 'judgments are the anchors of laws, as laws are of the state' (5. 103), and some legal principles 'run through the different matters of law, and act as its ballast' (106). Another type of Baconian image found here is that which develops a metaphor implied in a *sententia* and crosses it on to another plane, as in the fifty-third aphorism where Bacon uses almost his favourite quotation from the Vulgate, 'Pluet super eos laqueos' (Ps. xi. 6)—which he nearly always associates with obstructions in the law—and allows it to expand metaphorically the idea of obstruction:

The prophet says 'He shall rain snares upon them.' But there are no worse snares than legal snares, especially in penal laws; if being infinite in number, and useless through the lapse of time, instead of being as a lantern to the feet they are nets in the path. (5. 98.)

The movement is, as ever, from abstract to concrete, even when Bacon is being more ingenious: 'the proof is not to be sought from the words of the rule, as if it were the text of law. The rule, like the magnetic needle, points at the law, but does not settle it' (106). The effect of delayed illumination (and so persuasion) created by that pun is repeated in the only image not drawn from common experience, one which depends on the fact recorded by Erasmus (from Book 5 of Aristotle's *Ethics*) that on Lesbos men built with irregularly shaped stones, and so had to use flexible measuring rules: in Law those legal rules which, because of their 'concise and affected brevity', can be interpreted both ways are not to be copied 'lest by chance the law should become like a Lesbian rule' (5. 102). That witty analogy is a good example of Bacon's technique of using imagery to illuminate a particular context in such a way as to produce agreement, a technique which may now be familiar to us but which is always reapplied freshly.

A final way in which the use of imagery in the *De Augmentis* fits (and so validates) the patterns established earlier is in the creation of more fluid, self-developing metaphoric progressions. One result of dividing the *Advancement of Learning* into separate books is that he now adds an introductory paragraph to each book announcing the course he will take, and addressing praise to his 'most excellent King' (this is not such blatant flattery as it looks, for the two books of the *Advancement* originally had this feature). The reader certainly gains by it, for in these exordia Bacon writes with a confidence and imaginative power which even he seldom equals. As before, he shows considerable agility of mind by suspending an image through several layers of meaning with much witty play on resemblances, or else merging it into another image which carries on the movement. Such is the progression in the opening of the last Book of all, where the familiar image of his work as a 'globe of the intellectual world' changes into one of Bacon himself circumnavigating this globe, an idea which suggests in turn the necessary aids to navigation, in the intellectual as well as the physical sphere, and leads to the comparison of his progress towards Divinity, in this final stage of his journey, with the traditional thanksgiving service held after the successful completion of a sea-journey. And he adds, with a characteristic turn of wit, that, in dealing with a subject which the human mind cannot comprehend, it will be better for him to say little or nothing and to content himself with worship alone:

Seeing now, most excellent King, that my little bark, such as it is, has sailed round the whole circumference of the old and new world of sciences (with what success and fortune it is for posterity to decide), what remains but that having at length finished my course I should pay my vows? But there still remains Sacred or Inspired Divinity; whereof however if I proceed to treat I shall step out of the bark of human reason, and enter into the ship of the church; which is only able by the Divine compass rightly to direct its course. Neither will the stars of philosophy, which have hitherto so nobly shone upon us, any longer supply their light. So that on this subject also it will be as well to keep silence. I will accordingly omit the proper divisions thereof, contributing however a few remarks upon it, according to my slender ability, by way of paying my vows. (5. 111.)

The development of the 'imagery' here runs parallel to the 'thought' and constantly clarifies and extends it—in fact the two are inseparable. Many Renaissance writers use long, fully developed images, but few with Bacon's power to strike out fresh and illuminating analogies at every stage.

Bacon the Elizabethan sea-captain becomes Bacon the Homeric herald in another sequence of imaginatively fused images at the opening of Book 4, where he defends himself from critics' attacks by presenting the whole process in terms of a war, with his own scientific programme brought to a triumphant and inspiring conclusion:

If any one should aim a blow at me (excellent King) for anything I have said or shall hereafter say in this matter, (besides that I am within the protection of your Majesty), let me tell him that he is acting contrary to the rules and practice of warfare. For I am but a trumpeter, not a combatant; one perhaps of those of whom Homer speaks,

Hail, heralds, messengers of Jove and men!

and such men might go to and fro everywhere unhurt, between the fiercest and bitterest enemies. Nor is mine a trumpet which summons and excites men to cut each other to pieces with mutual contradictions, or to quarrel and fight with one another; but rather to make peace between themselves, and turning with united forces against the Nature of Things, to storm and occupy her castles and strongholds, and extend the bounds of human empire as far as God Almighty in his goodness may permit. (4. 372–3.)

There is an almost playful exercise of the imagination in the way Bacon takes up his initially simple metaphor—'aim a blow' and develops it into a Homeric contest, and with the same fluidity of analogy passing to the more serious and inspiring image of himself as the trumpeter heralding a new age in which man conquers the universe. The imagery of the *De Augmentis* may be judged, in the last analysis, as being less powerfully condensed than that in the *Advancement*, but it does show many of Bacon's most impressive qualities.

II

The nature of the revision of the *Essays* poses a slightly different problem from that of the *De Augmentis*, but it is in many ways an analogous one. The initial difference between the two works is that the alterations here were not made on one occasion only, and span almost the whole extent of Bacon's development. However, as the final version of the *Essays* belongs to the same period as the *De Augmentis* it will be of interest to discover whether the same tendencies are to be seen here and, if so, whether the earlier revision (of 1612) shows a similar progression. The general nature of the revisions can be briefly outlined, beginning with the changes in size of the *Essays*. The first edition of 1597 contained ten titles: the second edition, in 1612, expanded these essays, and added thirty new ones; the final edition, in 1625, expanded all forty essays from this volume, and added another eighteen. The process is always one of expansion, the only cuts being (as in the *De Augmentis*) of matter likely to cause offence on the Continent, or of a minor stylistic nature.[1] The small-scale expansions of phrasing are of the same order as those in the *De Augmentis*, giving a slightly fuller expression, though they are proportionally less numerous and important, and do not seem to be made with a view to being translated into Latin.[2] The additions are made generally in whole clauses, sentences, or larger units. The increase in number of essays is paralleled by the increase in length, as anyone willing to undertake the rather tedious task of counting them will find. The average length of the essays in 1597 is 325 words: in 1612 these ten essays now average 400 words; and in 1625 they average 550 words: the increase being of a quarter and a half respectively, rather as one might expect. What is remarkable, however, is that the new essays in the volume of 1612, which, at an average of 490 words, were a little longer than the revised ones in that volume, are expanded in 1625 to about 980 words each, exactly double their previous length, and far larger than the further expanded *Essays* of 1597 in this volume. The increase is so great that these revised essays are now larger than the average length (950 words) of the eighteen new essays added in 1625.

This is one case in which literary statistics are useful, for here they disclose an important fact about the structure of the *Essays*, which can be corroborated by a detailed examination of them. The conclusion to be drawn from both approaches is that the *Essays* in the 1597 volume, being of an aphoristic structure, were incapable of much expansion, without becoming shapeless or diffuse in the process. In the 1612 edition, though, it is notable that the new essays are mainly organised on the now customary basis of division, and could be expanded quite easily under their particular heads, in the same way that the *De Augmentis* was constructed from the *Advancement of Learning*. (I realise that this hypothesis begs the question of whether Bacon may not have had more *matter* to add on the newer topics—but I think it could be shown that the new material could often be placed just as fittingly under the 1597 'heads', and I feel that the fact that the discrepancy in size corresponds to the difference in structure shows that Bacon in 1625 is instinctively more at home with works built on a plan which he has been using on all kinds of topic for over thirty years). That the revised 1612 essays are slightly longer in 1625 than the new essays is not to be taken as proof that Bacon's literary powers were flagging, but rather that, divisions once being established, and a certain amount of substance added to them, it was easier to enlarge this from his now greater reading and experience than it was to establish new divisions for a subject, and find new material. A simple example of his method is the essay 'Honour and Reputation', which is unique in the 1597 volume in using a division, to distinguish five 'degrees of sovereign honour'; it was omitted, for some reason, from the 1612 volume, but when it reappeared in 1625 Bacon could now add eighteen examples of famous men under these heads.[1]

But, although it can be seen that the majority of the 1612 essays were constructed using division, the process is well below the surface, and only two of them have a statement of the heads ('Counsel'; 'Great Place'). The revisions of 1625, however, besides taking place under the heads already established, in many cases add an explicit statement of division marking the transitions, and summing up when all the parts have been dealt with.[2] In 'Seditions and Troubles' for example (which although written by 1612 was not included in the edition of that year), the original version had a simple distribution: 'But let us leave the part of predictions, and speake of the materialls, and the causes, and the remedyes' (6. 590). In 1625 this becomes a more elaborate *propositio*:

But let us pass from this part of predictions (concerning which, nevertheless, more light may be taken from that which followeth) and let us speak first of the Materials of seditions; then of the Motives of them; and thirdly of the Remedies. (6. 408.)

And in 'Judicature', we find an example of Bacon now numbering an already extant division similar to that noted in the *De*

Augmentis (6. 507–9). Bacon's tendency to develop and reapply a stylistic device once it is formed (he never abandons one) is shown in that the new essays of 1625 make still more use of *partitio*,[1] as a brief examination of two of them shows. 'Of Anger' begins with an aphorism and a *sententia*, and then has a most formal distribu-ion: 'We will first speak how the natural inclination and habit to be angry may be attempered and calmed, Secondly...Thirdly...' (6. 510), the division being carefully followed through: 'For the first'...'for the second'. Even clearer is 'Of Envy', which, after the introductory paragraph, announces its topics so: 'we will handle, what persons are apt to envy others; what persons are most subject to be envied themselves; and what is the difference between public and private envy' (6. 393). Under the first head six examples follow, and the familiar stages are carried through, complete even with a formal reminder that the promised contract has been fulfilled: 'And so much of public envy or discontent, and the difference thereof from private envy, which was handled in the first place.' Division is a simple enough method, but the persistent use that Bacon made of this 'singling out of parts' points to an overwhelming desire for clarity.

The search for clarity revealed in the increased use of *partitio* for the overall organisation of the *Essays* is seen again at the level of sentence structure, as Bacon gives more light to his writing by using the devices of syntactical symmetry. In this case the 1612 revisions of 1597 do not seem very significant but the 1625 revi-sions of both volumes certainly are. Such symmetries are to be found to a remarkable extent in the complete passages added, either in whole sentences or in longer sections, where Bacon seems to go out of his way to make exact and deliberate symmetries, for mnemonic clarity. Even extensive quotations could hardly do justice to the quantity of this sort of symmetry, and as this aspect has been perhaps adequately considered we can concentrate here on those very significant cases where a sentence has been rewritten in order to bring out its structure more clearly. So in the essay 'Of Death' Bacon adds a clause (here given in brackets) to balance the sentence:

A: Certainly the contemplation of death, as the wages of sin

                             and passage to another world,

B: but the fear of it,   (as a tribute due unto nature),

A: is holy and religious

B: is weak.   (6. 379.)

Later in this essay Bacon does not add a passage but cuts one so as to bring out its structure more clearly; in 1612 the sentence had read:

                Revenge   triumphs over death,

                Love   esteems it not,

                Honour   aspireth to it,

    delivery from Ignominy chuseth it,

                Grief   flieth to it,

                Feare   preoccupateth it. (6. 544.)

In 1625 one omission (the fourth clause) and one correction (the second) produces this absolutely symmetrical structure: 'Revenge triumphs over death; Love slights it; Honour aspireth to it; Grief flieth to it; Fear preoccupateth it' (380). By this means, the eye and the ear are not distracted by the difference between the verbal expression of the clauses, and can concentrate on the radical differences in sense.

In the essay 'Of Studies' Bacon adds two clauses to clarify and extend meaning. In 1597 the sentence had read:

          Reade not to contradict,

              nor to believe,

              but to waigh and consider. (525.)

In 1625 this becomes:

          Read not to contradict and confute;

              nor to believe and take for granted;

              nor to find talk and discourse;

              but to weigh and consider. (497–8.)

In addition to the slight gain in meaning, the sentence has a more satisfying growth to its climactic positive point. Similarly, in 'Of Counsel' the manuscript version (1607–12)[1] had a very careful symmetrical balancing of the respective advantages to a prince of advice given in public and in private: in the 1612 printed text

Bacon preserved the balance, but added to it two final clauses which expand the sense while keeping to the symmetry (here set out in brackets):

> therefore it is good to take both;
> and of the inferior sort rather in private, (to preserve freedom);
> of the greater   rather in consort, (to preserve respect).
>
> (6. 556.)

A still clearer example of revision in aid of symmetry can be seen in the essay 'Of Empire', where we find a double correction from the manuscript text. The relevant clause forms the completion of the sentence 'nothing destroyeth authority so much as the unequal and untimely interchange of':

pressing power and imbasing Majestie	MS
pressing power and relaxing power	1612; 6. 553
power pressed too far, and relaxed too much	1625; 6. 420

The improvement is partly towards more natural expression; but more interesting for our purposes is the growth of the desire for a balanced and expansive movement so easily expressed in the final version. Examples of syntactical revision are not numerous, but (like that more symmetrical version of the Lucretius quotation in the Essay 'Of Truth') they show Bacon once more using a stylistic device with increasing frequency.

But, although the move towards syntactical symmetry is the statistically dominant one in the development of the *Essays*, Bacon is not to be thought of as some mechanical pattern-builder. The aim of using these symmetries is, here as everywhere else, the clarification of meaning: by separating the parts of one's thought, so to speak, one points up similarities and distinctions and achieves clearer communication. However, in some cases an expansion or correction of an idea may not fit into a symmetrical mould, and, in complete consistency with his belief in the necessary coherence between expression and idea, we find Bacon deliberately abandoning a balanced structure in order to deepen meaning. So, in the most symmetrical essay of all in the earlier versions, 'Of Studies', Bacon makes a small change in the second sentence which ruins the careful balance (where 'judgment' is needed as a single item he now has 'judgment and disposition of Business'), and abandons the symmetries of the third sentence entirely:

1597: For expert men can execute,
    but learned men are fittest to judge or censure. (6. 525.)

1625: For expert men can execute, and perhaps judge of particulars, one by one;
    but the general counsels, and the plots and marshalling of affairs, come
    best from those that are learned. (6. 497.)

There the original thought has been deepened and qualified, so that the syntax cannot be reshaped into the original mould. A still more thorough-going discarding of a careful pattern can be seen in 'Of Followers and Friends', where both 1597 and 1612 versions preserved this balance:

        to be governed by one is not good, and
        to be distracted with many is worse
    but to take advise   of friends is ever honourable... (6. 528, 579.)

In 1625 Bacon keeps the outline of the distinction but adds so much new material that its structure is swamped:

To be governed (as we call it) by one, is not safe; for it shews softness, and gives a freedom to scandal and disreputation; for those that would not censure or speak ill of a man immediately, will talk more boldly of those that are so great with them, and thereby wound their honour. Yet to be distracted with many is worse; for it makes men to be of the last impression, and full of change. To take advice of some few friends is ever honourable... (6. 495.)

Bacon's willingness to jettison a neat structure in favour of a less tidy extension of meaning (seen again, 6. 432) is yet another factor which distinguishes his use of symmetry from the more obsessive patterns of a Nicholas Breton or a Lyly. Another form taken by this triumph of meaning over mere patterning is the addition of important new quotations or historical examples, which are also allowed to disrupt a pattern (e.g. for 1625 texts, 6. 380, 481). Although symmetry dominates over the complete work, Bacon is not a prisoner to it.

The desire for depth of meaning and truth is of course central to Bacon's whole work, as we have seen stylistically in his concept of the aphorism, and it finds further expression in the 1612 and 1625 *Essays*, appropriately enough, in the addition of many new aphorisms. In these versions the *Essays* are not aphoristic in structure, although not all of them are as tightly organised by *partitio* as I have perhaps suggested—indeed their form is fluid enough for Bacon to introduce aphorisms wherever they are needed. The 1612 version does not add many aphorisms (judging by the criteria established earlier), nor are they particularly condensed or stimulating, being nearer to the simple 'rule' or observation type:

For it is a secret both in nature and state, that it is safer to change many things than one. (6. 563.)

Certainly, he that hath a satirical vein, as he maketh others afraid of his wit, so he had need be afraid of others' memory. (6. 565.)

Only one of them contains an image: 'Speech of touch towards others should be sparingly used; for discourse ought to be as a field, without coming home to any man' (6. 565; not in MS). But, as in everything else, the older Bacon becomes, the more accomplished is his writing (there is no falling-off, rather—as with Verdi or Haydn—a constant development): thus the 1625 *Essays* add many more, and more brilliant aphorisms, which fall into some of the categories which I have distinguished. So we find Bacon choosing quite penetrating aphorisms as *sententiae*, often symmetrically arranged:

Cum non sis qui fueris, non esse cur velis vivere (When a man feels that he is no longer what he was, he loses all his interests in life). (6. 399.)

Qui de contemnenda gloria libros scribunt, nomen suum inscribunt (They that write books on the worthlessness of glory, take care to put their names on the title-page). (6. 504.)

The tendency towards clear symmetrical division as a means of definition is also seen, as in this uncompromising attack on vanity:

Glorious men are the scorn of   wise men,
the admiration of fools,
the idols of parasites,
and the slaves of their own vaunts. (505.)

We find, too, aphorisms condensing both Christian ethics and Renaissance policy: from the former this crushing image: 'The ways to enrich are many, and most of them foul' (6. 461); from the latter this reminder: 'And besides, to speak truth' (a frequent prelude to a *regola generale*): 'in base times active men are of more use than virtuous' (6. 495). Another Machiavellian aphorism uses that form whereby an image becomes the source for further metaphoric reflection: 'All rising to great place is by a winding stair; and if there be factions, it is good to side a man's self whilst he is in the rising, and to balance himself when he is placed' (401). An aphorism which also falls into that 'two-part' form, but with the image now placed in the second part, is this from 'Of Atheism': 'But the great atheists indeed are hypocrites; which are ever handling holy things, but without feeling; so as they must needs be cauterized in the end' (414). The surprise wit revealed there is another indication that, although Bacon is using certain stylistic devices more and more, he does not do so in any predictable way: we may expect an aphorism or an image, but we do not know what form it will take. Not only at the first reading but at many subsequent ones we are surprised by the condensation, the universality, and of course the aptness of this union of aphorism and image:

And money is like muck, not good except it be spread. (410.)

There at its most condensed (and ambiguous—does Bacon mean that money shares other attributes of muck?) is the metaphoric aphorism which has to be expanded to bring out its meaning, and Bacon's sense of the value of this type as a delayed-action summing-up is shown in that for the 1625 revision he several times adds such 'two-part' aphorisms to the very end of an essay,[1] leaving the reader with a thought which will take some time to develop:

In all negociations of difficulty a man may not look to sow and reap at once; but must prepare business, and so ripen it by degrees. (494.)

Men's behaviour should be like their apparel, not too strait or point device, but free for exercise or motion. (501.)

Bacon is equally sensitive to the importance of the first words of an essay, and uses a related technique for his famous surprise-openings:[1] 'Praise is the reflexion of virtue. But it is as the glass or body which giveth the reflexion' (501); 'Ambition is like choler' (465); 'Suspicions among thoughts are like bats amongst birds, they ever fly by twilight' (454); 'Deformed persons are commonly even with nature' (480). All of these paradoxical-aphoristic–metaphorical definitions need and receive immediate expansion, none more wittily than this very concrete embodiment of the obstructive effect of wealth on morality:

I cannot call Riches better than the baggage of virtue. The Roman word is better, *impedimenta*. For as the baggage is to an army, so is riches to virtue. It cannot be spared nor left behind, but it hindereth the march; yea and the care of it sometimes loseth or disturbeth the victory. (460.)

The close relationship between Bacon's aphorisms and his imagery is a sign of the imaginative life common to both. In expanding the *Essays* Bacon adds an enormous number of images, an *embarras de richesse* for the critic which it is impracticable to discuss in detail, and so I merely select a few categories. We find quite small revisions of extant images: in 1612 one of the causes of superstition is 'excess of outward holiness'; in 1625 it is 'outward *and pharisaical* holiness' (6. 416; my italics). Again the italicised words here represent a small but definite intensification of the image: 'glorious gifts and foundations are *like sacrifices without salt*; and but the painted sepulchres of alms, which soon will putrify and corrupt inwardly' (462). Similar moral contempt is expressed in other images added in 1625,[2] but is also seen in a remarkably witty image from the 1612 essay 'Of Vain Glory', where Bacon has considered how ostentation and vanity 'helpeth to perpetuate a man's memory'. He gives three examples of this, and sums up the process with a devastatingly pungent comparison:

Neither had the fame of Cicero, Seneca, Plinius Secundus, borne her age so well, if it had not been joined with some vanity in themselves; like unto varnish, that makes ceilings not only shine but last. (504.)

There too we see that conclusive effect which Bacon achieves by tying his image to an indisputable and recurrent natural pheno-menon—varnish is like that. Another characteristic of his imagery which appears in these revisions of 1625 is the tendency towards concrete reference to either natural or human situations. For the first source an example might be his revision of one of the attri-butes of 'Studies', that 'They perfect nature, and are perfected by experience', adding 'for natural abilities are like natural plants, that need proyning by study' (497). For the human source, very concretely realised, consider Bacon's illustration of his argument that men cannot retire from the world 'when they would, neither will they when it were reason; but are impatient of privateness, even in age and sickness, which require the shadow'—adding: 'like old townsmen, that will be still sitting at their street door, though thereby they offer age to scorn' (399).

Together with this feeling for the full realisation of the vehicle of an image goes Bacon's corresponding ability to develop a whole sequence of imagery on its own terms, as for an apparently unlikely topic for this sort of writing, the discussion of the duties of clerks and ministers of justice in 'Judicature'. This passage, with its extraordinarily nimble control of metaphor and its impressive application of quotations, may stand as an example of Bacon's writing at its best—one must quote the whole paragraph:

The place of justice is an hallowed place; and therefore not only the bench, but the foot-place and precincts and purprise thereof, ought to be preserved without scandal and corruption. For certainly 'Grapes' (as the Scripture saith) 'will not be gathered of thorns or thistles'; neither can justice yield her fruit with sweet-ness amongst the briars and brambles of catching and polling clerks and ministers. The attendance of courts is subject to four bad instruments. First, certain persons that are sowers of suits; which make the court swell, and the country pine. The second sort is of those that engage courts in quarrels of jurisdiction, and are not truly *amici curiae*, but *parasiti curiae*, in puffing a court up beyond her bounds, for their own scraps and advantage. The third sort is of those that may be accounted the left hands of courts; persons that are full of nimble and sinister tricks and shifts, whereby they pervert the plain and direct courses of courts, and bring justice into oblique lines and labyrinths. And the fourth is the poller and exacter of fees; which justifies the common resemblance of the courts of justice to the bush whereunto while the sheep flies for defence in weather, he is sure to lose part of his fleece. On the other side, an ancient clerk, skilful in precedents, wary in proceeding and understanding in the business of the court, is an excellent finger of a court; and doth many times point the way to the judge himself. (6. 509.)

At every stage of this analysis, Bacon's imagery, witty, ingenious, drawing on universal human experience yet still fresh and living, deepens and widens his meaning, and our understanding.

The imagery of the new essays of 1625 is, as we might expect, just as imaginative and convincing as that of the 1612 volume and of the 1625 revisions, and with more variety—for example, Bacon introduces a new technique by having an image-group recur through an essay, such as the analogy between conversation and dancing in 'Discourse' (455–6), or (more often, and more ingeniously) the coherent use of images of overshadowing and jealous looking in 'Envy' (392–7). Enough space has been given to the analysis of individual images, so I will end this discussion of the *Essays* by considering one essay as a whole. The essay I choose is no. 21, 'Of Delays' (6. 427–8), which is, as it happens, the shortest in the volume, and represents the associative type of development rather than the more expanded form which uses division and sequential progression, and also does not use much symmetry of syntax. But, if it is unrepresentative of the majority of the *Essays* on these grounds, it is certainly characteristic of Bacon's work at its most condensed and brilliant, particularly his way of concentrating an image so that it has to be re-expanded, thus giving an added tension to the thought. It opens with an abrupt analogy which reduces all human affairs to novel equality:

Fortune is like the market: where many times, if you can stay a little, the price will fall.

That is to say, 'If you can delay on one occasion, you will prosper'. Immediately this is answered by another elliptical analogy:

And again, it is sometimes like Sibylla's offer; which at first offereth the commodity at full, then consumeth part and part, and still holdeth up the price.

Or, 'if you delay here, you are lost'. Bacon could have stated the antithesis as clearly as this if he had wanted to, of course, but he instinctively chooses imagery which will make the meaning strike home: we see the two approaches in action, in perfectly realised human predicaments: to wait, or to act.

But, as if conscious of having been too 'dark', he now adds an explanation, though he does so, characteristically enough, by means of another image, the well-known 'catch time by the forelock':

For occasion (as it is the common verse) *turneth a bald noddle, after she hath presented her locks in front: and no hold taken.*

Here he achieves universality and surprise by the impudent colloquialism of 'noddle', which the *Oxford English Dictionary* defines as being 'usually playful or contemptuous' and often a dialect usage. The meaning of this advice is quite clear, but Bacon immediately makes the image even more concrete and tactile, by translating it into the familiar human action of grasping a bottle:

or at least turneth the handle of the bottle first to be received, and after the belly, which is hard to clasp.

Having led us to this position by a devious but illuminating route, he now sums up the experience so far with an aphorism which 'translates' the images, and which with its 'surely' appeals for our assent:

There is surely no greater wisdom than well to time the beginning and onsets of things.

We agree, and this ends the first movement.

The second movement sets off on another elliptical path, with a switch of direction to the cognitive process which determines our decision whether to commence or delay action, and a heightening of the necessity to act by presenting the situation as a dangerous one:

Dangers are no more light, if they once seem light; and more dangers have deceived men than forced them.

As he develops this rather gnomic observation, Bacon is led back to embodying the subject in fully defined human terms, with the chief objection to an extended wait being, ironically, man's inability to keep awake:

Nay, it were better to meet some dangers half way, though they come nothing near, than to keep too long a watch upon their approaches; for if a man watch too long, it is odds he will fall asleep.

The image is perhaps that of a sentry on duty, for the source of analogy now becomes that of soldiers in action, where the timing of 'beginnings and onsets' is peculiarly vital:

On the other side, to be deceived with too long shadows (as some have been when the moon was low and shone on their enemies' back), and so to shoot off before the time; or to teach dangers to come on, by over early buckling towards them; is another extreme.

Both situations are perfectly evoked, the premature buckling on of armour (which may represent a soldier's superstition, or else a psychological truth),[1] and, in a night encounter, the misleading effect of the giant shadows cast by the moon which produces a fatally early attack; these images convey, much more powerfully than any non-metaphorical language could, the crucial nature of decisions of this kind, for they dramatise it.

The third movement begins by recalling the conclusion of the first, so restoring the language of statement:

The ripeness or unripeness of the occasion (as we said) must ever be well weighed;

but again he moves off into metaphor, drawing on the insights of the 'military' analogy, but at the far higher level of mythological beings:

and generally it is good to commit the beginnings of all great actions to Argos with his hundred eyes, and the ends to Briareus with his hundred hands;

This is one of the most brilliantly apt of all Bacon's classical allusions, but, to be sure that his meaning has been taken, he translates it into human terms: 'first to watch, and then to speed'. Now he develops this double admonition with a further apt allusion, again classical and military:

> For the helmet of Pluto, which maketh the politic man go invisible, is secrecy in the counsel and celerity in the execution.

To make this point even more strongly, in the final sentence he cleverly combines this dichotomy in a paradoxical union, and expresses it with a very acute analogy, which, besides condensing much of the meaning of the essay and wittily completing the military image, enacts in its own syntax the movement of the thing compared:

> For when things are once come to the execution, there is no secrecy comparable to celerity; like the motion of a bullet in the air, which flies as it outruns the eye.

And, as the Essay itself recedes from us, here we are left, Bacon having compressed between the outer limits of two fine imaginative comparisons a remarkable amount of human experience, communicated by an exciting use of language and imagery.

These are the qualities of his writing which are found in their most concentrated form in the *Essays*, but the care with which Bacon revised them, extending, clarifying, and focusing both observation and expression, is not the care of a virtuoso working on a display piece, but that of a thinker who wants his meaning to be fully and deeply understood. The brilliance of style is due to his recognition that words, because they are a vehicle for thought, are important.

CHAPTER 8

JUDGMENTS OF BACON'S STYLE

The power of words in Bacon's hands is directly demonstrated by his dominance of seventeenth-century thought, the almost hypnotic way in which his view of the world and of the function of learning within it helped to mould English life, to an extent which no writer had achieved before and few since. His enormous influence is not explained by the actual detailed content of his scientific programme, as I suggested at the beginning of this study, but rather by the terms in which it was formulated and the imaginative eloquence with which these were transmitted. The terms were converted into images, and Anne Righter has well described their tenacity,

the transferred life of those Baconian phrases in which, miraculously, abstract ideas become available to the senses without relinquishing their basic character and precision: the clear and equal glass, the idols of cave, tribe, market-place and theatre, the instances of the lamp, the doctrine of scattered occasions, the branching candlestick of lights. Separated from their original context, they continue not only to live, but to articulate hypotheses and discoveries of which Bacon himself never dreamed. (B77, p. 7.)

Thus what Bacon said about the continuity of learning could well be applied to the effect of his own work:

the images of men's wit and knowledge remain in books, exempted from the wrong of time and capable of perpetual renovation. Neither are they fitly to be called images, because they generate still, and cast their seeds in the minds of others, provoking and causing infinite actions and opinions in succeeding ages. (3. 318.)

But while men in the seventeenth century and after were inspired by the terms in which he proclaimed the birth of the New Science, they were also critically aware of the language which carried this exciting programme and I shall end this study of Bacon by trying to trace the fluctuations in attitude to his style.

Such an outline of a writer's reception from the stylistic view-point might be useful on two counts. First, it could reveal critical reactions to his style which are valuable today, judgments which were produced either by readers close enough in time to Bacon to share his concepts of language or by readers of a later period who were perceptive in their observation. This type of sensitivity to language is always valuable, for its response is based on an intelligent, detailed analysis of a literary work, giving results which have a kind of accuracy and permanence—for this reason the first Shakespeare critics to respond to his language and atmosphere in detail, Coleridge and Hazlitt, are the first who can still be read for their direct illumination of the plays. The second fruit of this history of a writer's reception is less directly relevant to the writer himself, but may be a useful sidelight on cultural history. It is a commonplace that accepted ideas of what constitutes the proper language of poetry (or prose) change from age to age, but the corollary to this observation is that one of the best ways of study-ing 'the taste of the age' is by examining its attitude to style. Often a writer's deepest assumptions about language are shown by his judgment of somebody else's style, assumptions which are below (or above) the level of conscious formulation and which are revealed without choice: stylistic criticism is apparently objective but it constantly exposes the critic's own taste.

In trying to attempt this double task as far as it concerns Bacon (of course I cannot claim completeness and am sure that many more discussions of Bacon's style might be revealed by readers with more detailed knowledge) one possible way of organising it would be to group comments around the particular stylistic devices which have been distinguished here. Thus one might take the use of *partitio* on a large and small scale and juxtapose Rawley's praise of Bacon's ordered structure, or Archbishop Tenison's intro-ductory comment that 'These Speeches and Charges, are generally Methodically, Manly, Elegant, Pertinent, and full of Wise Ob-servations' with (say) George Saintsbury's criticism that 'The famous essay on "Studies" is like a mass of compressed meat or vegetables, sliced out into corresponding pieces of balanced clause'[1] (this comment is perhaps more revealing of Saintsbury's known gastronomic interests—also, he had just found that Bacon did not suit his 'scanning' method). But such an arrangement under constituent parts might produce merely sensational disagreements and would mean that the confrontation of completely opposed tastes would have to be repeated again and again. So it seems better to follow a loosely chronological sequence and relate reactions to the general changes of taste which are reflected here. There are nevertheless some surprising revelations.

I

Bacon's contemporaries (stretching that term to extend to the Restoration) were full of admiration for his writing, although the earliest allusions are extremely vague (such is generally the case with the growth of any great artist's reputation—compare Shakespeare, Berlioz). James Howell thought him 'the eloquentest that was born in this Isle', a 'Flexanious and Golden Tongued Orator'; Henry Peacham listed him among those who had used 'the best and purest English', while Walter Charleton gave him great credit for the 'carmination or refinement of English'. An anonymous writer in 1644 records that he 'taught us to speake the termes of Art in our own language', and Francis Osborn gives a vigorous account of Bacon's mastery of vocabularies as shown in conversation, '*treating with every man* in his respective *profession*...So as I have heard him entertaining a *Country Lord* in the proper *termes* relating to *Hawkes* and *Dogges*. And at another time out-Cant a *London Chirurgion*.' In 1653 Samuel Sheppard valued his style for being 'so succinct, elaborate, and sententious',[1] while Rawley anticipated the judgment of Bacon's other seventeenth-century editor in commenting on his 'weight and dignity of the style', leaving us a valuable account of Bacon's process of writing: 'In the composing of his books he did rather drive at a masculine and clear expression than at any fineness or affectation of phrases, and would often ask if the meaning were expressed plainly enough, as being one that accounted words to be but subservient or ministerial to matter, and not the principal' (I. 11).

The most interesting of these contemporary tributes is also the most tantalising, for the discovery that Ben Jonson's praise of Bacon in *Discoveries* is 'borrowed' from Seneca inevitably weakens our regard for it, but even though we shall never know just to what extent Jonson thought the account accurate ('Now that *really* fits Bacon', he might have said) his mere application of it to 'Dominus Verulanus' is proof of a very high esteem:

there hapn'd, in my time, one noble *Speaker*, who was full of gravity in his speaking. His language, (where hee could spare, or passe by a jest) was nobly *censorious*. No man ever spake more neatly, more presly, more weightily, or suffer'd lesse emptinesse, lesse idlenesse, in what hee utter'd. No member of his speech, but consisted of his owne graces: His hearers could not cough, or looke aside from him, without losse. Hee commanded where hee spoke; and had his Judges angry, and pleased at his devotion. No man had their affections more in his power. The feare of every man that heard him, was, lest hee should make an end.

This is a remarkable tribute, with its picture of a speaker hypnotising his audience, in ideally complete control over them, and one might suppose that this was fairly true of Bacon, given the respectful attitude to him as recorded in the parliamentary notebooks and in what little we know of his performance in the law-courts. Certainly many of his speeches have a compelling authority both in their grasp of the subject and in their economical, interwoven structure. We can also endorse Jonson's praise of the complete absence of self-regard in Bacon's writing, the objectivity with which he focused on the task in hand 'neatly', 'presly', quite devoid of 'emptiness' and 'idlenesse'. Jonson goes on to list the other great prose-writers of his time—including More, Sir Nicholas Bacon (who 'was singular, and almost alone, in the beginning of Queene *Elizabeths* times'), Sidney and Hooker, both 'great Masters of wit, and language; and in whom all vigour of Invention, and strength of judgement met', Sir Walter Raleigh, Savile, Sandys. It is a well-chosen list, one which modern criticism could largely support, and Jonson's comments on the writers are perceptive: thus it is still more significant that he should end the catalogue by placing Bacon at the head, and at the end, of an era. 'Sir Francis Bacon, Lord Chancellor', as the marginal note tells us, is he, who hath fill'd up all numbers; and perform'd that in our tongue, which may be compar'd, or preferr'd, either to insolent *Greece*, or haughty *Rome*. In short, within his view, and about his times, were all the wits borne, that could honour a language, or helpe study. Now things daily fall: wits grow downe-ward, and *Eloquence* growes back-ward: So that hee may be nam'd, and stand as the *marke*, and *akmè* of our language.

Although again partly dependent on Seneca, Jonson is not indulg-ing in idle praise here or playing games with his notebook: he places Bacon unequivocally at the top of a great succession of prose-writers, and it does not seem either accidental or inappropri-ate that the only other time that this prince of classicists should use the slighting epithets 'insolent *Greece*' and 'haughty *Rome*' to describe a modern writer's supremacy should be in his tribute to Shakespeare.

While of paramount interest for the reception of Bacon as a writer, Jonson's account also sets the tone for the seventeenth century's attitude to Bacon's scientific work and to his general stature. Thus he defends the *Novum Organum* (James I, to whom it was dedicated, had dismissed it with a cheap jest, saying that 'it was like the peace of God, which passeth all understanding'. Jon-son might almost be rebuking him):

Which though by the most of superficiall men, who cannot get beyond the Title of *Nominals*, it is not penetrated, nor understood: it really openeth all defects of Learning, whatsoever; and is a Booke,

Qui longum noto scriptori porriget aevum.

The quotation was prophetic: it is from Horace's *Art of Poetry* (v. 364), and in Jonson's own translation reads

This
Will passe the Seas, and long as nature is,
With honour make the farre-knowne Author live.

Jonson's final praise is more general and more absolute: 'hee seem'd to mee ever, by his worke, one of the greatest men, and most worthy of admiration, that had beene in many Ages'. If we are now tempted to discount these tributes because they are partially adapted from other sources, we should remember that Jonson's admiration for Bacon was genuine, as can be seen elsewhere (e.g. the *Poems* and in other places in *Discoveries*; Jonson also owned a copy of the *Novum Organum*) and that he would hardly be likely to transcribe and apply these passages in his notebook if they were not relevant. Furthermore, it is only in this century that the classical analogues have been discovered, and to readers of 1640 and afterwards such praise coming from the most-admired writer of the century must have seemed decisive.[1]

Certainly Bacon's status in the mid-century was supreme, and a chorus of admiration almost idolised him: 'the Master-Builder' of the new system, 'the Learned and incomparable Author', 'that Patriark of Experimental Philosophy', 'that Great Genius of Rational Nature', 'the Honour of our Nation'. He was praised not only by minor figures but by the leaders of the scientific movement associated with the Royal Society: Thomas Sprat, in his official *History* of that body gives Bacon the credit for inspiring its foundation: he 'had the true Imagination of the whole extent of this Enterprize as it is now set on foot', and Joseph Glanvill finds Bacon 'illustrious, immortal...that great Man...the noble *Advancer of Learning*, whose name and parts might give credit to any undertaking'.[2] In the frontispiece to the *History* Bacon shares pride of place with Charles II; in the *Ode to the Royal Society* Cowley describes Bacon as 'a mighty Man' who 'has broke that Scar-Crow Deitie' of reverence for past authority, brought the human mind back from 'words' to 'things', and 'like *Moses*, led us forth at last' to 'the very Border...Of the blest promis'd Land'; and, in his verses to Dr Charleton, Dryden confidently predicts that

> The World to Bacon does not only owe
> Its present knowledge, but its future too.

The praise continues from the mouth of distinguished scientists: the Frenchman Samuel Sorbière, who made a voyage to England in 1663 and liked little of what he saw, allows an exception here:

But to speak the Truth, the Lord Chancellor *Bacon* has surpassed all the rest in the Vastness of his Designs, and that Learned and Judicious Tablature he has left us... This undoubtedly is the greatest Man for the interest of Natural Philosophy that ever was, and the Person that first put the World upon making Experiments that Way.[1]

The most impressive testimony comes from the great scientist Boyle, and Professor Jones records that his every mention of Bacon 'is instinct with praise': 'that great Restorer of Physics...a great and candid philosopher...the great architect of experimental history' and so on. It is no wonder that one of the few opponents of the Royal Society should exclaim bitterly of the uniformity of 'this *Bacon-faced* generation' (Jones, B51, pp. 170, 258).

The shadow cast by Bacon was large and strong, but, although the majority of references to him in the later seventeenth century were to his philosophy, there are signs of a gradual awareness of the nature of his language. Archbishop Tenison collected some of Bacon's minor works into the *Baconiana* of 1679, and in rejecting a spurious scientific work he shows his sympathy with the style and with its ordered quality: 'His Lordship's Speeches were wont to be digested into more Method; his Periods were more round, his Words more choice, his Allusions more frequent, and manag'd with more decorum' (p. 97). Tenison does not mention Bacon's imagery, but other writers respond to it, and not always favourably. The Royal Society's effect on prose style has been well documented by R. F. Jones (B 52), and their known preference for a 'close, naked, natural way of speaking'; the language of Fact and 'mathematical plainness' inevitably legislated against metaphor,[2] and Sprat evidently appealed to a shared distaste: 'Who can behold, without indignation, how many mists and uncertainties, these specious *Tropes* and *Figures* have brought on our Knowledg?' The 'easie vanity of *fine speaking*', he writes, has often attained a specious facility in 'this Trick of *Metaphors*, this Volubility of *Tongue*', and thus the Society had rigorously resolved 'to reject all the amplication, digressions, and swellings of Style'.[3] In complete accordance with the manifesto Joseph Glanvill changed his mind about the style of his *Vanity of Dogmatizing* (1661) and in 1676 he transformed the old-fashioned imaginative wit of the first version into a more sober, scientific medium, explaining that he was now 'more gratified with manly sense, flowing in a natural and unaffected eloquence, than in the music and curiosity of fine metaphors and dancing periods'. The phrase 'dancing periods' may refer to the traditional syntactical symmetries (comments on syntax are always vaguer than on any other parts of style), but there is no doubt about the rejection of metaphor.

Given the presence of so much imagery in Bacon's writing, and given the Royal Society's twin positions of admiration for Bacon and opposition to metaphor, then it might be asked whether their members noticed Bacon's imagery, and if so whether it was an embarrassment to them. Sprat certainly noticed it, and commented on it twice. In the *History* he praised Bacon's style without reservations:

He was a Man of strong, cleer, and powerful Imaginations: his Genius was searching, and inimitable: and of this I need give no other proof, then his Style itself;...The course of it vigorous, and majestical; the Wit Bold, and Familiar: the comparisons fetch'd out of the way, and yet the most easie... (P. 36.)

This is a perceptive comment both on the overall control of Bacon's imagination and on the way his images are intellectually striking yet close to human experience ('Familiar' seems to have this sense—it is certainly true of the natural and human sources of his imagery). Better still is Sprat's comparison of Bacon with Hobbes, which is provoked by Sorbière's disparaging comment that Hobbes was much influenced by Bacon through having been his amanuensis, so much so that Hobbes has ' *Studied his manner of turning Things: That he just expresses himself in that Way of Allegory, wherein the other excell'd*' ('Allegory' is too strong, but it is still an intelligent observation on Bacon's thinking in images). In reply Sprat distinguishes between their use of imagery:

I scarce know Two Men in the World that have more different Colours of Speech than these Two Great Wits: The Lord *Bacon* short, allusive, and abounding with Metaphors, Mr. *Hobbs* round, close, sparing of Similitudes, but ever extraordinary decent in them. The one's Way of Reasoning proceeds on Particulars, and pleasant Images...The other's bold, resolv'd, settled upon general Conclusions... (*Voyage, ed. cit.* pp. 163–4.)

These comments by Sprat belong to my first category of useful allusions (giving direct illumination of the text) rather than to the second (revealing the taste of the age), for one would hardly imagine that the same writer could produce this account and the absolute attack on metaphor quoted earlier. It is again a perceptive description of Bacon's style—'abounding with metaphors'—even to the point of connecting these with his way of using analogies as arguments: his 'Way of Reasoning proceeds on Particulars, and pleasant Images'. Sprat's attack on metaphor in the *History* was certainly typical of the new taste, and he obviously has not forgotten it, for later on in this reply to Sorbière he complains that the French have not reformed themselves sufficiently, indeed '...there might be a whole Volume composed in comparing the Chastity, the Newness, the Vigour of many of our *English* Fancies, with the corrupt and the swelling Metaphors wherewith some of our Neighbours, who most admire themselves, do still adorn their books' (*ibid.* p. 172). Faced with this contradiction we can only conclude that Sprat's admiration for Bacon the scientist has overpowered his theoretical position—at all events, his comments are sympathetic as well as being accurate.

Later writers were not to be so tolerant, though, and, when the reaction against Bacon sets in, his imagery is one of the chief targets. The first sign of the reversal is a rather tentative one, as Gilbert Burnet notes (in the preface to his 1684 translation of More's *Utopia*) the remarkable change in style since 'the last age', one so marked that

even the great Sir *Francis Bacon*, that was the first that writ our Language correctly—in some places has figures so strong, that they could not pass now before a severe Judg. (Gibson, 498.)

Yet Burnet concludes that Bacon is 'still our best Author', a reconciliation of admiration and disapproval which it was not possible to maintain for long. One of the most subtle attacks (conducted largely, I think, by direct stylistic parody, and therefore rather hard to pin down) was that of Swift.[1] We know that Swift owned several copies of Bacon's works, and that he had made marginalia in them (none have as yet been rediscovered). We know too that Swift was strongly exposed to Baconian philosophy at two influential periods of his life, at Trinity College,

Dublin, and with his English patron Sir William Temple, and that
in both cases Swift did not exactly share his elders' tastes. It is
known that Swift expressed a lifelong contempt for the New
Science (most wittily seen in the parody of Baconian scientific
academies in Book 3 of *Gulliver's Travels*) and equally for most
systems; and, to one who took the traditional side in the Ancients
and Moderns controversy, Bacon the shining hero of the Moderns
would appeal as little as he did on the two previous points. From
an intellectual viewpoint, then, it is inevitable that Swift would
have disliked everything that Bacon stood for, and from a stylistic
position the antipathy would persist. Swift's distrust of metaphor
for its potential delusory power is another recognised feature of his
character, and equals that of Sprat in its violence—he had objected
to 'St Paul's allegories, and other figures of Grecian eloquence'
being taken as articles of faith.[1] Again, Swift shared a post-
Restoration dislike of the use of *sententiae* and all kinds of classical
tags,[2] writing in the Preface to his *Tritical Essay* that he had been
'*of late offended with many Writers of Essays and moral Discourses, for
running into stale Topicks and thread-bare Quotations*' (I, 246). Given
that the (functional, as opposed to the ornamental) use of quotations is one of the marked features of Bacon's style ('allusive', as
Sprat called it, 'his Allusions more frequent' than other writers',
according to Tenison) then it is hardly likely that Swift would
approve of this element either.

It is to be expected that Swift should want to mock Bacon, and
indeed some of his sarcastic allusions have already been noted:
editors of *The Battle of the Books* have recognised that the opening
of the first of Bacon's *Essays*, 'Of Truth' (and the most famous
opening words of any essay in English)—'*What is Truth?* said
jesting Pilate; and would not stay for an answer' (6. 377)—is
destructively applied by Swift to the dullard of criticism:
'MOMUS having thus delivered himself, staid not for an
answer' (I, 154).[3] But many more such allusions have not been
noticed, and, although it is impossible to be sure that Swift is
mocking Bacon when he uses some very common classical tags,
there can surely be no doubt about this example, say:

Bacon: For the truth and falsehood, in such things, are like the iron and clay in the toes of Nebuchadnezzar's image; they may cleave, but they will not incorporate. (6. 383.)

Swift: For such Opinions cannot cohere; but, like the Iron and Clay in the Toes of *Nebuchadnezzar's* Image, must separate and break in pieces. (I, 247.)

That is one of Bacon's most distinctive quotations, and Swift is not content with just repeating it but adds a new twist: the iron and clay do not merely not 'incorporate' (as in Bacon) but actually 'break in Pieces', thus casting doubt on the whole analogy. A subtle change in the sequence of one of Bacon's favourite tags (7. 158; also 3. 388; 4. 412, etc.) makes it ridiculous—where he has the order (*a*) the Oracle, (*b*) Socrates' disclaimer, Swift turns it upside-down: (*b*) '*Socrates*, on the other Hand, who said he knew nothing, (*a*) was pronounced by the Oracle to be the wisest Man in the World' (I, 247). Another tag is devalued by being slightly reworded:

Bacon: One of the Seven was wont to say: *That Laws were like Cobwebs; where the small Flies were caught, and the great brake through.* (7. 150.)

Swift: After which, Laws are like Cobwebs, which may catch small Flies, but let Wasps and Hornets break through. (I, 250.)

Both the throw-away start and the new precision of terms make the maxim—or the laws—look silly.

Many more such satiric allusions could be instanced with a fair degree of certainty. As for mockery of Bacon's imagery, it is harder to be sure, but one characteristic of his does seem to be undermined, and that is the quite explicit introduction of an analogy with an 'It is in / with *A* as it is in / with *B*'. Thus from works readily available to Swift (who concentrates mostly on the *Essays* and the *Advancement of Learning*) we might cite the following: 'For it is in knowledge as it is in plants...' (*Advancement*, 3. 404), and '...it is in praise as it is in gains...' (*Essays*, 6. 500); or more fully:

But it is in life as it is in ways; the shortest way is commonly the foulest, and surely the fairer way is not much about. (3. 472; also 7. 159; 6. 88.)

That dispassionate maxim can be juxtaposed with what seems to be Swift's *reductio ad absurdum* of it:

For in *Writing*, it is as in *Travelling*: If a Man is in haste to be at home...I advise him clearly to make the straitest and the commonest Road, be it ever so dirty... (1, 120—see the whole paragraph.)

Here not only the form of the analogy is mocked, but also—by its application to writing—its whole point. Elsewhere Swift also takes a serious-looking first term, and as the reader begins to assent to it he springs on him a quite ludicrous second part:

It is with *Wits* as with *Razors*, which are never so apt to *cut* those they are employ'd on, as when they have *lost their edge*. (1, 29.)

But, I believe, it is with Libraries, as with other Coemeteries...; For, I think, it is in *Life* as in *Tragedy*... (1, 144, 180.)

Of course, Swift's parodies are brilliant and often extremely funny, so that one does not mind that they are rather unfair. Another Baconian thumb-print which he seems to mock successfully is Bacon's favourite practice of introducing a maxim with 'for', which Swift deflates by making it seem banal: 'For, I have somewhere heard, it is a Maxim...', 'For, as it is the Nature, of Rags, to bear a kind of mock resemblance to Finery...so...' (1, 14, 128).[1]

Most of Swift's satiric allusions to Bacon come in his earliest and most 'literary' works, *A Tale of A Tub*, *The Battle of the Books*, and *A Tritical Essay*, but he had evidently been doing some careful reading for *Gulliver's Travels*, and amongst smaller allusions two particularly stand out, both in the description of the Royal Society of Laputa. One of the advantages of Bacon's programme for co-operation based on an agreed methodology was that it reduced the need for outstanding scientists: as he said, with perhaps unfortunate optimism, 'the course I propose for the discovery of sciences is such as leaves but little to the acuteness and strength of wits, but places all wits and understandings nearly on a level' (4. 62–3). On Swift's scale of satiric exaggeration this idea is immediately transformed by that mad professor with his random word-forming frame:

Every one knew how laborious the usual Method is of attaining to Arts and Sciences; whereas by his Contrivance, the most ignorant Person at a reasonable Charge, and with a little bodily Labour, may write Books in Philosophy, Poetry, Politicks, Law, Mathematicks and Theology, without the least Assistance from Genius or Study. (XI, 182–4.)

That is a dreadful prospect but, although Swift has distorted Bacon's point, we have to concede that the ridiculous was inherent in it. Last and most offensive is the reduction of Bacon the political theorist. In one of several similar passages he had given advice on how to study human nature:

The *knowledge of Men* six wayes may be disclosed and drawne out; by their *Faces* and *Countenances*, by *Words*, by *Deeds*, by their *Nature*, by their *Ends*, by the *Relations* of others (*De Augmentis*, tr. Wats; 5. 50–61 ff.; 6. 493–4, etc.).

However, Bacon had left out an important human function, of whose inescapable existence Swift never tired of reminding us. Thus in the 'School of political Projectors' a Professor has a sure-fire method of discovering plots:

He advised great Statesmen to examine into the Dyet of all suspected Persons; their Times of eating; upon which Side they lay in bed; with which Hand they wiped their Posteriors; to take a strict View of their Excrements, and from the Colour, the Odour, the Taste, the consistence, the Crudness, or Maturity of Digestion, form a Judgment of their Thoughts and Designs: Because, Men are never so serious, thoughtful, and intent, as when they are at Stool; which he found by frequent Experiment... (XI, 190.)

That devastating parody of Machiavellian 'observation of man' goes on with a further mock of Baconian language, as it had risen even to a Bacon-type maxim—'Because, Men are never so serious...' There is much more evidence for Swift's satiric attitude to Bacon, and, though the loyal Baconian may resent these attacks on what are after all perfectly acceptable features of Bacon's style, those who appreciate Swift's genius in satire and especially parody can only observe that they are clever and amusing, and could not have been written by anyone else. And they do not really damage Bacon.

Swift's dislike of Bacon may be expressed with added personal force but it is typical of the gradual hardening of opinion against Bacon's style, and later writers do not hesitate to criticise him openly (Swift's suppression of Bacon's name in these satiric attacks is not due to timidity on his part but probably to the playful secretiveness with which he conducted so much of his satire). Thus in 1713 Budgell, a general-purpose contributor to periodicals, launched a strong attack on *Henry VII*, and especially on its use of imagery, accusing Bacon of being

ever in the tedious style of declaimers, using two words for one; ever endeavouring to be witty, and as fond of out-of-the-way similies as some of our old playwriters. He abounds in low phrases, beneath the dignity of history, and often condescends to little conceits and quibbles.[1]

Budgell is so confident that his readers will grasp the point that he simply quotes some twenty images (ranging from the simplest, only a shade removed from 'prose usage', to quite splendid imaginative comparisons) with an off-hand dismissal: 'I leave the following passages to every one's consideration, without making any farther remarks upon them.' Here we find for the first time in connection with Bacon an explicit statement of post-Restoration neo-classicism, with its strong association between literary decorum and social decorum ('low phrases, beneath the dignity of history') and its scorn for the quibble or pun, as expressed so pungently in Dryden's criticism that Shakespeare 'is many times flat, insipid; his comic wit degenerating into clenches...',[2] a criticism which was echoed for over a century. Just as Budgell attacked Bacon's boldness of imagery (Sprat's qualificatory 'the comparisons fetch'd out of the way, and yet the most easie' now seems almost Jacobean in its sympathy), so, nearly fifty years later, Hume is still making the same point:

Bacon's style is stiff and rigid: his wit, though often brilliant, is also often unnatural and far-fetched; and he seems to be the original of those pointed similes and long-spun allegories, which so much distinguish the English authors.

To make Bacon the founder of such writing is obviously wrong, but Hume is right to see the presence of fully developed imagery in Bacon. Criticism of Bacon's impropriety in language was made

about the same time in a work long ascribed to Goldsmith, outlining a 'History of our own Language' in 1758, and which
attacked incorrect grammatical constructions:

Even the style of the great Sir Francis Bacon is far from being faultless in this
and many other respects. It is plain that he never is at a loss for matter, but that
he is often at a loss for *improper* words. His periods are sometimes strained, and
often twisted out of all natural order; and half the pains he took to be an
admired, would have rendered him a faultless writer.[1]

Criticisms of syntax, as I remarked earlier, are invariably vague,
and there seems little to be gained from enquiring what Hume
means by 'stiff', or Goldsmith by 'natural' other than saying that
the construction of sentences in Bacon seems to be the quality of
his style which reads most easily and naturally today—as F. P.
Wilson ironically observed of Dryden's style, 'If one hesitates to
call it "modern", that is only because it is so good.'[2]

Adverse criticism, though, is at least stimulating in that it
springs from a definite response to the writer. It is at all costs to be
preferred to the neutral making of quotations from Bacon or the
lip-worship of him that we find elsewhere in the eighteenth
century (Pope's many references hardly progress beyond this
level). Representative, no doubt, at the beginning of the period
are the periodicals: in both the *Tatler* and the *Spectator* Bacon is the
source of miscellaneous quotations, or is given quite commonplace
tributes, while later in the century Horace Walpole's many references are completely trivial, including two fictitious ones.[3]
Much more positive, as we could have expected, were the reactions
of Johnson, who read Bacon with some care for his *Dictionary*,
making extensive use of him, and informing Sir William Seward
that a Dictionary of the English Language might be compiled
from Bacon's writing alone, and that he 'had once an intention of
giving an edition of Bacon, at least of his English works, and
writing the Life of that great man'.[4]

Johnson quotes often from this 'favourite author', but never as
shallowly as Walpole or the periodicals—the quotations become a
source for further reflection.[5] Only once, however, does his

admiration take the form of a comment on a particular work, and that is in the judgment of the *Essays*, as recorded by Reynolds, that

their excellence and their value consisted in being the observations of a strong mind operating upon life; and in consequence you find there what you seldom find in other books.[1]

This description would have pleased Bacon, and seems to me true of the *Essays* still—clearly Johnson's own cast of mind is in sympathy with Bacon the moralist. If he never quite managed to escape from the literary assumptions of his age with respect to Shakespeare, Johnson is unique in the mid-eighteenth century in the independence of his reaction to Bacon, but his comments come as a reminder of how much has been lost. Since the early stages when the criticisms of Ben Jonson and Sprat were both in tune with Bacon's own attitude to language the enormous shift in taste after the late seventeenth century has contributed little if anything to the illumination of Bacon's style, even though it may have revealed the new assumptions. This sequence of understanding and sympathy being followed by ignorance and indifference might be called the first phase of the reception of Bacon as a writer, and the second phase produced a disappointingly similar pattern.

II

The second phase (this division is not an invention on my part—the publishing history bears it out)[2] begins towards the end of the eighteenth century, with a remarkable revival of interest at the beginning of the nineteenth. But in this period of rediscovery there are noticeable changes of attitude. Bacon is no longer important as a philosopher (the upgrading of his theories of induction does not occur until the 1840s), clearly because many other philosophical movements have replaced that pioneering revolution in natural science. There is the usual biographical squabble, Bacon being widely and indiscriminately criticised for his personal weaknesses, for his 'servile' relationship with James I, or for isolated remarks taken out of context. A greater change is that there is now no general hostility to his style, and a rather obvious explanation would be that, whereas for the Augustans he represented the style of an archaic, indecorous taste, and therefore had to be rejected, the Augustans themselves are now 'the last age' and young writers no longer sharpen their teeth on him, as Swift had done, but undermine the idols of classicism: universality and impersonality, the cult of a specifically 'literary' language, the 'rocking-horse' of the couplet. This is, as I say, not an original observation, but it does seem to explain the absence of animus to his style (especially the imagery) and the freedom and independence with which the critics from, say, 1790 to 1830 responded to his writing. There is, however, one point on which the Romantics did not totally succeed in freeing themselves from their predecessors, and that is in the disapproval of witty conceits.

The first signs of interest are to be seen in the work of Jeremy Bentham, who found Bacon a valuable model for his own programme of legal and political reform from his first published work, the *Fragment on Government* (1776), onwards. (This is another new reaction—instead of a general response to the major elements in Bacon's work, readers now seize on that aspect which suits their own specific interests. We see it again in Coleridge and Ruskin.) Most of Bentham's references reflect these concerns, but he was also very impressed with Bacon's technique of *partitio*, which he described as the 'precocious and precious fruit of the union of learning with genius', and on which, in preference to that of D'Alembert in the *Encyclopédie*, he based the curriculum for his 'Chrestomathic Day School'.[1] Bentham's attitude to Bacon was that of enthusiastic admiration shared by the majority of readers in this period, but there was one great exception in Blake, who apart from a single approving comment in an early letter regarded him with constant hatred as the co-founder (with Newton) of philosophical materialism. The key document here is Blake's copy of the *Essays*, which he annotated in about 1798,[2] in a vein of indignation and outrage directed against courts and kings, vigorously asserting the strength of Christ over all worldly and heathen philosophy: 'It was a common opinion in the Court of Queen Elizabeth that Knavery is Wisdom. Cunning Plotters were consider'd as wise Machiavels';—'A Lie! Every Body hates a King' (there is a scatological drawing connecting 'A King' with the devil's excrement);—'thought is Act. Christ's Acts were Nothing to Caesar's if this is not so'—and much more in this violently republican tone. Blake's objections were not literary, though, and, if his philosophy is so totally antipathetic to Renaissance policy—'Good advice from Satan's Kingdom', he wrote on the title-page—that nothing could bring them together, by contrast (had he known), his own belief in the necessity to consider 'minute particulars' is remarkably close to that of Bacon's, and they share a concept of fables and parables as being 'not too explicit' and therefore inviting men 'to enquire further'.

Blake's antipathy to Bacon is unique in this period, which witnessed a remarkable growth in interest: between 1800 and 1820 at least thirty-eight editions of works by Bacon appeared, the most for such a period since the heyday of the mid-seventeenth century, and in a rush which begins to resemble the earlier one he again becomes an important figure to literary men. Of the major Romantics (and I use this term as a convenient shorthand) there is no one who is not influenced by the revival, and many minor figures—Lamb, Southey, Godwin, Haydon, Crabb Robinson—all refer to Bacon with signs of having read him, if only because it was the done thing. Landor gives an *Imaginary Conversation* to Bacon, although it is a miserably crude pastiche, and Leigh Hunt is especially fond of quoting him, rounding off the final number of the *Companion* (23 July 1828) with a plea for the free expression of opinions:

All that I claim is a right to state them with decency, in vindication of the great human privilege which Bacon set free...the open, grave and sincere discussion of these and all other points interesting to the welfare of everyone of us.

It is hard to pin down what passage Hunt is referring to (if any), but we can see how Bacon is again of sufficiently high status, as he was for Glanvill, that his 'name and parts might give credit to any undertaking'. To this period belong the first serious estimates of Bacon as a philosopher, with Dugald Stewart's *Preliminary Dis-*

sertation (1815), and of his influence with Macvey Napier's excellent essay of 1818.[1] Indeed the interest is so great that the mere acquisition of editions becomes an event: Coleridge writes to Southey in 1799 to look for a 'Bacon's Works' for less than two guineas, Wordsworth asks De Quincey in 1808 to buy him 'Lord Bacon's Works, Milton's Prose Works—in short, any of the good elder writers', and Hazlitt records triumphantly how his copy of *The Advancement of Learning* passed through the suspicious French–Italian customs, to whom a box full of books 'was a contempt of the constituted Authorities'.[2]

Among the poets Byron takes a characteristically individual stand, leaving the social round in Ravenna in 1821 to correct some half-dozen of Bacon's *Apophthegms* (on the grounds of historical accuracy), and listing them with a flourish in a note to *Don Juan*. In complete contrast Shelley's interest in Bacon is lifelong and serious, and, in the words of a recent study by W. O. Scott, 'progresses from religious inquiry to historical speculations, and finally to a conception of Plato and Bacon as great poets', which is 'the highest praise he could have given anyone'. Here is a late instance of the persistence of Bacon's metaphors, for Scott argues that Shelley was influenced by Bacon in his own use of images of caves, mirrors, fountains, streams, veils and stars, and the list indeed includes most of the major categories which I distinguished earlier. Keats seems to be somewhat independent of the general movement, with two unimportant references only, but Wordsworth is right in it: according to his biographer he had been acquainted with Baconian philosophy since his schooldays, and later Bacon's portrait hung at Rydal Mount alongside those of Chaucer, Spenser, Shakespeare, and Milton. Wordsworth recommends a correspondent to read 'the best old writers, Bacon's *Essays*, his *Advancement of Learning*, for instance' and he shows a surprisingly wide knowledge by taking a quotation from Bacon's *Advertisement touching Church Controversies* which is to become the motto for his *Convention of Cintra* (1809).[3]

Bacon is undeniably a great source of interest for the early nineteenth century, for reasons which are not altogether easy to understand. But as well as this wide-ranging but indiscriminate enthusiasm we find evidence of a more intelligent understanding, and the reactions of Coleridge, De Quincey, and Hazlitt form the best account of Bacon's style yet produced—one, in fact, which has hardly been improved on since. Coleridge's chief interest in Bacon was in the philosopher, and like Bentham he focused on those aspects which were nearest his own thinking, especially the distinction between Reason and the Understanding (of which he thought Kant had merely provided an elaboration).[1] Happily Coleridge's interest extended to the style, and given his brilliance as a stylistic critic (of the 'impressionistic' type, not suitable to 'laboratory rigour' of course, but nevertheless remarkably perceptive) it is as much a matter of regret that he did not complete his proposed History of Prose as that Johnson did not make his edition and Life of Bacon. A convenient starting point amongst Coleridge's many references is the place where he detected an affinity between his own style and Bacon's (perhaps his way of paying a compliment—as again with *Hamlet*). He was replying to criticisms of *The Friend* in 1809 that found in his own writing

too often an entortillage in the sentences & even the thoughts, which nothing can justify; and, always almost, a stately piling up of *Story* on *Story* in one architectural period which is not suited to a periodical Essay or to Essays at all (Lord Bacon, whose style mine more nearly resembles than any other, in his greater works, thought Seneca a better model for his Essays)... (*Ed. cit.* pp. 426–7.)

To appreciate Coleridge's point it is necessary to make a distinction: Bacon did once mention Seneca as a model for the *Essays* in the cancelled dedication of the 1612 volume (they were to have been presented to the young Prince Henry, but he died just before publication), but it is clear that Bacon is referring to the general form of the work, that is, discursive observations on separate topics: these are 'certain brief notes, set down rather significantly than curiously, which I have called *Essays*. The word is late, but the thing is ancient. For Seneca's epistles to Lucilius, if one mark them well, are but *Essays*, that is, dispersed meditations, though conveyed in the form of epistles' (10. 340). Thus Coleridge is not describing Bacon's style as 'Senecan' (as we shall see, he thought it quite the opposite), although his distinction between the style of the *Essays* and that of 'the greater works' is a correct recognition of the presence of more aphorisms in that work. But he goes on to deny the presence of 'Senecan' style in Bacon (by implication from the analogy with himself), predicting sarcastically that his own way of writing is unlikely to please 'the present illogical age, which has in imitation of the *French* rejected all the cements of language; so that a popular book is now a mere bag of marbles, i.e. aphorisms and epigrams on one subject'.

The imagination and wit shown in that damaging analogy for the Senecan mode ('a mere bag of marbles'), is shown in still more ingenious attacks, where Coleridge's own felicity in metaphor produces a brilliantly impressionistic description of this 'asthmatic' style, in which, 'like idle morning visitors, the brisk and breathless periods hurry in and hurry off in quick and profitless succession', failing to catch in 'the hooks-and-eyes of the memory'. I know of few more imaginative descriptions of style than this—it ranks with Nashe's devastating accounts of Gabriel Harvey's clumsiness in writing hexameters, or Shakespeare's parody of Euphuism. Coleridge then contrasts this bitty style unfavourably with 'the stately march and difficult evolutions, which characterize the eloquence of Hooker, Bacon, Milton, and Jeremy Taylor' (*ibid*. pp. 425–6), and he elsewhere links these four writers as possessing power of language and strength of intellect, again distinguishing their style from Senecanism:

The unity in these writers is produced by the unity of the subject, and the perpetual growth and evolution of the thoughts, one generating, and explaining, and justifying, the place of another, not, as in Seneca, where the thoughts, striking as they are, are merely strung together like beads, without any causation or progression. (P. 414.)

That seems to me as good a description of Senecanism (if rather partisan) as of the unity of Bacon's style: Coleridge is unique both in his awareness of the existence of the two opposed theories of prose style, and in his placing of Bacon within the Ciceronian tradition.

Judgments of Bacon's Style

But not all of Coleridge's comments are favourable: he does not like Bacon's wit. His reaction is similar to that of Johnson on Shakespeare, and in his fullest critique he makes a neat variation on Johnson's image of the pun as being Shakespeare's 'fatal Cleopatra', having quoted a passage from the 'Distributio Operis':

> This last sentence is, as the attentive reader will have himself detected, one of those faulty verbal antitheses not infrequent in Lord Bacon's writings. Pungent antitheses, and the analogies of wit in which the resemblance is too often more indebted to the double or equivocal sense of the word, than to any real conformity in the thing or image, form the dulcia vitia for his style, the Dalilahs of our philosophical Samson. But in this instance, as indeed throughout all his works, the meaning is clear and evident. (P. 49.)

This is one point on which we can hardly agree with Coleridge—antitheses abound in Bacon, but few based on specious equivocation, and the objection seems to spring from a personal antipathy (as again on p. 211). However, if we disagree here, we 'rejoice to concur' with Coleridge in a final estimate of Bacon. A regrettably fragmentary and incoherent passage in a notebook attempts to define 'the character of Bacon's intellect' and traces two opposed tendencies:

> Generalization—a most active associative Power—an opulence in ramification —felicity in observation and the reduction of observances to the maximis & minimis and of particulars to their comprehensive & interpretive *Maxims*—n.b. seldom *Principles*—These are the Excellencies. (Pp. 56–7.)

Suspicious as one must remain of psychological stylistics, that is nevertheless a remarkable description of Bacon's imaginative power, of the pure intellectual grasp that must have existed to produce such a detailed and accurate revision of theories of knowledge and experiment. Coleridge's innate excellence as a reader is shown best of all, perhaps, in those occasional and disorganised comments on Shakespeare, but he was right about most of the major features of Bacon's style and displays more perception and imagination than any other reader known to me.

The achievement of De Quincey and Hazlitt is of a lower order, but by no means negligible. De Quincey is, for example, one of the first to recognise the importance of Solomon's House in the

New Atlantis as a model for the Royal Society, as he is certainly the first to comment on Bacon's Latin style, which, he says, was 'so much moulded by his own peculiar plastic intellect'. He acutely points to the initial advantages of Bacon's power in fully formed imagery—'being figurative and sensuous (as great thinkers must always be)'—and (in a passage that contradicts Coleridge's opinion that Bacon's 'illustrations have more wit than meaning') De Quincey affirms the validity and truthfulness of Bacon's images:

The reason is that, being always in quest of absolute truth, he contemplates all subjects not through the rhetorical fancy, which is most excited by mere seeming resemblances, and such as can only sustain themselves under a single phasis, but through the philosophic fancy, or that which rests upon real analogies.

If we assent to that judgment on Bacon's imagery we must have some reservations about this on his syntax: an

unfavourable circumstance, arising in fact out of the plethoric fulness of Lord B.'s mind, is the shorthand style of his composition, in which the connexions are seldom fully developed. It was the lively *mot* of a great modern poet, speaking of Lord B.'s *Essays*, 'that they are not plants, but seeds; not oaks, but acorns'.[1]

This does not distinguish between the styles as Coleridge had done nor does it seem true of the connected mode of the *Essays*, except in their first version—but the last comment (one would like to know who the poet was) does unwittingly hit on the very intention of the aphorisms there.

Hazlitt's comments on Bacon are more valuable than De Quincey's, and with a wider range. He refers to Bacon throughout his life, and in 1812 paid him a tribute as both poet and philosopher which seems to be echoed in Shelley's account of a few years later:

He united the powers of imagination and understanding in a greater degree than almost any other writer. He was one of the strongest instances of those men who by the rare privilege of their nature are at once poets and philosophers, and see equally into both worlds.[2]

Hazlitt's main discussion of Bacon as a writer comes in the seventh of his *Lectures on the Age of Elizabeth* (1820), and begins with a good account of the philosophical programme, which he actually illustrates by Bacon's own images of the 'vantage ground of genius and learning', the voyage of the human intellect, even 'the comparative anatomy' of the mind of man. Like all these Romantic critics Hazlitt is extremely sensitive to Bacon's use of imagery, praising especially his power of making analogies between 'any given result or principle' and 'others of the same kind scattered through nature or history', a power which works 'rather by intuition than by inference... or as he himself has finely expressed it, "by the same footsteps of nature treading or printing upon several subjects or matters"'. And, like his contemporaries, Hazlitt is also aware of the imaginative qualities revealed in Bacon's syntax, and his account of this sees more variety than De Quincey had and indeed surpasses Coleridge's:

His writings have the gravity of prose with the fervour and vividness of poetry. His sayings have the effect of axioms, are at once striking and self-evident... His style is equally sharp and sweet, flowing and pithy, condensed and expansive, expressing volumes in a sentence, or amplifying a single thought into pages of rich, glowing and delightful eloquence.

Hazlitt's enthusiasm almost runs away with him there into that gushing vein which mars some of his Shakespeare criticism, but it is a unique account of the presence of both concentration and expansiveness in Bacon's style. Like Coleridge he places Bacon with 'Ciceronian' writers such as Browne and Jeremy Taylor, all of whom share a 'pomp and copiousness of style'.

The comments of Coleridge, De Quincey and Hazlitt include some repetition, but it was worth quoting their most important judgments here, partly because their criticism of Bacon has never been discussed before, but also as it still forms an illuminating commentary on his style. The period 1790 to 1820 is one of great interest in Bacon, and these three critics achieved a major revaluation of his ability as a writer, but it was one which did not influence others. (Indeed, a disappointing feature revealed in this outline of Bacon's reception is that we do not find critics aware of previous judgments. But possibly this is typical of English criticism, in which a continuity or awareness of a critical tradition begins very late, perhaps not before this century.) I have called the period since Bentham the second phase of the reaction to Bacon the writer, and the same process of a growth of illumination leading to a decline can now be seen here, with the turning point of a Budgell now being filled by a much more dangerous opponent, Macaulay. His notorious essay in the *Edinburgh Review* for July 1837 had a considerable influence, with its sarcastic distortions of both Bacon's life and philosophy, but its failings are now generally appreciated[1] (although Spedding's masterly *Evenings with a Reviewer*, a vast Socratic dialogue which refutes Macaulay patiently, point by point, is not as well known as it should be). Macaulay gives only a little space to attacking Bacon's style, but uses considerable skill in distortion. Thus he grants Bacon the powers in analogy and imaginative thinking which the Romantic critics had argued for, but then rewords the definition of wit in the vein of Johnson attacking the Metaphysicals:

He had a wonderful talent for packing wit close, and rendering it portable. In wit, if by wit he meant the power of perceiving analogies between things which appear to have nothing in common, he never had an equal, not even Cowley, not even the author of *Hudibras*. Indeed, he possessed this faculty, or this faculty possessed him to a morbid degree.

This is a curious echo of post-Restoration taste, and in his other attacks on the pun the bracketing of Macaulay with Budgell does seem apt. Again in granting Bacon a 'poetical faculty', Macaulay does so only to undermine it: 'No imagination was ever at once so strong and so thoroughly subjugated. It never stirred but at a signal from good sense. It stopped at the first check from good sense', and so on. Macaulay has some praise for Bacon's style and for his philosophy, but it is both dwarfed by his abuse and made to seem hollow and insincere. Whereas one can accept Swift's resentment of Bacon for the wit and energy with which it is presented, Macaulay's piece is simply the result of a destructive intent which relies on cheap argument and specious insinuation. Unfortunately its influence in the nineteenth century seems to have been considerable, especially at the popular level, and parts of it have until quite recently been reprinted in a selection of Bacon's works—a publishing decision which was due either to ignorance or to malice. As Coleridge wrote in 1816, '"Lie boldly", says Lord Bacon in his aphorisms, "something will be sure to stick". "Lie boldly", said an Italian, "if it be only believed for a single day, it will not be without effect." The most ample confutation can only heal the wound, but not prevent a scar.'

Macaulay may not have been the sole cause of the decline of interest in the mid-century. One possible explanation is that whereas the Romantics themselves now become important influences (as in the general Victorian interest in both the style and ideas of Coleridge, Wordsworth, Keats, and Shelley) the writers they admired do not, and this is perhaps a common enough reaction. A more certain cause of the decline is, paradoxically, the growth of the specialised study of Bacon in the fields of science, philosophy and history, for a series of ever more technical studies removed Bacon from the province of the general reader and, more important, from that of the creative artist. Only specialists could have been attracted by the image of Bacon as seen in the row of books which begins with Whewell on the *History* (1837) and the *Philosophy of the Inductive Sciences* (1840) and continues with the studies of Bouillet, De Maistre, Rémusat, Kuno Fischer and S. R. Gardiner.[1] One unlooked-for good effect of Macaulay's essay was that it was said to have spurred James Spedding to begin his great edition of the works, but although this for the first time presented the full range of Bacon's achievement it cannot be said that there is much in those fourteen volumes to give any guide to Bacon's characteristics or excellence as a writer, and they do not seem to have had much influence except on other scholars—apart from accidental ones, such as the fact that Tennyson, who had known Spedding at Trinity, 'read aloud' from this edition 'with great enjoyment, as the Volumes came from the publishers'—he seems to have read Spedding's contribution, not Bacon's.

Elsewhere there is little sign of interest, and whereas a list of those of the Romantics who were interested in, and had read, Bacon would have included almost everyone of significance, now such a list would be just as thoroughly exclusive. Dickens makes some debating points with Bacon's name, George Eliot has a few insignificant allusions in the Letters (Bacon figures on a stock list of improving authors for Gwendolyn Harleth), Carlyle has even less to say. Reference to Bacon has again declined to the level of mere name-dropping, for the major novelists and poets seem indifferent, and there is not even any disapproval—apart from Trollope, who fills his copy of the *Essays* with indignant comments. On the academic side there are some traces of interest: Hopkins at Balliol in 1865 drew up a reading list which began with the *Essays*, noted that he would have to read the *Novum Organum* for Greats, and in his undergraduate essays compared Bacon and Plato. Arnold made notes from Fischer's book on Bacon, and occasionally refers to the *Essays* and *Advancement*, while Gladstone at twenty-five made a 'Digest' of Bacon's works. One of the few references to Bacon that I have come across in the novels of this period occurs in *The Way of all Flesh* and besides recording the decline of Bacon to the level of an 'improving author' Butler's reference to the physical nature of the edition concerned is, by comparison with the enthusiasm of Wordsworth, Hazlitt or Coleridge in actually acquiring a copy of his works, symbolic of the decline: Mr Pontifex senior wished to reward Theobald for having taken a good degree,

and told his son he would present him with the works of any standard writer whom he might select. The young man chose the works of Bacon, and Bacon accordingly made his appearance in ten nicely bound volumes. A little inspection, however, showed that the copy was a second-hand one.[1]

Thus, unless my impression is a very false one, there is little evidence that in the mid and late nineteenth century Bacon was important either as a figure to be mentioned or as a writer to be appreciated for his style. The only exception comes in the first category, and that is Ruskin, who refers to Bacon frequently, and in all his major works from 1841 to 1887. Too often Bacon is merely a name to be set against other great men, and on one occasion he is used for a grossly distorted comparison with Pascal, to show the influence of environment, especially mountains, on the human character, but Ruskin's more pertinent references are usually to 'the father of modern science', who 'unsealed the principles of nature', and is 'the master of the science of *Essence*'. Ruskin is untypical in his knowledge of *The Wisdom of the Ancients*, but even more so in his fascination with the *New Atlantis*, to which he makes increasingly eloquent reference, from *Munera Pulveris* (1862–3) to *Fors Clavigera* (1871–87), being especially fond of the quotation 'God's first creature, which was light', these being 'the words of the wisest of Englishmen'. The work's real significance for him, though, was as a portrait of an ideal community, and he invariably links it with Plato's *Critias* and More's *Utopia* as great precursors of his Guild of St George, in which Bacon's social system would be partly adopted. His last reference is characteristic, as he returned to the editor his copy of the *Pall Mall Gazette* which had included Sir John Lubbock's '100 Best Books' with the whole of the section on philosophy heavily erased but for the name of Bacon, to which is added 'Chiefly the *New Atlantis*'.[1]

Ruskin's interest in Bacon is personal and rather eccentric, and certainly not literary, but Bacon is still for him a living force, which cannot be said for any other Victorian. With his segmentation into the various specialised and technical interests Bacon the writer is left for the literary historians, with depressing results. Thus Hallam's long chapter in the *Introduction to the Literature of Europe* discusses the style only briefly, and then simply takes over from Macaulay, finding that one of Bacon's 'petty blemishes' is that he is 'too metaphorical and witty', his analogies often being 'fanciful and far-fetched'. It is curious that a cautious Victorian should resemble an average Augustan, but Hallam's comments return us firmly to Budgell. Some of the literary historians disagree: Professor Earle had found that Bacon's *Essays* were remarkable for showing 'the true English tradition', but Professor Saintsbury, on the other hand, having described Bacon's dangerous preference for Latin, observes with some satisfaction that as a consequence he is little read: 'But the English language which he thus despised had a noble and worthy revenge on Bacon.' That is a fatuous and irresponsible comment, but it could be duplicated—a distinguished foreign critic, for example, writes that 'His *New Atlantis* is a scientific Utopia, curious in matter, clumsily written, and painfully didactic'.[2] It would be easy to go on amassing hostile and ill-informed comments, but the point has already been taken: the decline in Bacon's reputation as a writer that set in after Macaulay has only recently been reversed, and it is only in the last ten years or so that there has been any revaluation of his stylistic theory or practice. And the ebbing of interest amongst creative writers has continued—E. M. Forster must surely be the last major novelist to quote from Bacon, when in *The Longest Journey* Mrs Failing is teasing Stephen Wonham about his agnosticism:

Suddenly she stopped, not through any skill of his, but because she had remembered some words of Bacon: 'The true atheist is he whose hands are cauterized by holy things.'[1]

★　　★　　★

This survey of changing attitudes to Bacon's style has probably been too long for some tastes, and too limited in scope for others. It has certainly been anticlimactic—or rather, it has had two climaxes, both tailing off into ignorance and disinterest. I think that it has been worth doing for the second main purpose: the light that has been shed on significant changes of taste, even though I am not competent to evaluate some of them, e.g. the reasons for the two extremes of reaction in the nineteenth century. I am sure that it was worth while for the first purpose, because in the two climactic periods the analyses of Bacon's style made by such well-qualified contemporaries as Jonson and Sprat and by such sensitive later readers as Coleridge, De Quincey, and Hazlitt still give more illumination than anything produced up to very recently. There is no need to recapitulate their findings, but it is significant that their response definitely focuses on the major elements in Bacon's style which were distinguished by my own analysis (imagery, Ciceronian syntax, the condensation of the aphorism), and that it resulted in an estimate of the imaginative value of Bacon's writing much higher than that made elsewhere or indeed generally today.

Every writer hopes that his work will have a wider significance than its chosen field, and I would wish that this book might provide a useful framework for the revaluation of other major Renaissance prose-writers: the outlines given earlier of the traditional symmetries of syntax and of the local argumentative power of imagery could well be applied to the work of Shakespeare, Sidney, Raleigh, Nashe, Hooker, Sir Thomas Browne and others. No other language can boast such an incidence of great prose-writers over such a short period, and, if this study both helps to further the recognition that the years from 1580 to 1660, say, are the richest in English prose and also provides some tools with which to evaluate its work, then I shall be additionally pleased. But its main purpose is to reinstate Bacon as a writer, and looking at that list he seems to me, with the exception of the first named and possibly of the second, to have the greatest range and power, in intellect as in all the resources of language. So perhaps it is fitting to end this book by endorsing an estimate of him made at the end of that period,[1] one which will be found, I think, to justify the vigour of its challenge:

A man so rare in knowledge, of so many severall kinds, endued with the facility and felicity of expressing it all, in so elegant, significant, so abundant, and yet so choise and ravishing a way of Words, of Metaphors, and Allusions, as perhaps, the World hath not seen, since it was a World. I know this may seem a great Hyperbole, and strange kind of riotous excesse of speech; but the best means of putting me to shame, will be, for you to place any other man of yours, by this of mine.

APPENDIX
NOTES
BIBLIOGRAPHY
INDEX

APPENDIX

CHART OF EDITIONS OF BACON'S WORKS, 1597–1967

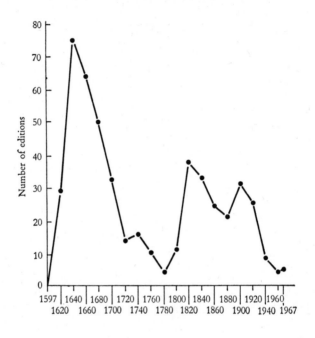

NOTES

1 A running commentary on Bacon's sources (of intermittent value) is provided by the notes of Ellis and Spedding; see also the edition of the *Novum Organum* by T. W. Fowler (Oxford; second, revised edition, 1889). The study by Emil Wolff (B104) is weakened by an over-simple concept of 'sources'. More valuable studies are those by V. K. Whitaker, *Francis Bacon and the Renaissance Encyclopedists* (Ph.D. thesis, Stanford, 1933; microfilm copy in Cambridge University Library) and B99, Lemmi (B61), Thorndike (B89), Rossi (B78) and Larsen (B60).

1 For a long enough list, see Spedding's preface to the *De Interpretatione Naturae* (3. 510 ff.).

2 *Astronomical Thought in Renaissance England* (Baltimore, 1937), especially pp. 245–6.

3 See, for example, A. R. Hall, *The Scientific Revolution, 1500–1800* (London, 1962), pp. 164–9. Marie Boas, *Scientific Renaissance* (London, 1962), pp. 247–60.

4 B12; his account has been challenged by Hardin Craig, *New Lamps for Old* (London, 1960), pp. 5–10, and Benjamin Farrington (B28).

1 The most influential critic of the half-century, Mr T. S. Eliot, has one reference only, to 'the heavy sententiousness of Francis Bacon', *The Use of Poetry and the Use of Criticism* (London, 1933), p. 54. I shall be considering the assessments of Bacon's prose by M. W. Croll, G. Williamson, C. S. Lewis, and L. C. Knights, below. The most detailed study of Bacon as a writer yet performed arrived after this book had been completed: Sister M. A. Bowman, B.V.M., *The English Prose Style of Sir Francis Bacon* (Ph.D. Thesis, Univ. Wisconsin, 1964: Xerox copy in Cambridge University Library). This study is divided into five chapters: the first two discuss the 'doctrine of rhetorical memory' found in classical and Renaissance rhetoric and Bacon's relation to it, the third chapter attempts to make a connection between memory and 'invention', while the last two chapters discuss 'Variety of Style' in *The Advancement of Learning* and the *Essays*. The first two chapters are unexceptionable as far as they go, but the third seems to claim too much significance for the verbal repetition in Bacon's work: 'What looks like mere repetition will soon be seen for what it is: linguistic frames holding arguments in readiness: Prenotions and

Emblems of Bacon's intentions of memory' (p. 85). Dr Bowman performs a useful service in showing how the ideas presented in seminal form in Bacon's early oration *In Praise of Knowledge* recur and are expanded in later work, but it is difficult to see how these ideas can be thought of as 'structural patterns' or 'Promptuary' of Emblems. Her discussion develops into an account of some of the recurrent image patterns, and, although she has not always chosen the most fruitful images nor seen the connections between them and Bacon's concept of knowledge, she does bring out successfully the significance of individual images (e.g. the cluster connected with 'clouds of error', p. 123, or the marriage metaphor, pp. 134–7).

Chapter 4 deals with the *Advancement* in some detail, although some of the stylistic factors chosen for inspection are not of much literary significance (e.g. the use of transitions and conclusions), and the application of statistical analysis here and elsewhere results in a quantification but not an evaluation of literary data. Her account of the forensic quality of Bacon's similitudes (p. 166) is a valuable support to my own findings, but she does not discuss the function of the images, only their general types. Dr Bowman's final chapter analyses the *Essays* and their revision in considerable detail (some 30,000 words), and seems to have fallen into the trap open to any thorough stylistic analysis (I may not have escaped it either), where the sheer weight of analytic process makes consecutive reading a wearying if not an impossible task. Beyond a certain point detailed stylistic analysis should be reserved for a commentary accompanying a text: Dr Bowman's one-at-a-time analyses of the *Essays* would be an admirable foil to an edition. The assumptions and methods used here are not free from question: the tabulation of data is used too frequently, as in checking the length of sentences in the various revisions of the *Essays*, and the similar mechanical process of counting how many times an essay uses its title-word (e.g. p. 221) rests on the dubious assumption that such 'repetition of key-words' gives an essay a 'structural unity'. Most disappointing is the fact that though Dr Bowman often presents evidence of Bacon's deliberate use of symmetrical syntax (e.g. pp. 209–11) she professedly accepts the Croll–Williamson theory that he is a Senecan writer, and is even compelled by it to find traces of 'imbalance' and 'asymmetry' in passages which are structurally symmetrical (pp. 210, 211, 275).

These objections may sound like Momus carping at a rival thesis, but I hope that they have been arrived at in an objective not a destructive spirit; Dr Bowman does not seem to have worked with much rigorous literary method from her stylistic analysis. However, I am glad to agree with her in several perceptive comments, such as that 'In neither the *Essays* nor in Bacon's projection for the advancement of learning are we dealing so much with ideas that change as with ideas that acquire new fullness under various lights of observation' (p. 193), or with her valuable analysis of the structure of argument in some essays (pp. 214–

17), or the point that 'the development of the thought-groups' here is often that of 'a general statement...repeated in a figurative translation and a conclusion' (p. 238), or especially with her demonstration of how Bacon's plane of statement is characteristically 'converted to figurative terms', with such an organic connection that it is frequently difficult to state his argument 'without recourse to his image, so closely identified are statement and illustration' (p. 256).

2 In the Renaissance debate between the active and the contemplative life Bacon is unambiguously on the side of action, though with a characteristically new twist. See the admittedly unsympathetic placing of Bacon in this debate by H. Schultz, *Milton and Forbidden Knowledge* (New York, 1955), pp. 32–42, and for the wider context Fritz Caspari, *Humanism and the Social Order in Tudor England* (Chicago, 1954).

PAGE 4

1 The following quotations are from T. Fowler, *Novum Organum* (1878 ed.), pp. 127–8; H. Baker, *The Wars of Truth* (London, 1952), p. 307; H. Haydn (B45), p. 263; D. G. James (B50), p. 18; H. Fisch (B32), p. 86; cf. also W. H. Greenleaf's estimate that Bacon described his scientific enterprise 'in matchless language and with measured but contagious enthusiasm' (B39), p. 212, and Elizabeth Sewell's conclusion that Bacon's work 'vibrates with a passion of excitement which he communicates, unexplained, to his reader. On one point all those who write about him agree: he has a marvellous power of words' (B80), p. 61.

PAGE 5

1 These discussions of stylistics are listed here and numbered, to avoid cumbersome footnotes; references to them in the text are by authors' surnames with the numbers italicised—e.g. (Spitzer, *16*, p. 18). Items marked with an asterisk have further bibliographies.

1 Alonso, Amado, 'The Stylistic Interpretation of Literary Texts', *Modern Language Notes*, LVII (1942), 489–96.

2 Enkvist, Nils Erik, 'On Defining Style: an Essay in Applied Linguistics', in *Linguistics and Style*, ed. J. Spencer (London, 1964), pp. 1–56.

3 Gray, Floyd, *Le Style de Montaigne* (Paris, 1958).

4 Gregory, Michael, and Spencer, John: 'An Approach to the Study of Style', in *Linguistics and Style*, ed. J. Spencer (London, 1964), pp. 57–105.

5 Hatzfeld, Helmut, *A Critical Bibliography of the New Stylistics* (Chapel Hill, 1952).

6 Hatzfeld, Helmut, and Le Hir, Yves, *Essai de Bibliographie de Stylistique Française et Romane (1955–1960)* (Paris, 1961).

7 Ohmann, Richard, 'Prolegomena to the Analysis of Prose Style', in *Style

in Prose Fiction, English Institute Essays, 1958; ed. H. C. Martin (New York, 1959), pp. 1–24.

8 Ohmann, Richard, 'Generative Grammars and the Concept of Literary Style', *Word*, xx (1964), 423–39.

9 Riffaterre, Michael, *Le Style des Pléiades de Gobineau: Essai d'Application d'une Méthode Stylistique* (Paris, 1957).

10 Riffaterre, Michael, 'Criteria for Style Analysis', *Word*, xv (1959), 154–74.

11 Riffaterre, Michael, review of (*17*), *ibid.* pp. 404–13.

12 Riffaterre, Michael, 'Stylistic Context', *Word*, xvi (1960), 207–18.

13 Sayce, R. A., *Style in French Prose* (Oxford, 1953).

14 Sayce, R. A., 'Literature and Language', *Essays in Criticism*, vii (1957), 119–33.

15 Sebeok, Thomas A. (editor), *Style in Language* (New York, 1958): collected papers and discussions from 'an interdisciplinary Conference on Style', held at Indiana University, 1958.

16 Spitzer, Leo, *Linguistics and Literary History: Essays in Stylistics* (Princeton Univ. Press, 1948); other works on style by Spitzer are referred to by Riffaterre (*9*), Ullmann (*19*).

17 Ullmann, Stephen, *Style in the French Novel* (Cambridge, 1957).

18 Ullmann, Stephen, *The Image in the French Novel* (Cambridge, 1960).

19 Ullmann, Stephen, *Language and Style* (Oxford, 1964).

20 Wellek, René, 'Closing Statement: From the Viewpoint of Literary Criticism', in (*15*), pp. 408–19.

21 Wellek, René, *Concepts of Criticism*, ed. S. G. Nichols (Yale Univ. Press, 1963).

22 Wellek, René, and Warren, A., *Theory of Literature* (1949; quotations from Penguin ed., 1963).

23 Wimsatt, W. K., *The Prose Style of Samuel Johnson* (Yale Univ. Press, 1941; 2nd ed., 1963).

PAGE 13

1 B102, p. 31; for similarly confusing attempts at inter-discrimination of 'schools' of style see pp. 15, 21, 30, 35, 52, 103, 119, 129, 134, 148, 180, 185, 187, etc.

PAGE 24

1 See Rosamund Tuve's *Elizabethan and Metaphysical Imagery* (Chicago, 1947), especially ch. viii, 'The Criterion of Rhetorical Efficacy'. I have outlined the Classical and Renaissance concepts of the functional nature of rhetorical figures (that is, to their ability to re-create psychological effects in verbal forms) and attempted to apply the principle to literary analysis in my *Classical Rhetoric in English Poetry* (Macmillan, London, in the press).

Notes, pp. 30–34

1 *Coleridge on the Seventeenth Century*, ed. R. F. Brinkley (Duke Univ. Press, North Carolina, 1955), p. 414. This unity of thought and style, Coleridge says, which Bacon shares with Hooker, Milton, and Jeremy Taylor, is quite different from the style of Seneca, 'where the thoughts, striking as they are, are merely strung together like beads, without any causation or progression'.

1 All quotations from Plato are from the translation of Benjamin Jowett, *The Dialogues of Plato* (Oxford, 1875; 2nd ed.). On Plato's use of *diaíresis* see W. Lutoslawski, *The Origin and Growth of Plato's Logic* (London, 1897), pp. 340 ff., 445; F. M. Cornford, *Plato's Theory of Knowledge* (London, 1935), pp. 170 ff., 186; R. Robinson, *Plato's Earlier Dialectic* (Oxford, 1953), pp. 52, 62–7 (a valuable discussion of Plato's concept of method), 280; and W. G. Runciman, *Plato's Later Epistemology* (Cambridge, 1962), pp. 59–62.
2 *Plato's Phaedrus* (Cambridge, 1952), p. 134.

1 *The Works of Aristotle*, trans. W. D. Ross (Oxford, 1926–).

1 For particular discussions of division which are relevant to Bacon's use of it, see Gilbert (B37), pp. 22, 109, 119, 155–7, 166, 177, 190 and 227.

1 W. S. Howell documents some of the outraged reactions to Ramus in his *Logic and Rhetoric in England, 1500–1700* (New York, 1956). The most thorough and sympathetic study of Ramus, his immediate predecessors (such as Rudolph Agricola), and his many successors is that by W. J. Ong, *Ramus, Method, and the Decay of Dialogue* (Harvard, 1958). However, it seems to me that Father Ong's enormous knowledge of Ramism makes him too tolerant of the weaknesses of the system, and his account of Ramus's influence on what he calls 'the spatialization of knowledge' has a fatal touch of the wild theories of Marshall McLuhan.
2 By K. R. Wallace (B93), p. 140; G. Williamson (B102), p. 156 n. 1, and by H. Fisch (B32), p. 26 n. 1: 'In Bacon's case, the influence of Ramus's technique is clear in the use of dichotomies—the seemingly endless bifurcation and selection of subject matter which we note for instance in *The Advancement of Learning*.' A more searching account of Bacon's debt to Ramus, mainly in the classification of logic, is given by Paolo Rossi (B78).
3 Some popular encyclopedias which use division (often with a tabular analysis of their contents, sometimes arranged on the trivium–quadrivium

Notes, pp. 34–36

basis) are: *Martiani Minei Capellae de nuptiis philologiae et Mercuri* (ed. seen: Basilae, 1532); Gregor Reisch, *Margarita Philosophica* (1496); *Georgii Vallae... De Expetendis, et Fugiendis Rebus* (1501), etc. For the use of division in fifteenth- and sixteenth-century Italy, see B. Weinberg, *A History of Literary Criticism in the Italian Renaissance* (Chicago, 1961), especially ch. 1, 'The Classification of Poetics among the Sciences', vol. 1, pp. 1–37; also *ibid.* pp. 47, 82. For its important role in the development of the sermon, see K. Polheim, *Die Lateinische Reimprosa* (Berlin, 1925), pp. 456–9, on 'Die gereimte *Partitio*' as it appeared in sermons (some of which in the sixteenth century were set out in tabular form) and J. A. Blench, *Preaching in England in the late Fifteenth and Sixteenth Centuries* (Oxford, 1964), especially ch. 2, pp. 71–112. On the significance of division in the Hellenistic and Classical periods of Roman law see Fritz Schulz, *History of Roman Legal Science* (Oxford, 1946), pp. 62–8, 76, 129, 339; for the twelfth-century glossators' use of it see H. Kantorowicz, *Studies in the Glossators of the Roman Law* (Cambridge, 1938), pp. 42, 97; and for its use and misuse in Renaissance Germany see R. Stintzing, *Geschichte der deutschen Rechtswissenschaft* (München und Leipzig, 1880), pp. 104–15. Finally, for the enormous occurrence of division in gnomic wisdom, see E. R. Curtius on 'Numerical Apothegms', *European Literature and the Latin Middle Ages* (New York, 1953), pp. 510–14.

PAGE 35

1 This work is available in a modern translation by Benjamin Farrington (B29), but a more vigorous and aptly colloquial version of this passage is that of Peter Shaw: 'I have no affection for that *sculking-Hole of Ignorance*, that destructive *Book-worm of Learning*, that *Father of Epitomes*, who, when he wrings and presses things with the *Shackles of his Method, and Contraction*; the Substance, if there was any, immediately starts out, and escapes him; whilst he grasps nothing but the empty Chaff, and exhausted Carcass' (*Philosophical Works of Francis Bacon* (London, 1733), II, 52).

2 W. J. Ong has said that 'the interest in method which marks Ramus' age... is generated not out of a logical or scientific context, but out of rhetoric' (*op. cit.* p. 230), but he does not make the connection with Bacon.

3 For an analysis of the various lists, see H. Lausberg, *Handbuch der literarischen Rhetorik* (München, 1960).

PAGE 36

1 See Cicero, *Topics*, iii. 13 and v. 17; Quintilian, *Institutes of Oratory* (ed. H. E. Butler, Loeb Library, London, 1921), v. x. 63 and VII. i. 1.

2 Translated by H. M. Hubbell, Loeb library (London, 1944). On Cicero's use of *partitio* in his own speeches, see Quintilian, IV. v. 12–21.

3 Puttenham records that 'I have come to the Lord Keeper Sir *Nicholas*

Notes, pp. 36–39

Bacon, & found him sitting in his gallery alone with the works of Quintilian before him, in deede he was a most eloquent man, and of rare learning and wisedome, as ever I knew England to breed...' (*The Arte of English Poesie*, ed. G. D. Willcock and A. Walker, Cambridge, 1936, p. 140).

PAGE 37

1 For evidence of the rhetorical basis of English education see T. W. Baldwin, *Shakespere's Small Latine and Lesse Greeke* (Urbana, 1944), *passim*; and M. H. Curtis, *Oxford and Cambridge in Transition, 1558–1642* (Oxford, 1959), pp. 85–95. Dr Bolgar informs me that Quintilian is not specified in the following school curricula: Ipswich (1528), Eton (1528), Winchester (1529), Canterbury (1541), Sherborne (1550), Eton (1560), Westminster (1560), Sandwich (1580), St Bees (1583), Durham (1593), Uppingham (1598), Camberwell (1625), Rotherham (1630), Newcastle (before 1634), Winchester (1647); nor is he recommended by the leading contemporary writers on grammar-school education, Kemp, Brinsley, and Hoole.

PAGE 38

1 For the clearest signs of the debt to Cicero see the edition by R. H. Bowers (Scholars' Facsimile Reprints; Florida, 1962), pp. 131–3, 177, 179.
2 Puttenham, *op. cit.* p. 222; Peacham, *The Garden of Eloquence* (1593), ed. W. G. Crane (Florida, 1954), pp. 123–5; for related figures pp. 129, 192–3.
3 *Elizabethan and Metaphysical Imagery* (Chicago, 1947), pp. 120, 299–309; her list of the many poems constructed on the basis of 'definition and division' could be considerably extended, and of course similar techniques were applied in dramatic verse and in prose.

PAGE 39

1 After the sudden death of Sir Nicholas Bacon in February 1578–9 Bacon returned from his diplomatic career in France having to learn a profession to earn a living. He entered Gray's Inn in 1579, and his father's eminence as a lawyer undoubtedly helped in his extraordinarily fast rise: he became an utter barrister in 1582, a bencher in 1586, a reader in 1588, double reader (a rare distinction) in 1600, and Treasurer from 1609 to 1617, in which last office he had an important administrative task (see *The Pension Book of Gray's Inn*, ed. R. J. Fletcher (London, 1901), *passim*). The association was very close, being only ended by his appointment as Attorney-General in 1613: between 1587 and 1613 he attended no less than 141 of the Pensions, or council-meetings; he had rooms in Gray's Inn for over forty years, and did much of his work there. As he wrote in dedicating his *Arguments in Law* to the members of Gray's Inn, 'therefore few men, so bound to their societies by obligation, both ancestral and personal, as

I am to yours' (7. 524). A recent study which begins to compensate for the neglect of this aspect is P. Kocher, 'Francis Bacon on the Science of Jurisprudence', *Journal of the History of Ideas*, XVIII, 3–26.

2   2 *Henry IV*, III, ii, 8–12. A. R. Ingpen, *Master Worsley's Book* (London, 1910), p. 41, quotes Stow's *Survey of London* and Coke as evidence that this was the normal sequence. Coke elsewhere said that it was indeed necessary 'that our students should (as Littleton did) come to the study of the common law from one of the universities, where he may learn the liberall arts, and especially logick...' Quoted by C. D. Bowen, *The Lion and the Throne* (London, 1957), p. 50.

PAGE 40

1   *Pension Book, ed. cit.* pp. 4 and 5, citing the description of the method compiled in 1547 for Henry VIII's information (and drawn up, incidentally, by Sir Nicholas Bacon amongst others).

2   The presence of this 'modesty formula' here shows the continuing mutual influence between rhetoric and law: E. R. Curtius notes it first in Cicero (*De. inv.* I. 16. 22), it being 'expedient for the orator to show submissiveness and humility ("prece et obsecratione humili ac supplici utemur")...The orator's referring to his feebleness (*excusatio propter infirmitatem*), to his inadequate preparation ("si nos infirmos, imparatos...dixerimus": Quintilian, IV. i. 8) derives from judicial oratory, it is intended to dispose the judges favorably. But it is very early transferred to other genres', (*op. cit.* p. 83 and pp. 83–5 *passim*).

3   *Origines Juridiciales* (London, 1666), p. 286.

4   Sir James Whitelocke recorded the events of his 1619 Reading in his diary, first published in 1858. After his statute was read, he 'first made a speeche, and then went to the statute, proposed my divisions, and put upon the division of that day ten cases, of whiche the puisne cubberd man chose one, and began *pro* and so *contra, alternatim*'. He gives a more exact account of the recapitulation on the final evening: 'I went to my place, and red my division, and put my cases; then the two puisnes spoke to a case. I toke it of them, went thoroughe the case, breefly opening the poynts only, whiche being done, I uttered my conceits' (*The 'Liber Famelicus' of Sir James Whitelocke*, ed. J. Bruce, London, 1858; Camden Society Publications, no. 70, pp. 74–5). See also *A Just Vindication of the Questioned Part of the Reading of Edward Bagshaw* (London, 1660), pp. 7, 9, 14.

PAGE 41

1   Sir William Stamford, in his *Crowne plees*, says Fraunce, divides and propounds, 'And so goeth on forward, defining, devideing, and making playne by example all the speciall sortes of offences against the crowne. *Bracton* foloweth

the order of the civill law altogether, in so much that he that hath seene the one, may easily judge of the other. *Perkins* in every of his severall tractates doth, as *Stamford*, propounde, divide, and add examples. Lyttleton in like manner, by definitions, divisions, and induction of speciall cases insteade of so many examples, made up his booke' (fo. 118v). Bacon held Stamford to be 'the best expositor of a statute that hath been in our law; a man of reverent judgment and order in his writings' (7. 676). A last detail on legal division is given by Sir Edward Coke, who in the preface to his *Institutes* defends Littleton's division of his work on tenures with a quotation from Bracton—'For *Res per diuisionem melius aperiuntur.*'

2   *A Direction or Preparative to the study of the Law* (London, 1600), fo. 24r. For proof that this criticism is not exaggerated see Sir John Doderidge's tedious display of logical division in his *English Lawyer* (1631), pp. 66–93.

3   See K. O. Myrick, *Sir Philip Sidney as a Literary Craftsman* (Cambridge, Mass., 1935).

PAGE 42

1   More's *Utopia*, trans. R. Robinson; Everyman ed. (London, 1923), p. 26; the 'Old' *Arcadia*, in *Works*, ed. A. Feuillerat (2nd ed., Cambridge, 1963), IV, 361, 362, 366–7, 375 (Evarchus' summing-up also uses partition), and p. 289 for the pun, used as a contemptuous dismissal for the injured rebel who protests loquaciously against Musidorus until 'muche loss of blood helped on with this vehemency choked up the spirits of his lyfe leaving hym to make betwixt his body and his sowle an evill favoured partition'.

PAGE 43

1   See also his *Argument in Chudleigh's Case* (1594), where he began the division: 'And in confutation I will not bind myself to Mr Attorney's order, but pursue my own course, which is the order the matter itself more aptly induces for resolution and decision' (7. 618). And in the Essex trial of 1600: 'I keep order of matter, and not of circumstance' (9. 179).

PAGE 46

1   An honourable exception is Karl Wallace (B95). However, in his book on Bacon's theory of rhetoric he does not discuss the importance of division, nor Bacon's contribution to rhetorical theory here (see B93, pp. 212–14). A brief account of the use of *partitio* in the *Advancement of Learning* is given by M. B. McNamee (B67). R. Hannah (B42) has argued that Bacon's speeches conform to the seven-part oration: while he is right in so far as *partitio* is involved, Bacon deliberately abandoned the other sections (and often comments on so doing), subsuming them all under *partitio*.

Notes, pp. 48–56

1 10. 347–60; see also 10. 327; 11. 228; 11. 314; 14. 174.

1 See 8. 98; 9. 42–3, 99, 198; 10. 46; 11. 369; 12. 24, 176, 268; 13. 17; 14. 115, 155.

2 See 8. 79 ff.; 8. 150 ff.; 10. 103; 11. 116 ff.; 7. 47 ff.; 7. 11 ff.; and 14. 469 ff.

3 As Edward Fueter put it, 'Man glaubt eine Debatte des Parlaments zu hören, in der der Kanzler persönlich Stellung zu nehmen hatte' (*Geschichte der Neueren Historiographie*, München and Berlin, 1936, p. 169).

1 See Fowler's introduction to his edition of the *Novum Organum*; R. L. Ellis, 'General Preface to Bacon's Philosophical Works' (1. 22–67), and B. Farrington (B27). Summaries of the divisions, with some discussion of their contents but none of the form itself, are provided by C. D. Broad (B12), F. H. Anderson (B3), especially pp. 144–80, and P. Rossi (B78a), especially chs. 4, 'Logica Retorica e Metodo', and 6, 'La Tradizione Retorica e il Metodo della Scienza'. Rossi often concludes that the methods and terms Bacon uses are 'typically rhetorical'.

1 See *Valerius Terminus* (3. 229, 234, 239, 241, 243); *Descriptio Globi Intellectualis* (5. 503); *Commentarius Solutus* and its notes on Motion (11. 67 ff.); the *Historia Ventorum* (5. 141, 146, 184); *Historia Vitae et Mortis* (5. 221–2); *Cogitationes de Natura Rerum* (5. 425); *De Fluxu et Refluxu Maris* (5. 443); *Thema Coeli* (5. 551); *De Principiis atque Originibus* (5. 494–5); *Sylva Sylvarum* (2. 643, 654, 656, etc.).

1 See also 6. 526, 527, 528–9, 533–4.

1 Aldis Wright provides tabular analyses (or reconstructions) of the divisions in Books 1 and 2 in his edition of the *Advancement of Learning* (Clarendon Press, 1880, etc.), pp. 1, 75. On the tradition of faculty psychology behind the division of Book 2 see G. K. Shepherd's edition of Sidney's *Apology for Poetry* (London, 1965), p. 166, and for criticism of the grounds on which Bacon makes his divisions see Kuno Fischer, *Francis Bacon of Verulam: Realistic Philosophy and its Age* (London, 1857; translated J. Oxenford), pp. 231–2.

Notes, pp. 62-65

1 *The tragicall Historie of Doctor Faustus*, in Marlowe's *Works*, ed. C. F. Tucker Brooke (Oxford, 1910), ll. 42–50. The emendation of '*sound* Aphorismes' (1604 Quarto) to *found*, as proposed by various editors, is supported by the usage in the following quotations from Lodge ('held an Aphorisme') and Mulcaster ('may stand').

2 *Wits Miserie* (1596) in *Complete Works*, ed. A. Grosart (1883; reprinted New York, 1963), IV, 24.

3 *Positions* (1581), ed. R. H. Quick (London, 1888), p. 292, ch. 45, 'The Peroration'. Mulcaster also uses *partitio* to organise his work, heading ch. 7 'The Braunching, Order, and Methode, kept in this Discours of Exercises' (p. 49).

1 *Riders Dictionarie Corrected...* by Francis Holyoke (Oxford, 1612); T. Thomas, *Dictionarium Linguae et Anglicanae* (London, 1587). Renaissance dictionary makers were unashamedly eclectic, and these definitions can be traced back through Cooper's *Thesaurus* (1565) to Elyot's *Dictionary* (1538). For the traditional terminology, equating *pronunciatum* and *effatum* with *axioma*, see e.g. Cicero, *Tusc. Disp.* i. 7. 14 and *Acad.* ii. 29. 95. Hobbes in 1651 still makes the equation: 'general rules, called *theorems* or *aphorisms*', *Leviathan*, ed. M. Oakeshott (Oxford, 1946), p. 27.

2 Quoted in the study of Coke by C. D. Bowen, *The Lion and the Throne* (London, 1957), p. 441. See also Curtius, *op. cit.* ch. 6, n. 32.

3 *Euphues, The Anatomy of Wit* (1579), ed. E. Arber (London, 1919), p. 100.

1 *Op. cit.* pp. 6–7. For a comparison of Bacon's use of the term 'axiom' with Aristotle's, see R. E. Larsen (B60), who finds difficulty in defining what Bacon means by 'axiom' and finally convicts him of 'muddle-headed thinking' for his confusion of 'propositions (his *axioms*) with predicates or concepts (his *notions*)...' (*ibid.* pp. 438–40). Some light might be gained from a historian of the language, who concluded that Bacon 'endeavoured, but failed, to alter the meaning of "axiom" itself from "a self-evident proposition" to "a proposition established by the method of experimental induction"'. See Owen Barfield, *History in English Words* (London, 1954), p. 145.

1 See 3. 356, 373, 433; 4. 376, 384; 5. 20, 217, 285; 6. 750; 7. 25, 312. In the *Sylva* he singles him out for special praise: 'Hippocrates' aphorism, "in morbis minus", is a good profound aphorism' (2. 367; *Aphorisms*, II, 34).

Notes, pp. 65–68

2 *Opera*, ed. Kühn (Lipsiae, 1830), XIX, 349. Liddell and Scott also records a definition by Isidore: 'Aphorismus est sermo brevis, integrum sensum propositae rei scribens' (*Origines*, 4. 10).

3 The editor of the Loeb edition, from which quotations are taken, summarises its manuscript tradition with some impressive figures: 'The Greek MSS (140) are more numerous than those containing any other work, while there are translations into Hebrew (40), Arabic (70), Syriac (1) and Latin (232).' (See Hippocrates, *Works*, ed. W. H. S. Jones (London, 1931), vol. IV, p. xxxiii). For a full account of manuscripts and translations up to 1500 see George Sarton, *A History of Science* (London, 1953), I, 374–5, and for a large, but doubtless incomplete, list of editions after 1500, see the great edition of Hippocrates by Émile Littré (Paris, 1839–61), IV, 446–57. Interesting evidence of its popularity with the medical leaders of Bacon's day is provided by the bequest to the Cambridge University Library in 1591 by Thomas Lorkin, M.D., Regius Professor of Physic, which contains at least five different copies of the *Aphorisms*, one of which (edited by Rabelais (12°, Paris, 1543), shelf-mark Adv. e. 12. 1) is completely covered with annotations, presumably from Lorkin's own experience.

PAGE 66

1 *Regulae Iuris. From Juristic Rules to Legal Maxims* (Edinburgh, 1966). Professor Stein also provides a survey of Bacon's theory of the legal maxim (pp. 170–4).

PAGE 67

1 Christopher St Germain, *Dialogue between a Doctor of Divinity and a Student of the Common Law* (1523, Latin; 1532, English), ch. 8; quoted and translated by Stein, p. 160. Also on this page Professor Stein cites a description of the maxim which seems to be the direct source of that quoted from Bacon in the text (7. 509): Serjeant Morgan, in a case in 1551 reported by Plowden, wrote that 'maxims are the foundations of the law, and the conclusions of reason, and therefore they ought not to be impugned but always to be admitted'.

PAGE 68

1 W. S. Holdsworth, 'The Elizabethan Age in English Legal History', *Iowa Law Review* (1927), p. 329. And Roscoe Pound has described the work as 'a long step forward...in legal science', quoted by Stein, p. 174.

2 Much useful information about the use of gnomic wisdom in Renaissance political writing can be found in some of the standard works on Machiavelli and Guicciardini, e.g. A. H. Gilbert, *Machiavelli's 'Prince' and Its Forerunners* (Durham, N.C., 1938); *Il Principe*, ed. L. A. Burd (Oxford, 1891); H. Butterfield, *The Statecraft of Machiavelli* (London, 1955), especially ch. II, section 2, 'The rise of the inductive method'; Felix Gilbert, *Machiavelli and Guicciardini* (Princeton, 1965); N. Orsini, 'I *Ricordi* del Guicciardini nell'Inghilterra Elisabettiana' in his *Studii sul Rinascimento Italiano in Inghilterra* (Florence, 1937), pp. 77–99 (I am grateful to L. G. Salingar for drawing my attention to this essay and for kindly providing me with a summary of it); G. K. Hunter's article on Marston in *Jacobean Theatre*, ed. J. R. Brown and B. Harris (London, 1960), pp. 84–111, has a good account of how Italian *Ragione di stato* was imported into sixteenth-century England.

PAGE 69

1 See *A Discourse upon the Meanes of Wel Governing*...trans. S. Patericke (London, 1602) on the inductive method as used in Machiavelli, 'from particulars to general maxims' (Sig. Aiv) and on the corrupt nature of these maxims (which Gentillet equates with axioms): 'he hath taken Maximes and rules altogether wicked, and hath builded upon them, not a Politicke but a Tyrannical Science' (Sig. Aiir).

2 *The Prince*, trans. Edward Dacres (1640), reprinted in the 'Tudor Translations' series (London, 1905), p. 272.

3 See Dacres, pp. 277, 280, 292, 297, 313, 321. Machiavelli even repeats his favourite maxims: L. A. Burd, in his great edition (*op. cit.* p. 188), noted six uses of the maxim 'gli uomini si debbono o vezzeggiare o spegnere' ('men must either be flattered with all, or else be quite crushed', Dacres, p. 267). Cf. also Butterfield, *op. cit.* p. 20: 'this science of statecraft existed as a collection of maxims in Machiavelli's own mind'.

4 *Advancement*, 3. 430. For an admirable account of the dialectic between 'what men do' and 'ought to do', see Hiram Haydn's book on the *Counter-Renaissance* especially the section on Guicciardini, and for the rise of the empirical attitude to history see W. H. Greenleaf (B39) especially ch. x, 'Francis Bacon: The Empirical Science of Politics'.

PAGE 71

1 'Those who exalt themselves into the chair of instruction, without inquiring whether any will submit to their authority, have not sufficiently considered how much of human life passes in little incidents, cursory conversation, slight business, and casual amusements; and therefore they have endeavoured only to inculcate the more awful virtues, without condescending to regard those petty qualities, which grow important only by their frequency, and which, though they produce no single acts of heroism, nor astonish us, by great events, yet are every moment exerting their influence upon us, and make the draught of life sweet or bitter by imperceptible instillations' (*Rambler*, no. 72).

Notes, pp. 73–77

PAGE 73

1 Letter of 23 August 1799; *The Complete Writings of William Blake*, ed. G. Keynes (London, 1966), p. 793.

PAGE 75

1 *Daniel Deronda*, pt 1, ch. 5. There is an even harsher attack in *The Mill on the Floss*, Book 7, ch. 2, last paragraph, but it serves usefully to highlight those potential weaknesses of the aphorism which Bacon's theory avoided.

2 *Aphorisms* (Oxford, 1903), no. 41; cited by J. P. Stern, *Lichtenberg: A Doctrine of Scattered Occasions* (Indiana Univ. Press, Bloomington, 1959; London, 1963), p. 219.

3 Baldwin, *Shakespere's Small Latine and Lesse Greeke* (Urbana, Illinois, 1944), I, 1; Frye, *Fearful Symmetry* (Princeton, 1947), p. 82.

PAGE 76

1 *Carnets 1942–1951*, trans. P. Thody (London, 1966), p. 176. Cf. also the entry for 27 May 1950: 'After *The Rebel*, creation in freedom.'

2 *English Literature in the Sixteenth Century* (Oxford, 1954), p. 537.

3 In an essay on 'English Literature of the Renaissance', in *The Renaissance*, ed. T. Helton (Madison, Wisconsin, 1961), p. 147.

PAGE 77

1 See his admirable book *The Classical Heritage* (Cambridge, 1958), especially pp. 268–75, 297–301 (on Erasmus and 'imitation'), 321–9 (on the effects of imitation on Rabelais and Shakespeare); see also F. L. Schoell, *Études sur l'Humanisme Continental en Angleterre* (Paris, 1926) on Chapman; P. Porteau, *Montaigne et la Vie Pédagogique de son Temps* (Paris, 1935); P. M. Schon, *Vorformen des Essays in Antike und Humanismus* (Wiesbaden, 1954), and R. W. Dent, *John Webster's Borrowing* (California, 1960).

2 See G. K. Hunter, 'The Marking of Sententiae in Elizabethan Printed Plays, Poems and Romances', *Library*, ser. 5, VI (1951), 171–8.

3 See *The Historie of Guicciardin*, trans. G. Fenton (London, 1579), e.g. pp. 32, 189, 245, 252, 263, 268, 283, 298, 388–94, etc. R. Gottfried, 'Geoffrey Fenton's *Historie of Guicciardin*', *Indiana Univ. Pub. Humanities Ser.* no. 3 (1940), lists all the additions but does not see the significance of the marginal commas. However, his comment on the tone of the additions is valuable: what Fenton adds 'reveals his complete acceptance of the picture which the *Storia* gives of human baseness. He more than doubles the generalisations on ambition: victory, prosperity, and glory all feed men's overweening aspirations' (p. 29). The note of disillusionment which is often felt in aphorisms on man and society (it is there in Bacon too) seems to be closely tied to the form: cf. J. P. Stern's descrip-

tion of 'the tradition of the *moralistes*. Gracián, Le Rochefoucauld, Vauvenargues
—and Lichtenberg—tell us (among other things) that the world is not what it
seems: that men are selfish, impious, and deceitful: that honour is vain and dis-
honour always close at hand, and both relative and adventitious: and, since
unhappiness is loath to boast of its coherence, they tell us all this in scattered
reflections' (*op. cit.* p. 260). In Bacon's own history, *Henry VII*, the maxims are
mainly disillusioned, as e.g.: 'And as Kings do more easily find instruments for
their will and humour, than for their service and honour' (7. 217); or 'For
although the French seemed to speak reason, yet arguments are ever with multi-
tudes too weak for suspicions' (p. 81); or this comment on why a nobleman of
great merit, indeed 'over-merit', did not have an offence pardoned by the
King: 'for convenient merit, unto which reward may easily reach, doth best
with Kings' (p. 150).

PAGE 78

1 Roger Ascham, *English Works*, ed. W. A. Wright (Cambridge, 1904),
pp. 214–15.
2 See G. K. Hunter, 'Isocrates' Precepts and Polonius' Character', *Shakespeare
Quarterly*, VIII (1957), 501–6; also earlier discussions *ibid.* IV, 3–9, 362–3; VI,
362–4; VII, 275–6. Incidentally, Professor Hunter notes that he has found no
parallels for Polonius's final '...to thine owne self be true', and takes it as 'a
mere summing-up' (p. 505 n.). Bacon's closeness to the advice tradition is
shown by the fact that he uses the phrase, or one similar to it, several times,
usually equating it with 'self-interest': in the 1595 Device of 'Love and Self-
Love' the Statesman's speech to the Squire includes this politic advice: 'To
conclude, let him be true to himself, and avoid all tedious reaches of state that
are not merely pertinent to his particular' (8. 383). In the 1612 addition to the
1597 Essay 'Of Faction' Bacon writes, 'The even carriage between two factions
proceedeth not always of moderation, but of a trueness to a man's self, with end
to make use of both' (6. 499); in the 1612 Essay 'Of Wisdom for a Man's Self'
he gives the rule: 'Divide with reason between self-love and society, and be so
true to thyself, as thou be not false to others; specially to thy King and country'
(6. 431–2); and in 'Of Suspicion' (1625) he attacks those who are over-suspicious
of their servants: 'What would men have? Do they think those they employ and
deal with are saints? Do they not think they will have their own ends, and be
truer to themselves than to them?' (6. 454).
3 For the 'Advice to Princes' tradition see A. H. Gilbert, *op. cit.* in note 2, p. 68
above, and for bourgeois guides to improvement see L. B. Wright, *Middle Class
Culture in Elizabethan England* (Chapel Hill, N.C. 1935), pt II, especially ch. v,
'Handbooks to Improvement'.
4 The Essay 'Of True Greatness of Kingdoms and Estates' is 'an argument fit

for great and mighty princes to have in their hand' (6. 445). Bacon seems loath to discuss 'Masques'—'But yet, since princes will have such things', he does so (467). One of the chambers projected in 'Building' must be kept as an infirmary, in case 'the prince or any special person should be sick' (484): this Essay sets out to describe 'a princely palace' (482), and 'Of Gardens' likewise assumes the subject to be 'a princely garden' (485, 488, 492).

PAGE 79

1 I hope to produce the evidence of this connection in a later article. Dr Stern's study has been valuable not only for its account of Lichtenberg but also for stimulating my own thinking on the aphorism. Perhaps I should add that from his rich discussion I summarise only those points which make for the most suggestive comparison with Bacon.

PAGE 80

1 J. P. Stern, *op. cit.* pp. 189–226; and especially as regards the maxim and the reflection, pp. 196, 197, 200, 262–3.

PAGE 91

1 An important recent article which proposes categories for the aphorism is H. E. Pagliaro, 'Paradox in the Aphorisms of La Rochefoucauld and some representative English Followers', *PMLA*, LXXIX (March, 1964), 42–50. Although Mr Pagliaro gives a superficial account of Bacon as an exponent of the purely 'expository' aphorism (p. 44), his distinction of the main categories of the 'paradoxical aphorism' is a useful one, and can be summarised as follows, with all the examples drawn for convenience from the best-known of Mr Pagliaro's English examples, Swift's *Various Thoughts, Moral and Diverting* (in *The Prose Works*, ed. Herbert Davis, vol. IV). He divides the paradoxical aphorisms into two main groups, Polar (divided into two parts) and Non-Polar (i.e. those 'that do not employ grammatically balanced elements to express the paradox', p. 45 n. 11) and under the first and more important head distinguishes five categories by which the two parts are connected:

I By *antithesis*, 'stimulating an initial opposition and subsequent fusion of disparates': 'Every Man desires to live long: but no Man would be old' (Swift, p. 246).

II By *analysis*, in which 'the first element presents a generalisation and the second an elucidation by particulars': 'A very little wit is valued in a woman; as we are pleased with a few words spoken by a parrot' (Swift, p. 247)—although this is perhaps nearer to the fifth category.

III By *synthesis*, those which 'adduce particulars in the first polar member and the generalisation inferred from them in the second': 'No Man will take Counsel, but Every Man will take Money; therefore Money is better than Counsel' (Swift, p. 253).

IV By *equation*, that is 'metaphors of one sentence in which a copulative verb joins two nouns': 'Vision is the Art of seeing Things invisible' (Swift, p. 252).

V By *comparison*, 'an aphorism in which all the elements are part of a comparison', sometimes joined by a simile: 'Some People take more Care to hide their Wisdom than their Folly' (Swift, p. 244).

These are useful categories and could well be applied to Bacon's aphorisms (indeed some of them I had established before reading Mr Pagliaro's article), and if I have preferred to leave this section as it stood without applying them that is simply because I did not want to enlarge further what is already a sufficiently long discussion.

PAGE 96

1 The main studies to which I am indebted are: R. C. Jebb, *The Attic Orators* (2 vols. London, 1893); Edward Norden, *Die antike Kunstprosa (vom VI. Jahrhundert v. Chr. bis in die Zeit der Renaissance)* (2 vols. 1898; 5th ed. Stuttgart, 1958); Karl Polheim, *Die Lateinische Reimprosa* (Berlin, 1925); A. D. Leeman, *Orationis Ratio: The Stylistic Theories and Practice of the Orators, Historians and Philosophers* (2 vols. Amsterdam, 1963), and L. P. Wilkinson, *Golden Latin Artistry* (Cambridge, 1963), with a useful bibliography, pp. 271–8; *q.v.* for details of work by H. Bornecque, H. D. Broadhead, A. C. Clark, J. D. Denniston, A. W. de Groot, L. Laurand, J. Marouzeau, F. Novotný, and W. Schmid.

2 Wilkinson, *op. cit.* p. 144. Successors to Saintsbury include A. C. Clark, *Prose Rhythm in English* (1913); N. R. Tempest, *The Rhythm of English Prose* (Cambridge, 1930), and books with similar titles by J. H. Scott (Iowa, 1925), A. Classe (Oxford, 1939); also O. Elton, 'English Prose Numbers', *Essays and Studies*, IV (1913), 29–54; M. W. Croll, 'The Cadence of English Oratorical Prose', *Studies in Philology*, XVI (1919), 1–55.

3 I limit the following discussion (which is based largely on Norden and Leeman) to the question of symmetry, omitting two topics which are not relevant ultimately to Bacon, although they had considerable importance both in Antiquity and in the Renaissance, the use of specifically 'poetic' words or metaphors in prose, and the technique of the *clausula*.

PAGE 98

1 Eric Laughton, in an illuminating article, 'Cicero and the Greek Orators', *American Journal of Philology*, LXXXII (1961), 27–49, has shown that Isocrates' style is characterised by the simplest types of balance (usually two-member

antithesis and parallelism) within a paratactic structure: the combination of these simple patterns and a loose co-ordination produces a 'rocking movement' with only a 'gentle progress' within the period, and the ultimate effect is 'cloying and monotonous' (pp. 42–3). In contrast both Demosthenes and Cicero (who has obviously learned from him) use a 'progressive rhythm', in which the symmetries of the individual clauses are arranged so that the 'successive members...increase in weight and length, and certainly that the last member should be noticeably the heaviest', this climactic movement being geared to the logical and emotional development of the argument. Laughton also refers to the study by Gilberte Ronnet, *Étude sur le style de Démosthène* (Paris, 1951), which stresses the rhetorical structure of the prose. See also E. Lindholm, *Stilistische Studien zur Erweiterung der Satzglieder im Lateinischen* (Lund, 1931).

PAGE 99

1 *Pro Marcello*, 5; quoted by Laughton, *op. cit.* p. 44. On Cicero's use of rhetoric to underline thought see also Norden, pp. 231–3, Polheim, *op. cit.* p. 184 n. (quoting Laurand: in the later works 'la symétrie des constructions est au service d'une pensée plus ferme; on ne trouve plus ce contraste entre le pauvreté de l'idée et la recherche de l'expression qui choquait quelquefois dans les premiers discours').

PAGE 100

1 Having made this point about the more noticeable effect of symmetry within a smaller syntactical mould I was pleased to find support from Leo Spitzer, in his discussion of this aspect of Diderot's style: 'Here, for the first time, we find a rhythm which will recur many times in our paper: this "style coupé" (the term Diderot himself applied, in a laudatory vein, to Seneca's writing), which is produced by a sequence of short sentences, gives a mechanical effect—which is never likely to be achieved with the longer periods, however artificially they may be composed'. *Linguistics and Literary History* (Princeton, 1948), p. 176 n. 8.
2 Norden writes: 'Theatralisch ist auch sein Stil: es genügte ihm nicht, das, was er fuehlte, in schlichter Form zu bieten, sondern er hat das rhetorische Pathos in einer uns oft verletzenden Art walten lassen. Er hat dadurch erreicht, dass wir nur zu häufig das Gefühl haben, als wenn er zufriedener ist, wenn wir ein geistreiches Aperçu beklatschen, als dem der umgebenden Phrase entkleideten Gedanken wegen seines innern Gehalts folgen. Er versichert uns freilich oft genug des Gegenteils:... *haec sit propositi nostri summa: quod sentimus loquamur, quod loquimur sentiamus: concordet sermo cum vita* (ep. 75, 4), aber wird es uns nicht schwer, einem zu glauben, der eben diese *propositi summa* in ein pointiertes *schema* kleidet?' (pp. 306–7). K. Polheim says that Seneca 'must be given an

important place in the history of prose rhyme', and shows that he uses every variety of sound-echo, particularly to end symmetrical clauses (*op. cit.* pp. 196–7).

PAGE 101

1 Cited by Polheim (*op. cit.* p. 244), who shows how Augustine's style is dominated by parallelism to a remarkable extent.

PAGE 102

1 Cited by M. W. Croll, Introduction to Lyly's *Euphues*, ed. Croll and Clemons (London, 1916), p. xxx. See this essay pp. xv–lxiv for further examples of symmetry in medieval Latin, also M. B. Ogle, 'Some Aspects of Medieval Latin Style', *Speculum*, I (1926), 170–89.
2 Cited by William Ringler, 'The Immediate Source of Euphuism', *PMLA*, LIII (1938), 678–86, at p. 680.

PAGE 103

1 *English Works* (Selections), ed. P. and H. Allen (Oxford, 1924), pp. 81–2.
2 *The Scholemaster*, ed. cit. pp. 188–9.

PAGE 104

1 Cf. Professor John Earle's description of Bacon's *Essays*: 'As English prose it is indeed a very remarkable book, especially as it lets us see through the now prevailing and rampant classicism to some select retreat where the true English tradition flourishes with its native vigour.' *English Prose* (London, 1890), p. 442.
2 *Dialogus de oratoribus*, 18, 4–5; translated by G. M. A. Grube, *The Greek and Roman Critics* (London, 1965), pp. 181–2; in the *Orator* Cicero described the Asiatics as using 'a fatty kind of diction' (*tamquam adipatae dictionis genus*). (*Ibid.* p. 184.)
3 Norden, pp. 251–300, 355–92, 777–8; Laughton (*op. cit.* p. 27) writes that 'The attitude of the Atticist reactionaries at Rome was plainly wrong-headed'; see also U. Wilamowitz, 'Asianismus und Atticismus', *Hermes*, XXXV (1900), 1–52; A. D. Leeman, *op. cit.* vol. I, ch. 6, 'Cicero and the Atticists'.
4 I find only Cicero commenting on symmetry, in his distinction between the two types of Asianism: 'the one sententious and studied, less characterized by weight of thought than by the charm of balance and symmetry...The other type is not so notable for wealth of sententious phrase, as for swiftness and impetuosity—a general trait of Asia at the present time—combining with this rapid flow of speech a choice of words refined and ornate', lacking 'elaborate symmetry of phrase and sentence'. (*Brutus*, 325–6; Loeb translation).

Notes, pp. 105–106

1 See Izora Scott, *Controversies over the Imitation of Cicero* (New York, 1910), II, 36 (Erasmus), I, 99 (Landi), 72 (Dolet), 49 (Scaliger).

2 For Erasmus's praise of Cicero's style, see Scott, I, 26, 27; II, 57, and, for Ramus, *ibid.* I, 102–3 (though he complains of Cicero's 'long and involved sentences', p. 101). See also 'Gabriel Harvey's *Ciceronianus*', ed. H. S. Wilson, with an English translation by C. A. Forbes, *University of Nebraska Studies in the Humanities*, no. 4 (Lincoln, 1945), pp. 46–55 (text) and pp. 14–15 (comment).

1 Erasmus's chief speaker, Bulephorus, offers this example: 'This thought, "Jesus Christ, the Word, and Son of the Eternal Father, according to the prophets came into the world and was made man; of his own will he suffered death and redeemed his church; turned the wrath of the offended father from us; reconciled us to Him so that, justified by the grace of faith and freed from tyranny, we are brought into the church and, persevering in the communion of the church, after this life we reach the kingdom of heaven", a Ciceronian would express thus: "The interpreter and son of most excellent and mighty Jove, preserver and king, in accordance with the response of the soothsayer, flew down from Olympus to earth and, assuming the shape of man, sacrificed himself voluntarily to the shades below for the safety of the Republic and thus freed the state; he extinguished the lightning of most excellent and mighty Jove which flashed about our heads, restored us to his favor so that we, rendered innocent by the wealth of persuasion and freed from the mastery of a deceiver, are admitted into the state; and if we persevere in the fellowship of the Republic we shall gain the highest happiness, when the fates shall have called us from this life, into the society of the Gods"' (Scott, *op. cit.* II, 67–8).

2 'Juste Lipse et le mouvement anti-cicéronien', *Revue du seizième siècle*, II (1914), 200–42; Introduction to *Euphues, ed. cit.*; '"Attic" Prose in the Seventeenth Century', *Studies in Philology*, XVIII (1921), 79–128; 'Attic Prose: Lipsius, Montaigne, Bacon', *Schelling Anniversary Papers* (New York, 1923), pp. 117–50; 'Muret and the History of "Attic" Prose', *PMLA*, XXXIX (1924), 254–309; 'The Baroque Style in Prose', *Studies in English Philology*, ed. K. Malone and M. Ruud (Minneapolis, 1929), pp. 427–56: these articles will be referred to here in an abbreviated form, respectively: *Lipsius*; *Attic*; *Montaigne*; *Muret*; *Baroque*. These are now conveniently collected in book form with the title *Style, Rhetoric, and Rhythm*, ed. J. M. Patrick *et al.* (Princeton, New Jersey, 1966), to which page references will be given in the abbreviated form *SRR*.

3 *Lipsius*, 211 n., 218–19; *Muret*, 286, 296 (*SRR*, 17 n., 23–5, 139, 149).

1 *Lipsius*, 208 n., 225, 232, 238; *Attic*, 79 n., 80, 93, 97, 103, 106, 113; *Muret*, 256, 259, 302; *Montaigne, passim*; *Baroque*, 444, 455 (*SRR*, 13, 14, 30, 41, 51, 69, 76, 79, 81, 94, 99, 109, 112, 119, 155, 167–202 *passim*, 230, 243, 285, 325). It is worth noting that Croll has lumped together his leaders with little care: Montaigne can hardly be said to have 'led' an anti-Ciceronian movement (he took no part in literary controversies), except in the sense that his style may have exerted an influence, and there seems little evidence for that. Bacon only referred to the movement once, and it is hard to see how Muret (who died in 1585, and produced little during his last years) can be claimed as aiding a movement in the generation following his own (I owe some of these points to the suggestions of Dr R. R. Bolgar).

2 The fullest exposition of the philosophical thesis is in *Muret*, especially pp. 257–72 (*SRR*, 111–25); but significant supporting references will be found at *Lipsius*, 203, 206, 207, 222, 242; *Attic*, 90, 92, 94, 95, 101, 103, 112–16; *Muret*, 277, 303; *Montaigne, passim*; *Baroque*, 427–9, 436, 455–6 (*SRR*, 10, 12–13, 27, 44, 62–4, 66–7, 74, 76, 85–90, 130–1, 156, 167–202 *passim*, 207–8, 215, 231–3.

3 René Wellek has pointed to that naïve assumption of an organic relation between style and psychology in a literary movement which overlooks the simple possibility of imitation: 'For example, in the discussion of the Baroque, most German scholars assume an inevitable correspondence between dense, obscure, twisted language and a turbulent, divided, and tormented soul. But an obscure, twisted style can certainly be cultivated by craftsmen and technicians. The whole relationship between psyche and word is looser and more oblique than is usually assumed' (*Theory of Literature*, ed. cit. p. 184). George Orwell noted the contradiction between Yeats's 'tendency' towards fascism and his style, and commented: 'No one has succeeded in tracing the connection between "tendency" and literary style. Texture cannot seemingly be explained in sociological terms' (*Critical Essays*, London, 1946, p. 114). He went on to protest that 'there must be some connection', but the tracing of a connection between a writer's ideology and his style is an extremely difficult task, and—in my experience, at least—when it is done it is usually done crudely.

4 See the admirable analysis by P. A. Duhamel, 'The Ciceronianism of Gabriel Harvey', *Studies in Philology*, XLIX (1952), 155–70.

1 Duhamel, *op. cit.* p. 164, also notes that Ramus's *Rhetorica* 'exhibits a more extensive and precise knowledge of the Ciceronian cadences than any other Renaissance rhetoric'. For examples of English Ramists on this topic, see Dudley Fenner, *Artes of Logike and Rhetorike* (1584), Sig. D 3; Charles Butler,

Rhetoricae Libri Duo (1597), ch. 15 (1629 ed. seen); Abraham Fraunce, *Arcadian Rhetoric* (1588), ed. E. Seaton (Oxford, 1950), p. 34.

2 *Op. cit.* in note 30, p. 85.

3 See *Lipsius*, 226–7 (*SRR*, 30–1) for such sequences: 'Atque ut venena vinis admixta, medicorum consilio, perniciter et perniciose penetrant; sic peccata haec adsita virtuti...Ut pictor, levi manu, et volante penicillo, rugas, verrucas, naevos in facie exprimit, haud tam facile ipsam...' or 'In Italia tota tria haec mihi serva. Frons tibi aperta, lingua parca, mens clausa.' Of Muret Croll only quotes from his earlier Ciceronian style (*Muret*, 273–4; *SRR*, 127), and nothing from his later 'Attic'. For Croll's references to their 'rough' style see *Lipsius*, 224; *Muret*, 282–3 (*SRR*, 28–9, 136–7).

4 *Baroque* (the best of the articles for English prose, and the only one to use any analysis), *passim*, but especially pp. 432–40, 445–52 (*SRR*, 211–19, 222–9).

5 *Ben Jonson and the Language of Prose Comedy* (Harvard Univ. Press, 1960), especially ch. 2 (pp. 41–89).

6 *Attic, passim*, especially pp. 88, 96–9, 101–5, 116–17, 126–8 (although on p. 98 he admits that no real discrimination can be made, and begins and ends by conceding that 'Attic' is a vague term; *SRR*, 60–1, 68–72, 73–8, 89–91, 99–101; 71).

PAGE 109

1 *Muret*, 283; *Lipsius*, 218; *Attic*, 95 and 19 (*SRR*, 137, 23–4, 67 and n. 21). The quotations in the following paragraph are, respectively, from *Muret*, 269; *Lipsius*, 217; *Attic*, 95, 84; *Baroque*, 437; *Montaigne*, 134 (*SRR*, 123, 22, 67, 56, 216, 185).

PAGE III

1 *Op. cit.* p. 49. Mr Barish must be given credit for being the first critic to note, albeit briefly, that 'asymmetry, where it occurs in Bacon, remains tangential' (*ibid.* p. 56). See also pp. 57–60 for an analysis of the structural symmetries (though not of the expressive function) of the passage in the *Advancement* where Bacon attacks Ciceronianism, and for an excellent comparison with Ben Jonson, who quotes this passage (*Discoveries*, 2116–24) almost verbatim, but subconsciously rearranges it into a much more asymmetrical pattern.

PAGE II2

1 *Of the Advancement and Proficience of Learning; or, the Partitions of Sciences* (Oxford, 1640), p. 29.

PAGE II3

1 *Op. cit.* p. 65. Mr Barish goes on to suggest that these 'are questions that Renaissance authors did not raise', and he is surely right, although he elsewhere accepts Croll's thesis that the anti-Ciceronians had 'a highly articulate rhetorical theory' (p. 48), for which I have tried to show there is little evidence. Nor can I agree that Renaissance authors 'assumed that regularity was artful, irregularity natural and spontaneous, and they wrote accordingly' (p. 65). However, these are tiny points, and one must be grateful to him for his fine comparison between the prose of Shakespeare and Jonson—a classic of stylistic criticism.

2 P. A. Duhamel, *op. cit.* p. 162.

PAGE 115

1 Preface to *The History of the World* (1666 ed., p. 16).

PAGE 116

1 *Euphues*, p. xvii; *Baroque*, 441–3 (*SSR*, 243, 220–2).

PAGE 117

1 *Senecan Amble*, pp. 116–18.
2 For symmetry in the *New Atlantis* see, for example, 3. 130, 134, 136, 139, 152, 156, 157, 162; and for *Henry VII* see 6. 27–8, 32, 36, 39, 50, 59, 77, 85, 87, 94, 103–6, 118–20, 138–45, 149–56, 182–5, 217, 243–5.

PAGE 127

1 Dryden, *Absalom and Achitophel*, pt 1, ll. 585–92; Pope, *Moral Essays*, Epistle III, 'Of the Use of Riches', ll. 385–92. My italics throughout.

PAGE 128

1 On the disyllabic pronunciation of *-ion* see H. Koekeritz, *Shakespeare's Pronunciation* (London, 1953), pp. 293–4; E. A. Abbott, *A Shakespearian Grammar* (London, 1884), § 479, and E. J. Dobson, *English Pronunciation 1500–1700* (Oxford, 1957), II, §§ 270, 276, 277, 281, 292, 387: there seems to be evidence for the disyllabic usage outside the exigencies of verse form.
2 For other uses of *gradatio* in the *Advancement* see 3. 373, 388, 457, 476, 483; another favourite figure is *antimetabole* or *chiasmus*, used for subtle distinctions: see 3. 269, 273, 276 (twice), 281, 292, 332 (twice), 343–4, 345, 348, 350, 351–2, 371, 382, 384, 447, 468, 486.

PAGE 129

1 Other instances of this rhyming of *sententiae* will be found at 3. 279, 290, 315, 324, 340, 353, 383, 396, 413, 421, 427, 432, 447, 460, 463, 473, 478, 482.

PAGE 134

1 For other examples of symmetry sharpening the classification of human behaviour see 6. 380, 385, 389, 391, 393–6, 402, 405, 426, 433, 436, 455, 466, 470, 477–8, 493, 494, 496, 501, 505.

2 As, for example, 'Of Parents and Children', 'Of Simulation and Dissimulation', 'Of Adversity', 'Of Usury', 'Of Youth and Age', 'Of Envy', and others.

3 Compare the paraphrase of this quotation as used in the *Advancement* (*a*) with its appearance in the Essay 'Of Truth' (*b*): *Suave mari magno, turbantibus aequora ventis* (2. 1)—(*a*) 'It is a view of delight' (saith he) 'to stand or walk upon the shore side, and to see a ship tossed with tempest upon the sea; or to be in a fortified tower, and to see two battles join upon a plain. But it is a pleasure incomparable, for the mind of man to be settled, landed, and fortified in the certainty of truth; and from thence to descry and behold the errors, perturbations, labours, and wanderings up and down of other men' (3. 317–18). (*b*) 'It is a pleasure to stand upon the shore and to see ships tossed upon the sea; a pleasure to stand in the window of a castle, and to see a battle and the adventures thereof below: but no pleasure is comparable to the standing upon the vantage ground of Truth' (a hill not to be commanded, and where the air is always clear and serene), 'and to see the errors, and wanderings, and mists, and tempests, in the vale below' (6. 378). For other examples of symmetrical quotations in the *Essays*, see 6. 431, 399, 423, 437, 480, 448, 386, 393, 385, 412, etc.

PAGE 137

1 Hazlitt frequently criticised this aspect of Johnson's prose, and though his own effusive style exaggerates the charge he does make a fair comment on the occasional triumph of manner over matter in Johnson: 'All his periods are cast in the same mould, are of the same size and shape, and consequently have little fitness to the variety of things he professes to treat of' (*Works*, ed. P. P. Howe, London, 1930–34, VI, 101–2); and again: 'There is a tune in it, a mechanical recurrence of the same rise and fall in the clauses of his sentences, independent of any reference to the meaning of the text, or progress or inflection of the sense... his periods complete their revolutions at certain stated intervals, let the matter be longer or shorter, rough or smooth, round or square, different or the same' (*ibid.* XII, 6. Quoted by W. K. Wimsatt, *The Prose Style of Samuel Johnson*, Yale Univ. Press, 2nd ed. 1963, p. 32 and note).

PAGE 141

1 The closeness of poetry to prose has often been recognised: see Curtius, *op. cit.* chs. 4 and 8; Norden, *op. cit.* pp. 30–41, 160–1; M. B. Ogle, *op. cit. passim*; Puttenham, *Arte of Poesie*, ed. Willcock and Walker, p. xxxiv. Some representative statements, which often say that rhetoric is in fact the province of oratory/ prose (so perpetuating Gorgias' reversal of the original situation) can be simply listed: (1) Cicero, *De Oratore* 1. 70: 'The poet is closely akin to the orator, being somewhat more restricted in rhythm, but less restricted in his choice of words, and in many kinds of embellishment his rival and almost equal' (cited in John Rainolds, *Oratio in Laudem Artis Poeticae*, ed. W. Ringler and W. Allen, Princeton, 1940, pp. 20–1; also *ibid.* pp. 49, 66, 74). (2) John of Garland, in his thirteenth-century treatise *Poetria*, 'thought that rhetorical ornament was as necessary in metre as in prose' (K. G. Hamilton, *The Two Harmonies: Poetry and Prose in the Seventeenth Century*, Oxford, 1963, p. 78). (3) Erasmus, Letter to Andrew Ammonius, 21 December 1513: 'What especially delights me is a rhetorical poem and a poetical oration, in which you can see the poetry in the prose and the rhetorical expression in the poetry' (*Epistolae*, ed. P. S. Allen, I, 545; cited and translated by Ringler and Allen, *op. cit.* p. 20). (4) Gascoigne, 1575: 'You may use the same Figures or Tropes in verse which are used in prose, and in my iudgement they serve more aptly and have greater grace in verse than they have in prose' (in *Elizabethan Critical Essays*, ed. G. G. Smith, Oxford, 1904, I, 52; cited by Hamilton, *op. cit.* pp. 10–11).

PAGE 142

1 *The Verbal Icon* (Kentucky, 1954), p. 128.

2 Hulme continues in the same derogatory vein: 'Images in verse are not mere decoration, but the very essence of an intuitive language. Verse is a pedestrian taking you over the ground, prose—a train which delivers you at a destination' (*Speculations*, ed. H. Read, London, 1924, p. 135); cf. also Middleton Murry (who throughout his book on style shows a strong distrust of imagery in prose): 'Metaphor, if regarded by a prosaic eye, or analysed by a mind which has lost a certain keenness of intuition, does tend to look like ornament' (*The Problem of Style*, Oxford, 1922, p. 12).

3 The discussions or demonstrations of the critical analysis of imagery to which I am most indebted are: A. D. Leeman, *Orationis Ratio*, I, 125–32; E. R. Curtius, *European Literature and the Latin Middle Ages*, especially ch. 7 ('Metaphorics'), ch. 16 ('The Book as Symbol'), and Excursus III; R. A. Foakes, 'Suggestions for a New Approach to Shakespeare's Imagery', *Shakespeare Survey*, V (1952), 81–93; and S. L. Bethell, 'Shakespeare's Imagery: The Diabolic Images in *Othello*', *ibid.* especially pp. 62–5; I. A. Richards, *The Philosophy of Rhetoric* (New York, 1936) for the now familiar distinction between the 'tenor' and the 'vehicle' of the image (that is, between the thing itself and that to which it is compared); W. K. Wimsatt, 'Symbol and Metaphor', in *The Verbal Icon*, pp. 119–30; R. Wellek and A. Warren, *Theory of Literature* (New York, 1949), ch. 15 (by Warren), 'Image, Metaphor, Symbol, Myth' (though I find this discussion confused by some critical jargon); and, above all, Rosemond Tuve, *Elizabethan and Metaphysical Imagery* (Chicago, 1947). Miss Tuve's epoch-making book establishes with great precision and detail the variety of functions to which imagery was applied in the Renaissance, and several of the points I make (and the

quotations I use) have been anticipated by her. Although it is possible to disagree with her interpretation of the effects of logic on images (most of all her too positive equation of Ramist logic with Metaphysical imagery), her book is a splendid union of critical and historical method. If her constant oscillation between Renaissance and modern attitudes may result in some duplication and even confusion, it has certainly clarified the assumptions of both periods.

4 (B55). Professor Knights may have misunderstood the nature of Renaissance imagery, but elsewhere in this essay he is guilty of associating Bacon with the *bêtes noires* of a sensitive, conscientous pre-war English liberal: scientific materialism, industrial civilisation, soil erosion, the internal-combustion engine, and America. It is a pity that this non-literary animus should have been allowed to colour his account of Bacon's prose style. Some sensible arguments in defence of Bacon's imagery have been made by J. B. Leishmann, *The Monarch of Wit* (London, 1951), pp. 138–9; J. Andrews (B5), and Anne Righter, *op. cit.* A brief and laudatory general assessment of Bacon's imagery was made by H. W. Wells, *Poetic Imagery Illustrated from Elizabethan Literature* (New York, 1924), but applied to a rather obscure category.

PAGE 143

1 Quotations from the *Poetics* are from the translation by L. J. Potts, *Aristotle on the Art of Fiction* (Cambridge, 2nd ed. 1959); and from the *Rhetoric* from the Loeb translation by J. H. Freese (London, 1947).

PAGE 146

1 Longinus, *On the Sublime*, ch. 32 (§ 66); translated by A. H. Gilbert, *Literary Criticism: Plato to Dryden* (New York, 1940), p. 183.

2 According to J. J. Mangan, *Erasmus of Rotterdam* (London, 1927), II, 395 ff., there were at least 64 editions of Erasmus's *Similia* by 1669; for evidence of its use in English education see T. W. Baldwin, *op. cit.* and W. G. Crane, *Wit and Rhetoric in the Renaissance* (New York, 1937). Besides Erasmus, other continental collections, such as the *Polyanthea* of Nannius Mirabellius and the *Officina* of J. R. Textor, were used to form English versions—the latter work is the main source for Meres's *Palladis Tamia* (1598), as D. C. Allen has shown. The major English collections of similitudes up to 1600 are: William Baldwin, *Treatise of Morall Phylosophye* (1547); Thomas Palfreyman, *A Treatise of Heavenlie Philosophy* (1578); Anthonie Fletcher, *Certaine Very Proper and Most Profitable Similes* (1595); Robert Cawdrey, *A Treasurie or Storehouse of Similes* (1600).

PAGE 147

1 The quotations in this paragraph are respectively from Wilson's *Arte of Rhetorique* (1553), ed. G. H. Mair (London, 1909), pp. 190, 188 (my italics);

Coke, cited by C. D. Bowen, *op. cit.* p. 247; Meres, *op. cit.* Sig. A2v; Puttenham, *ed. cit.* pp. 240–3.

PAGE 148

1 Wilson, *ed. cit.* pp. 172–3; Puttenham, *ed. cit.* Book 3, ch. 16, pp. 178, 180; Peacham, *The Garden of Eloquence, ed. cit.* p. 13; Hoskins, *ed. cit.* p. 8 (my italics).

PAGE 153

1 The explicit connection between communication in fables and the techniques of alchemy has been shown by C. W. Lemmi (B61), especially pp. 77–120. Bacon describes his *Philosophia prima* as 'the Persian magic', mentioning Zoroaster (4. 339) and in a later reference to it using the terminology of Paracelsus (4. 366–7). For an excellent account of Bacon's views on fables and related topics, see J. L. Harrison (B44).

PAGE 159

1 On this and on several other points the analysis of Bacon's images by C. F. E. Spurgeon, *Shakespeare's Imagery and What It Tells Us* (Cambridge, 1935) is simply wrong (although she was right to point out Bacon's fondness for images from light). My analysis of Bacon's imagery (even though it does not claim to be complete—no such analysis ever is, for some images can be taken for a variety of applications) shows that the dominant image-group (amounting to a tenth of the whole) is that from nature, especially the processes of growth and cultivation. Bacon also draws many images from sources which Miss Spurgeon denies him (the stars; storms and shipwrecks; bowls, etc.).

PAGE 170

1 Cf. Anne Righter's acute comment on this sentence from the *Historia Densi et Rari*: 'Wine and beer in frost lose their vigour; yet in thaws and south winds they revive, relax, and as it were ferment again' (5. 370): 'The strange animism of this latter remark, in which the single technical term is handled far more diffidently than those which seem to endow the inanimate with a soul, is altogether characteristic of Bacon, and worlds away from what we ordinarily regard as dispassionate, scientific observation' (*op. cit.* p. 20).

2 A happy exception is Mrs Righter, who quotes that passage from the *Advancement* on 'the same footsteps of nature, treading or printing upon several subjects or matters', which includes this sentence and the quotation from Virgil: 'Is not the delight of the quavering upon a stop in music the same with the playing of light upon the water? *Splendet tremulo sub lumine pontus* (Beneath the trembling light glitters the sea.)' (349) and comments: 'This Virgilian glittering of light on the sea must be valued for itself or not at all. As for its presence in

Bacon's mind, and on his page at this particular moment, it has clearly been evoked by that sensuous procession of love, music, the arts of language and the beauty of the natural world which it crowns' (*op. cit.* p. 16).

1 Caroline Spurgeon, *Shakespeare's Imagery and What It Tells Us* (Cambridge, 1935). The main weaknesses of this approach were well exposed by Lilian Hornstein, 'Analysis of Imagery: A Critique of Literary Method', *PMLA*, LVII (1942), 638–53. An important recent demonstration of this method is that by Paul Fussell, *The Rhetorical World of Augustan Humanism* (Oxford, 1965), and, although sometimes the literary and philosophical conclusions drawn from the stylistic evidence seem too far-reaching, the analyses are highly perceptive and coherent. The literary evaluations behind the method which I have used in this chapter have been acutely described by Mr Fussell, first the 'critical assumption ...that, the mind being a thing that must work by means of metaphors and symbols, imagery is the live constituent in that transmission of shaped illumina-tion from one intelligence to another which is literature'; and, secondly, that 'habitual recourse to certain image-systems and a preference—however uncon-scious—for them over others seems almost to shape the mind itself, or at least to predispose it towards certain equally habitual objects of concern' (Preface, p. viii).

1 Translated by Spedding. The principle on which I use this translation will be explained in the notes to the next chapter. Whatever other objections there may be to his work (and they are slight), Spedding is particularly good at preserving Bacon's images faithfully in his translation and he even reproduces this image, unconsciously perhaps, in accounting for the presence of the *De Augmentis* as the first part of the Instauration, instead of the completed *Descriptio Globi Intellec-tualis*: 'he found he had not time to finish it on so large a scale, and therefore resolved to enlarge the old house instead of building a new one' (1. 147).

2 This image of intellectual excavation is found throughout Bacon's work, from the *Valerius Terminus*—'digging further and further into the mine of natural knowledge' (3. 219), through the *Filum Labyrinthi* (3. 503) and the *Novum Organum* ('arts and sciences should be like mines, where the noise of new works and further advances is heard on every side'—4. 89–90; also 4. 50) to the *Historia Vitae et Mortis* (5. 267), the *New Atlantis* (where those 'that try new experiments' are called 'Pioners or Miners', 3. 164) and the *De Augmentis*, where the division between Speculative and Operative is summed up in this image: 'The one searching into the bowels of nature, the other shaping nature as on an anvil' (4. 343).

PAGE 178

1 Similarly we find 'threshold of the work' here (4. 13), and in the *Thema Coeli* Bacon describes himself as 'standing...on the threshold of natural history and philosophy' (5. 559). He applies the idea to create the powerful image of the 'Porches of Death', the 'Atriola Mortis' of the *Historia Vitae et Mortis* (5. 217, 222, 311), also found in a letter to Gondomar in 1621 (14. 285) and the *Wisdom of the Ancients* (6. 763).

PAGE 179

1 In outlining the plan of the *Instauratio Magna* he even sees his work as a source of refreshment for other travellers on the same road. Apologising for the incompletion of the fifth part, he hopes that his speculations, although unfinished, may 'serve in the meantime for wayside inns, in which the mind may rest and refresh itself on its journey to more certain conclusions' (4. 32)—the image is both definitely localised and witty.

PAGE 180

1 Connected with this image of finding the right path is that of knowledge as a hunt to track down an elusive prey. So Bacon's method of 'Experientia Literata' is called 'The Hunt of Pan' (see 3. 331; 4. 413; 5. 122; 6. 713), which is 'rather a sagacity and a kind of hunting by scent, than a science' (4. 421).

PAGE 183

1 See, for example, 6. 99; 4. 8; 3. 293; 4. 101–2 (and in the related form of gaining the heights).

PAGE 184

1 Another image for fruitlessness is the often repeated 'veluti via navis in mari', as in the *Wisdom of the Ancients*: 'anything that yields no fruit, but like the way of a ship in the sea passes and leaves no trace, was by the ancients held sacred to the shades and infernal gods' (6. 706).

PAGE 185

1 For other images of shipwreck see 6. 722, 755; 3. 334, 418; 5. 466.

PAGE 186

1 4. 17, 30; see also 3. 279, 437.
2 See, for example, 4. 190; 5. 103, 106.
3 *De Augmentis* (4. 283); *New Atlantis* (3. 141). The *Redargutio Philosophiarum*, characteristically enough, expresses the idea in a defiant spirit: 'Nos nostrum *plus ultra* antiquorum *non ultra* haud vane opposuimus' (3. 584).

4 Daniel xii. 4. The English translation of the *De Augmentis* (1640) repeated image and motto, and the title-page of the *Sylva Sylvarum* (1626) has the Pillars of Hercules with the 'Mundus Intellectualis' suspended between them, being struck by a light from heaven (Gibson, 103, 131, 170).

PAGE 187

1 Connected with this idea is that of confluence, of the fruitful union of smaller streams in a larger one (or sometimes a vessel), which may suggest the scientific co-operation that Bacon so strongly advised; see, for example, 3. 487; 4. 258, 293; 5. 123, 141, 160, 504.
2 3. 349; see also the *Instauratio Magna* (4. 7); the *De Augmentis* (4. 336); and the *Novum Organum* (4. 99).
3 For the *Advancement* see 3. 262, 263, 367, 373, 434, 475, and for the later scientific works see, for example, 3. 218, 501; 4. 16, 293, 364; 5. 6, 105, 183, 323, 435, 496, 504, 536, 555; 6. 735, 751.

PAGE 188

1 See 3. 227, 292, 503; 4. 15, 72; 6. 502. Both Miss Spurgeon and Professor Knights objected to this image, but in Bacon's defence it must be said that, although Time the river has brought down to us many of the great monuments of humane learning, from the point of view of natural philosophy at the beginning of the seventeenth century the fact that the extant concepts of science and even its observations were hardly improved beyond Aristotle (with the exception, as Bacon so often reminds us, of purely technological inventions such as printing, the compass, and gunpowder) is such a disastrous fact that it deserved the most vigorous attacks. Nor was Bacon original, even though he did the job with absolute finality as far as the English seventeenth century was concerned—in opposing Aristotle he followed such forward-looking Renaissance minds as Ramus, Giordano Bruno, Telesio, Patrizi and others. See, for example, P. O. Kristeller, *The Classics and Renaissance Thought* (Harvard, 1955), ch. 2.

PAGE 192

1 For images of gloom and shadow see 4. 65; 3. 475; 6. 730; 5. 496; 4. 59; 6. 738; of vaults and caves: 3. 396; 4. 54; 6. 725; 5. 131; of the sight being 'veiled': 5. 461; 6. 695; 6. 387; 3. 500; 4. 317; or covered by clouds and vapours: 3. 316; 3. 231; 3. 332; 3. 362; 4. 448; of men groping in the dark: e.g. *Novum Organum*, 4. 95, 159–60, 199; and of blindness: 3. 239; 3. 273; 6. 731; 4. 224; 4. 406.
2 2. 377; for other images of the eye and perception see 3. 137; 4. 19, 302, 435; 5. 121.

PAGE 195

1 See also 5. 199—'it will be enough to have sown a seed for posterity and the Immortal God'; also 3. 406, 415, 470, 490; 5. 127.

PAGE 196

1 See, for example, 3. 220, 227, 276, 346, 404, 421, 430, 475; 4. 412, 449; 5. 54, 477.

PAGE 197

1 3. 294–5, repeated 3. 222, 232; other fruit-images in the *Advancement*: 3. 305, 321, 363, 406. The presentation of fruitlessness in human terms is managed even more scathingly in the Preface to the *Instauratio Magna*, where Bacon writes that the 'wisdom which we have derived principally from the Greeks is but like the boyhood of knowledge, and has the characteristic property of boys: it can talk, but it cannot generate; for it is fruitful of controversies but barren of works' (4. 14; also 4. 73).

PAGE 199

1 The persistence of Baconian images has been noticed in general terms, though a detailed analysis would be valuable, and would probably be the best way of organising a history of Bacon's influence. Cf., for example, Anne Righter, *op. cit.* p. 7 (quoted in the text above, p. 232) and the concluding words of Paolo Rossi (B 78a), p. 513, 'Bacon, imbued with a rhetorical culture, unable to understand the works of Copernicus, Galileo and Gilbert, nevertheless put forward problems in a way which had deep echoes in the later formation of the logic of scientific thought. So we see that Newton, in opposition to Galileo and Descartes, did not believe mathematics to be the "queen of all sciences" but a *method*, an *instrument* with which to explain experience. He refuted Plato's vision of a nature which was *itself* mathematical, and said that the task of science was to *explore* an *unknown endless ocean*. Thus he brought back to life (although at a different level) some of the typically "Baconian" images' (see G. Preti, *Newton*, Milan, 1950, pp. 56, 100, 112); I am grateful to Mrs Maria Pollard for help with this translation.

A recent analysis by W. R. Davis (B24) of image-groups in the *Novum Organum* supports some of the main categories which I have distinguished (those of architecture, the mirror, 'wandering', light and fruit), while making rather more than I do of the image of Bacon as a priest officiating at the wedding of the Sciences, and even awaiting the coming of the bride (pp. 171–2)—a characteristically concrete and fully acted metaphor.

PAGE 202

1 For Glanvill's revisions see R. F. Jones (B 52), especially pp. 88–97; for James's, see H. Harvitt, *PMLA*, XXXIX (1924), 203–27, corrected by R. D. Havens, *ibid.* XL (1925), 433–4, and further corrected by O. Cargill, *The Novels of Henry James* (New York, 1961), pp. 32–3.

PAGE 205

1 He announces his wish for clarification before almost every one of the new sections (see 4. 318, 424; 5. 36, 58, 79, 88).

2 This fullness is often achieved by adding more examples to a particular head, e.g. 4. 430; 5. 31, 66. But often long sequences of *sententiae* and comments on them will remain unchanged, while much around them is altered, e.g. 4. 381, 408–10; 5. 22, 76.

3 The work also marks the period of time which has elapsed since the *Advancement*, and there is something of the old man's awareness of the changes which have taken place within his own life-span in remarks such as 'The pleasure of the ears is Music, with its various apparatus of voices, wind and strings; water instruments, once regarded as the leaders of this art, are now almost out of use' (4. 395). Some other added comments mark scientific advance—Copernicus's theory of the earth's rotation 'has now become prevalent' (4. 478) while others record linguistic fashions: a saying new at the time of the *Advancement* 'has now grown into a commonplace' (4. 456) or 'is commonly said' (4. 457).

PAGE 208

1 For examples of new divisions see 4. 374–5, 396–7; 5. 35, 89–90, etc.

2 For the numerical listing of divisions see also 5. 25, 32, 71–5, etc.

PAGE 209

1 *Propositio*: 4. 300, 303, 309–10; 5. 37, etc.; transitions: 4. 355, 493, 497, etc.; summing-up: 4. 298, 301, 371, 448; 5. 6, 12, etc.; repetition of a division: 4. 347, 493.

2 Opening division: 5. 88–90; transitions and further divisions: 5. 94, 97, 98, 101, 103.

PAGE 210

1 See Spedding's Preface (1. 420), and the letter entitled 'Bacon's Literary Methods' by R. F. Young, *TLS*, 9 Oct. 1930 (p. 810), which prints a Latin letter from Joachim Huebner of Cleves (1600–65) to Comenius, written 7 Oct. 1638 while he was engaged in research at the Bodleian for Hartlib. Young argues that it can be taken as accurate despite its late date because it represents 'the oral traditions of Oxford Common-rooms'. In translation it reads as follows: 'It is said that the incomparable Bacon religiously observed the follow-

ing procedure: when he had expressed his thoughts as exactly as possible in the vernacular, he passed them over to some of the finest minds for translation and assessment. Out of the different translations of all these men he himself finally produced one in a consistent style. By this means he easily outclassed most of the writers of our age' (I am grateful to A. E. Alexander, Classical Scholar of Downing College, for this translation).

2 As a translator, Spedding seems both accurate and authentic in that he preserves Bacon's own terminology. A small fault is his tendency to paraphrase or expand *sententiae* so that they seem part of the original text (cf., for example, 1. 489 and 4. 287; 1. 617 and 4. 408; 1. 622 and 4. 412). But, unlike Wats, Spedding is particularly good at preserving the exact form of Bacon's images: where the Latin text has 'omnem lapidem in natura moveas' (1. 632) and Spedding rightly translates 'the leaving...of no stone in nature unturned', Wats has 'trie nature every way' (*ed. cit.* p. 235). Where Bacon expands the image of the 'muster-roll of sciences' from the *Advancement* (3. 402) to read in Spedding's translation: 'It may be suspected perhaps that in this enumeration and census as I may call it, of arts my object is to swell the ranks of the sciences thus drawn up on parade' (1.661,4.447), Wats falls tamely back on the original image (p. 227). Other examples of Wats toning down or removing an image will be found on pp. 30 (1. 453; 3. 285), 412 (1. 781; 5. 68), 415 (1. 784; 5. 71) and 417 (1. 786; 5. 73).

3 Of the many hundreds of examples of piecemeal improvement which could be quoted, particularly detailed ones will be found at 4. 303–5, 310, 313, 455–6; 5. 54–5.

4 So 'a rude stone' in the *Advancement* (3. 442) becomes 'a rude and unshaped stone' (5. 28) to create this pleasing and uniquely Latin effect of balance: 'rude permanet et informe saxum' (1. 741). Latin double-negatives are also preferred: 'well expressed' becomes 'not inelegantly' (3. 332; 4. 297), and 'non insulse' or 'non inelegans' is often found (e.g. 4. 307, 398; 5. 41, etc.).

PAGE 211

1 Examples where the English of the *Advancement* creates effects not possible or not wanted (often these are of repetition, especially doublets) in the Latin of the *De Augmentis* (and hence often wisely not attempted) will be found by comparing 3. 261 and 1. 431; 3. 262, 1. 432 (three good examples); 3. 263, 1. 432; 3. 264, 1. 433; 3. 267, 1. 436; 3. 276, 1. 444; 3. 283, 1. 451; 3. 285, 1. 453; 3. 286, 1. 454; 3. 292, 1. 461; 3. 293, 1. 461; 3. 318, 1. 483, etc. For cases where the Latin possibly improves on the English text in terms of precision and mimetic effect in symmetry cf. 3. 268, 1. 437; 3. 273, 1. 442; 3. 282, 1. 450; 3. 284, 1. 453; 3. 289–90, 1. 457; 3. 290, 1. 458; 3. 295, 1. 463; 3. 295, 1. 464; 3. 316, 1. 481; 3. 323, 1. 486, etc.

PAGE 214

1 Other images from water range from the very title of the work ('the Fountains of Equity') to Bacon's declaration that its intention is 'to go to the fountains of justice and public expediency' (5. 88) and to avoid the 'three fountains of justice' (88; also 105), and to his image for statutes which obstruct by being too verbose: 'An explanatory statute stops the streams of the statutes which it explains' (5. 91–2).

2 Further images which present abstract qualities of the Law include these for conflict: the people are 'guarded by the shield of the laws against civil discords and private injuries' (5. 89), but even the courts 'fence and dispute about jurisdiction' (109), so that it is not surprising that in a law which is verbosely formulated justice is soon lost in the 'noise and strife of words' (102). Justice must be sternly administered, it being extremely important 'that the way to a repeal of judgments be narrow, rocky, and as it were paved with flint stones' (108), but the areas of justice must be carefully enlarged: to try to extend the jurisdiction of Courts, for example, 'stimulates the disease and applies a spur where a bit is needed' (109).

PAGE 218

1 These cuts, not amounting to a hundred words in all, consist of removing redundancies and clarifying expression. See, for example, 1625 revision of 1597 'Faction'; 1625 revision of 1612 'Unity of Religion'; 'Marriage and Single Life'; 'Great Place'; 'Greatness of Kingdoms and Estates'. The only cut which *may* be significant, is in 'Regiment of Health', where 1625 revises the 1612 addition to the advice given in 1597: 'Discerne of the comming on of yeares, and think not to doe the same things still.' 1612 adds: 'Certainly most lusty old men catch their death by that adventure; For age will not be defied.' In 1625 Bacon has only 'For age will not be defied'.

2 See, for example, 6. 477, 407–12, 495–6, 500–1, for the most concentrated examples of this piecemeal type of revision.

PAGE 219

1 The large-scale addition of examples in 1625 can be seen in several places, e.g. 'Of Death', 6. 379–80; 'Of Empire', 6. 419–23; 'Of the true greatness of kingdoms and estates', 6. 445–52; 'Of Youth and Age', 6. 477; 'Of Beauty', 6. 479; 'Of Deformity', 6. 481; 'Of Honour and Reputation', 6. 505–6. And also in 1625, for the first time, Bacon is prone to indicating that he could quote many more examples if he wanted to—see 'Of seditions and troubles', 6. 412; 'Of the true greatness...', 6. 445 and 451; 'Of Deformity', 6. 481; and 'On Fame' (a fragment), 6. 520, where the attitude is stated rather pungently;

'There be a thousand such like examples, and the more they are, the less they need to be repeated; because a man meeteth with them everywhere'.

2 See 'Unity in Religion' (6. 381): 'Empire' (6. 420); 'Counsel' (6. 424); 'Ambition' (6. 466); 'Friendship' (6. 440–1); and 'Nobility', which has the barest opening announcement possible: 'We will speak of Nobility first as a portion of an estate: then as a condition of Particular Persons' (6. 405).

PAGE 220

1 See 'Truth' (6. 378); 'Simulation' (6. 387–8); 'Usury' (6. 474); 'Building' (6. 482); 'Gardens' (6. 488); 'Vicissitude' (6. 514); and 'Fame', which announces 'We will therefore speak of these points' (6. 519–20). There are, of course, many other instances of Division within the *Essays*.

PAGE 221

1 On the Manuscript collection see Spedding's note, 6. 535–6, and also E. Arber, *A Harmony of Bacon's Essays* (London, 1871), from which the following quotations are taken.

PAGE 225

1 Images are used to complete an essay with particular effectiveness in 'Suitors' (497), 'Friendship' (443), 'Of Nature in Men' (470), 'Of Faction' (500), 'Of Superstition' (416) and 'Of Adversity' (386); Bacon reused this last image at 2. 470 and 7. 160.

PAGE 226

1 Cf. the comments by Douglas Bush: 'And along with his genius for pithy and proverbial expressions goes a full share of the "wit" of his age; many of his opening phrases remain as arresting as those of Donne's poems' (*English Literature in the Earlier Seventeenth Century*, Oxford, 1945, p. 184); and Anne Righter: 'The rifle-shot of this opening, the little imaginative explosion, is a familiar Baconian technique and frequently imitated' (*op. cit.* p. 27).

2 Added contemptuous images include this from 'Cunning': 'And because these cunning men are like haberdashers of small wares, it is not amiss to set forth their shop' (428) or this description of misanthropes: 'Such men in other's calamities are as it were in season, and are ever on the loading part: not so good as the dogs that licked Lazarus' sores; but like flies that are still buzzing upon anything that is raw' (404).

PAGE 230

1 Perhaps the latter, for he observes of infections in 'Envy' that 'if you fear them, you call them upon you' (6. 396).

Notes, pp. 233–238

PAGE 233

1 Tenison, *Baconiana* (1679), p. 62; Saintsbury, *History of English Prose Rhythm* (London, 1912), p. 164.

PAGE 234

1 These allusions are drawn from R. W. Gibson's *Bibliography* (B 36), items 447, 448a, 521, 429*, 626**, 511, 567*; the asterisks denote entries in the *Supplement* to the Bibliography (1959).

PAGE 237

1 See Ben Jonson, *Works*, ed. Herford and Simpson, VIII, 590–2, for the text, and XI, 241–4, for the notes; for the translation of Horace see VIII, 328–9. Evidence of the period's respect for Jonson's eulogy is easily found (no doubt more could be discovered): thus Aubrey's biography of Bacon referred to it (*Brief Lives*, ed. O. L. Dick, Peregrine ed., 1962, p. 118), and seventeen popular editions of the *Essays* between 1680 and 1715 included these excerpts from *Discoveries* together with the first five stanzas of Cowley's *Ode to the Royal Society*, that is, those referring to Bacon (Gibson, 24 to 30).

2 These quotations are cited by R. F. Jones, *Ancients and Moderns*, pp. 89, 161, 191, 221, 260, 234, 239, 240, 305.

PAGE 238

1 Samuel Sorbière, *A Voyage to England* (London, 1709 ed., reprinted with Thomas Sprat's *Observations on the Voyage...*), p. 32. For a brief account of the voyage and the controversy following the publication of Sorbière's book see T. Sprat, *History of the Royal Society*, ed. J. I. Cope and H. W. Jones (London, 1959), Introduction, pp. xvi ff.

2 The generally accepted view of the diminished use of metaphor in prose after the Restoration has been challenged by Paul Fussell (*op. cit.* pp. 139–41), who calls it a 'vulgar error'. He is certainly right to say that 'the nature of language is inseparable from symbolic conventions', and there is no doubt that some crude versions of the change underrate the extent of imagery in prose from Swift to Burke (his own excellent analysis has established the width and thematic reference of imagery in the prose of this period). But there does seem to me to be a definite change in the way images are used, and it is not explained by his hypothesis that 'Augustan imagery operates generally as polemic rather than as revelation or epiphany' (p. 140), for the polemical function of imagery was prominent in classical and Renaissance theory, as we have seen. The nature of the change is in fact clarified by a statement which he makes elsewhere, defining the 'dualistic' mode of thought common to the orthodox Augustan humanists as it is seen in their 'general theory of metaphor': 'To the humanist, metaphor, which

operates like rapid or almost instantaneous simile, does not actually assert that "a *is* b"; instead it suggests that "a is *like* b". Tenor and vehicle are never thought to interfuse; regardless of closeness of resemblance, the two terms in a comparison remain ultimately distinct', a thesis which he illustrates with examples of Johnson's 'distrust of the "reality" of metaphor' and his 'conception of the ultimate frivolity of metaphor' (p. 120). This may seem a rather specious explanation, but at least Mr Fussell recognises the nature of the separation. Images are used in Augustan prose, then, but they approach simile much more often than metaphor, and the general 'orthodox Augustan humanist' fear of giving the imagination power to subvert rational processes and actually think in metaphor results in a tendency to keep analogy at a cautious distance (the deference to this concept of the dangers of metaphor can be seen in the much increased use in Dryden and beyond of introductory formulae such as 'If I may be pardoned the metaphor' or 'If I may be allowed so bold a figure'). On both counts Renaissance prose had access to a richer imaginative source, and critics contrasting the two modes are surely right to prefer pre-Restoration prose for this reason (e.g. Hugh Macdonald and Joan Bennett in *Review of English Studies*, 1941 and 1942).

3 *History, ed. cit.* pp. 112–13. But the manifesto against metaphor did not entirely succeed: see G. Watson, 'Dryden and the Scientific Image', *Notes and Records of the Royal Society of London*, XVIII (1963), 25–35, and W. P. Jones, *The Rhetoric of Science* (London, 1966), p. 38 and note.

PAGE 240

1 I have presented the evidence for this connection more fully in an article, 'Swift and the Baconian Idol' in the collection of essays which I have edited, *The World of Jonathan Swift* (Basil Blackwell, in the press).

PAGE 241

1 *Prose Works*, ed. Herbert Davis (Oxford, 1939–), IX, 262. All subsequent references to this edition. Cf. also, for example, Martin Price's summing-up: 'Propriety, then, for Swift is not simply a principle of exclusion. The plainness of his style comes of the rejection of expansive imagery and analogical turns, of elaborated schemes and tropes' (*Swift's Rhetorical Art*, Yale, 1953, p. 22), and Paul Fussell's comment on 'Swift's mockery throughout *A Tale of a Tub* of the intellectual technique of ready and complacent analogy' (*op. cit.* p. 10).

2 The New Science certainly objected to excessive quotation: in his first version of the *Vanity of Dogmatizing* (1661) Joseph Glanvill attacked 'this vain Idolizing of Authors, which gave birth to the silly vanity of *impertinent citations*; and inducing Authority in things neither requiring, nor deserving it. That saying was much more observable, *That men have beards, and women none*; because quoted from *Beza*; and that other *Pax res bona est*; because brought in with a,

said St. Austin.' By 1678 he could write that 'the custom is worn out every-where except in remote, dark corners'. See Jones (B52), p. 84 n. For an illumi-nating account of Swift's characteristic mockery of classical tags see E. W. Rosenheim, *Swift and the Satirist's Art* (Chicago, 1963), p. 234.

3 See *The Tale of A Tub*, etc. ed. A. C. Guthkelch and D. Nichol Smith (2nd ed., Oxford, 1958), p. 241, and for identification of other unannounced allusions to Bacon, pp. 32, 134, 172.

PAGE 243

1 For more examples of the 'It is with' construction, cf. Bacon 11. 404; 12. 317; 14. 17, and Swift, I, 100, 133, 128; and for other mocking examples of clauses introduced by 'for' see Swift I, 62, 91, etc. This is a remarkably frequent device in Bacon, as—to take one example only—in the Essay 'Of Envy', where, of seventy-six head clauses in all, no less than twenty-one begin with the explanatory 'for': see R. Tarselius (B85).

PAGE 245

1 *The Guardian*, no. 25 (9 April 1713). I have been directed to some of these eighteenth-century allusions by R. C. Cochrane (B19), an article which traces both the general decline in Bacon's reputation parallel to that of the Royal Society and also the increasingly vague laudatory elevation of Bacon to the status of 'the British Plato'. (A small point is that the list of 'attacks' given by Mr Cochrane, p. 68 n. 17, seems to be erroneous.)

2 Dryden, *Essay of Dramatic Poesy* (1668), ed. G. Watson (London, 1962), I, 67. Against punning cf. also Addison, *Spectator*, no. 71, and John Oldmixon, *The Arts of Logick and Rhetorick* (1728), p. 164, on how Lancelot Andrewes and other Jacobean divines 'reduc'd Preaching to Punning'. Earlier, however, Oldmixon had said that 'My Lord Bacon's Writings are full of just and beautiful Comparisons' (p. 121).

PAGE 246

1 Hume, *History of England* (1754–7), quoted by Fowler, *Novum Organum* (1878 ed.), p. 136; Goldsmith, *Works*, ed. J. W. Gibbs (London, 1885), IV, 451. Six years later, however, Goldsmith described Bacon's style as 'copious and correct' (V, 309), while elsewhere he praises him as 'perhaps the greatest philosopher among men' (*ibid.*; also V, 88; V, 146; III, 274). The first work of Goldsmith quoted here is not included in the recent *Collected Works*, ed. Arthur Friedman (5 vols. Oxford, 1966), but whether because he thinks it is not authentic or because he groups it with those 'compilations' also omitted (vol. I, p. xi) I cannot discover. For the case for authenticity, see Gibbs, II, 456.

2 *Seventeenth Century Prose* (Cambridge, 1960), p. 11.

3   See *Tatler*, nos. 17, 108, 133, 149, 168, 213, 239, 267; *Spectator*, nos. 10, 19, 68, 160, 177, 388, 411, 447, 500, 554; *Letters of Horace Walpole*, ed. Mrs Paget Toynbee (Oxford, 1905), I, 271, and XIV, 360; also II, 335; IV, 159; VII, 51; X, 39; XIII, 53, and XIV, 238.

4   Boswell, *Life of Johnson* entry for Monday, 22 September 1777 (Johnson also criticised Mallet's *Life of Bacon* because the biographer's mind 'was not comprehensive enough to embrace the vast extent of Lord Verulam's genius and research'). See G. S. Haight's study of Johnson's method in using Bacon for his *Dictionary*: 'Johnson's Copy of Bacon's Works', *Yale University Library Gazette* (1932), pp. 67–73.

5   See, for example, Boswell's *Life* (London, 1957; Oxford Standard Authors edition), pp. 674, 871, 1226, 1280, 1283; *Rambler*, nos. 106, 137, 140; *Adventurer*, no. 85.

PAGE 247

1   *Johnsonian Miscellanies*, ed. G. B. Hill (Oxford, 1897), II, 229.

2   See the Appendix, 'Editions of Bacon, 1597–1967'. This publishing analysis is based on R. W. Gibson's *Bibliography* to 1750, and thereafter on the study by J. Spurrell, *The Writings of Sir Francis Bacon Published in the British Isles between 1750 and 1850* (Diploma in Librarianship, London University, 1955). From 1850 I have used the British Museum catalogue of 1934, the Cambridge University Library catalogues, Whitaker, and the *British National Bibliography*. In this last period I have omitted the many and various selections from the *Essays* published between 1903 and 1910 for professional and 'Certificate' examination purposes, which would otherwise have given that period an unreal importance. The popular demand for Bacon's *Essays* (which have always been amongst the first few titles in any series of 'English Classics') explains the bulge noticeable at this time—indeed, in the last hundred years, the *Essays* have accounted for over two-thirds of the published editions of Bacon. An analysis of the titles would show a steep decline since the seventeenth century in the range of works available.

PAGE 248

1   *Works of Jeremy Bentham*, ed. J. Bowring (Edinburgh, 1843), VIII, 73, 6–7, 99, and see the index to this edition for some thirty more references.

2   Geoffrey Keynes printed the full text for the first time (B54); see now his *Complete Writings of William Blake* (London, 1966), pp. 396–410.

PAGE 250

1   See *Leigh Hunt's Literary Criticism*, ed. L. H. and C. W. Houtchens (New York, 1950), p. 268, and further references in the same editors' collection of

Political and Occasional Essays (New York, 1962). Napier's essay appeared in the *Transactions of the Royal Society of Edinburgh*, and was reprinted in 1853.

2 Coleridge, *Letters*, ed. E. L. Griggs (Oxford, 1956), p. 530; Wordsworth, *Letters, Early Years*, ed. E. de Selincourt (Oxford, 1937), p. 233; Hazlitt, *Works*, ed. A. R. Waller and A. Glover (London, 1906), IX, 186.

3 Byron: *Don Juan*, Canto 5, stanza cxlvii; see his *Letters and Journals*, ed. R. E. Prothero (London, 1904), V, 153, 220, 351, 597. Shelley: see W. O. Scott (B79), especially pp. 229, 232. Keats: *Letters*, ed. M. B. Forman (Oxford, 1952), pp. 233, 284; Wordsworth: see M. Moorman, *The Early Years of William Wordsworth* (Oxford, 1957), pp. 56–7, and the reference to Bacon in the 'School Exercise' of 1784–5, ll. 55–6; *Letters of H. C. Robinson*, ed. E. J. Morley (Oxford, 1927), II, 859; Wordsworth, *Letters, Early Years*, p. 559; *Letters, Middle Years*, p. 297; *Prose Works*, ed. A. Grosart (London, 1876), I, 357. Further references in M. L. Peacock, *The Critical Opinions of William Wordsworth* (Baltimore, 1950), pp. 179–80.

PAGE 251

1 See the convenient collection by R. F. Brinkley, *Coleridge on the Seventeenth Century* (Duke, North Carolina, 1955), pp. 41–58 and 110–16. Subsequent page-references to Coleridge in the text are from this edition, and for further evidence of his dislike of punning see his *Unpublished Letters*, ed. E. L. Griggs (London, 1932), II, 364. Anne Righter in her essay has replied convincingly to Coleridge's specific attack: *op. cit.* p. 11.

PAGE 254

1 References to De Quincey are to the *Works*, ed. D. Masson (Edinburgh, 1890), XIII, 429–30; V, 95, 144; X, 109 n. (with a sensitive comment on Raleigh's prose).

2 Hazlitt, *Works*, ed. Waller and Glover, XI, 25. This passage was later incorporated in a review article in the *Morning Chronicle* (3 Feb. 1814), when Hazlitt expanded the end of the sentence to read: 'and see equally in both worlds, the individual and sensible, and the abstracted and intelligible form of things'. See the index to this edition for some forty more references to Bacon; the quotations from the *Lecture* are from Vol. 5, pp. 327–8 and 333. Hazlitt's own copy of the *Advancement of Learning* (1629 ed.) has recently been discovered, closely annotated and including this perceptive comment on Bacon's powers as a critic of extant systems and his deficiencies as an inventor of new ones: 'when he goes from contemplation of what others have done to projecting himself into future science, he becomes quaint & conceipted instead of original. His solidity was in reflection, not in invention.' See P. G. Gates (B35), p. 333.

PAGE 256

1   Thus for his influence: 'I read today with very great pleasure Macaulay's article on Bacon in the last *Edinburgh Review* in which the personal character of Bacon is very ably reviewed, and his philosophy admirably characterized' (entry for 9 Aug. 1837 in Henry Crabb Robinson, *On Books and Writers*, ed. E. J. Morley, London, 1938, II, 533). A convenient modern statement of its deficiencies is by S. C. Chew: 'The account therein of Platonic doctrine is of a superficiality to shame Macaulay's own proverbial "school-boy"; and Bacon's achievement in inductive science is magnified beyond all reason, as is, antithetically, his moral turpitude' (*A Literary History of England*, ed. A. C. Baugh, New York, 1948, p. 1328). Quotations from the *Essay* are from his *Works* (London, 1897), VIII, 637, 639. Elsewhere Macaulay was nastier still, recalling Addison: 'The King quibbled on the throne...the chancellor quibbled in concert from the woolsack' (VII, 134). The quotation from Coleridge at the end of the paragraph is from his *Letters*, ed. E. L. Griggs, IV, 675.

PAGE 257

1   T. W. Fowler's edition of the *Novum Organum* gives an impressive list of the more technical works on Bacon up to 1877 (*ed. cit.* pp. 146–51). It might be an interesting project for a historian of science to consider nineteenth-century attitudes to Bacon in the light of developing ideas about physics, say, or scientific method.

PAGE 258

1   Tennyson's reaction is recorded in Charles Tennyson's biography *Alfred Tennyson* (London, 1949), p. 303; other references from *Speeches of Charles Dickens*, ed. K. J. Fielding (Oxford, 1960), pp. 4, 54, 245; M. Sadleir, *Trollope* (London, 1927), pp. 352–4 (Trollope used Aldis Wright's edition); *Journals and Papers of Gerard Manley Hopkins*, ed. H. House and G. Storey (Oxford, 1959), pp. 56, 49, 116, 119; Arnold, *Notebooks*, ed. H. F. Lowry *et al.* (Oxford, 1952), pp. 6, 48, *Lectures and Essays in Criticism*, ed. R. H. Super (Michigan, 1962), p. 15, and *On the Classical Tradition* (same edition, 1960), p. 179; British Museum, Gladstone Papers, no. 44723, fos. 196–231, 260, and no. 44724, fo. 70; and *The Way of All Flesh*, ch. 8.

PAGE 259

1   Ruskin, *Works*, ed. E. T. Cook and A. Wedderburn (London, 1909): on Bacon and Pascal, VI, 439–40; on Bacon the scientist, XI, 67; XII, 128; V, 387; on the *New Atlantis*, XVIII, 513–14; XVII, 282; XX, 367, XXII, 206; XXVIII, 23; XXIX, 242; XXIX, 600; XX, 290; *Pall Mall Gazette*, 19 Jan. 1886: XXXIV, 583. The other philosophers were Mill, Darwin, Adam Smith, Berkeley, Descartes, Locke, and Lewes.

2 Hallam, *Introduction* (6th ed., London, 1860), III, 65; Saintsbury, *A History of Elizabethan Literature* (8th ed., London, 1887), p. 209; Emile Legouis, *A Short History of English Literature* (Oxford, 1934), p. 117.

PAGE 260

1 *The Longest Journey*, ch. 10 (Penguin ed. 1960), p. 97. The quotation is from the Essay 'Of Atheism', and is not quite accurate: 'But the great atheists indeed are hypocrites; which are ever handling holy things, but without feeling; so as they needs must be cauterized in the end' (6. 414). Lawrence refers to Bacon (quite accurately) as 'a magician on the verge of modern science', but in a critical essay on Hawthorne, *Studies in Classical American Literature* (London, 1933), p. 100.

PAGE 261

1 *A Collection of Letters made by Sr Tobie Matthews Kt*, ed. J. Donne (London, 1660), Sig. B7r.

BIBLIOGRAPHY

NOTE. There seems to be no detailed analytical bibliography of modern Bacon criticism, and the following list attempts to fill this gap, subject to certain restrictions: (i) I have omitted a number of ephemeral articles, reviews, etc., together with such as are demonstrably inaccurate or so biased as not to represent even a reaction worth discussing. (ii) Unpublished doctoral theses are not included, and only those articles and excerpts from books which offer a fairly substantial assessment of Bacon. (iii) Some omissions may simply be due to ignorance on my part, and others are certainly due to my incompetence to evaluate them (e.g. a number of pre-war books in Italian).

Items have been indexed under their main subjects as a help to workers in those fields. I have collected what seems to me the best of modern criticism for a volume on Bacon in the 'Essential Articles' series (Archon Books, Connecticut; Frank Cass, London, in the press).

Alphabetical List of Items
1 Adams, R., 'The Social Responsibilities of Science in *Utopia, New Atlantis, and after*', *Journal of the History of Ideas*, x (1949), 374–98.
2 Anderson, F. H., 'Bacon on Platonism', *University of Toronto Quarterly*, xi (1942), 154–66.
3 Anderson, F. H., *The Philosophy of Francis Bacon*. Chicago, 1948.
4 Anderson, F. H., *Francis Bacon, His Career and Thought*. Univ. S. Carolina, 1963.
5 Andrewes, J., 'Bacon, Hazlitt, and the "Dissociation of Sensibility"', *Notes & Queries*, cxcix (1954), 484–6, 530–2.
6 Beckingham, C., 'Parallel Passages in Bacon and Fuller', *Review of English Studies*, xiii (1937), 449–53.
7 Bierman, J., 'Science and Society in the *New Atlantis* and Other Renaissance Utopias', *PMLA*, lxxviii (1963), 492–500.
8 Blodgett, E., 'Campanella and the *New Atlantis*', *PMLA*, xlvi (1931), 763–80.
9 Boas, M., 'Bacon and Gilbert', *Journal of The History of Ideas*, xii (1951), 466–7.
10 Boulton, J. T., 'Bacon and Aesop', *Notes & Queries*, ccii (1957), 378.
11 Bowers, R., 'Bacon's Spider Simile', *Journal of the History of Ideas*, xvii (1956), 133–5.
12 Broad, C. D., *The Philosophy of Francis Bacon* (Cambridge, 1926),

Bibliography

reprinted in *Ethics and the History of Philosophy* (London, 1952), pp. 117–43.

13 Brown, C., 'Lucan, Bacon, and Hostages to Fortune', *Modern Language Notes*, LXV (1950), 114–15.

14 Bullough, G., 'Bacon and the Defence of Learning', *Seventeenth Century Studies presented to Sir Herbert Grierson* (Oxford, 1938), pp. 1–20.

15 Busch, W., *England under the Tudors* (tr. A. Todd). London, 1895.

16 Cawley, R. C., 'Bacon, Burton, Sandys on Coffee', *Modern Language Notes*, LVI (1941), 271–3.

17 Cochrane, R., 'Bacon, Pepys, and the *Faber Fortunae*', *Notes & Queries*, CCI (1956), 511–14.

18 Cochrane, R., 'Francis Bacon and the Architect of Fortune', *Studies in the Renaissance*, V (1958), 176–95.

19 Cochrane, R., 'Bacon in early Eighteenth Century English Literature', *Philological Quarterly*, XXXVII (1958), 58–79.

20 Cohen, M. R., 'Bacon and Inductive Method', *Studies in Philosophy and Science* (New York, 1949), pp. 99–106.

21 Colie, R. L., 'Cornelius, Drebbel and Salomon de Caus: Two Jacobean Models for Salomon's House', *Huntington Library Quarterly*, XVIII (1954), 245–60.

22 Craig, H., *The Enchanted Glass*. Oxford, 1936.

23 Crane, R. S., 'The Relation of Bacon's *Essays* to his Programme for the Advancement of Learning', in *Schelling Anniversary Papers* (New York, 1923), pp. 87–105.

24 Davis, W. R., 'The Imagery of Bacon's Late Work', *Modern Language Quarterly*, XXVII (1966), 162–73.

25 Dean, L. F., 'Sir Francis Bacon's Theory of Civil History-Writing', *ELH*, VIII (1941), 161–83.

26 Ducasse, C. J., 'Francis Bacon's Philosophy of Science', *Structure, Method and Meaning*, ed. P. Henle *et al.* (New York, 1951), pp. 115–44.

27 Farrington, B., *Francis Bacon, Philosopher of Industrial Science*. London, 1951.

28 Farrington, B., 'On Misunderstanding the Philosophy of Francis Bacon', *Science, Medicine and History*, ed. E. A. Underwood (Oxford, 1953), I, 439–50.

29 Farrington, B., *The Philosophy of Francis Bacon*. Liverpool, 1964.

30 Fisch, H. and Jones, H., 'Bacon and Sprat', *Modern Language Quarterly*, XII (1951), 399–406.

31 Fisch, H., 'Bacon and Paracelsus', *Cambridge Journal*, V (1952), 752–8.

32 Fisch, H., *Jerusalem and Albion*. London, 1964.

33 Freeman, E. L., 'Jeremy Collier and Francis Bacon', *Philological Quarterly*, VII (1928), 17–26.

34 Fussner, F. S., *The Historical Revolution: English Historical Writing and Thought, 1580–1640*. London, 1962.

35 Gates, P. G., 'Bacon, Keats and Hazlitt', *Fifty Years of the 'South Atlantic Quarterly'*, ed. W. B. Hamilton (Durham, N.C., 1952), pp. 331–43.

36 Gibson, R. W., *A Bacon Bibliography and Allusion Book, 1597–1750* (Oxford, 1950), *Supplement* (1959).

37 Gilbert, N. W., *Renaissance Concepts of Method*. New York, 1960.

38 Greene, G., 'Bacon a source for Drummond', *Modern Language Notes*, XLVIII (1933), 230–2.

39 Greenleaf, W. H., *Order, Empiricism and Politics*. London, 1964.

40 Griffiths, G., 'The Form of Bacon's Essay', *English*, V (1944), 188–93.

41 Hannah, R., *Francis Bacon, the Political Orator*. New York, 1925.

42 Hannah, R., 'Bacon the Orator', in *Studies in Rhetoric Presented to J. A. Winans* (New York, 1925), pp. 91–132.

43 Harrison, C. T., 'Bacon, Hobbes, Boyle, and the Ancient Atomists', *Harvard Studies and Notes, Philological and Literary*, XV (1933), 191–218.

44 Harrison, J. L., 'Bacon's View of Rhetoric, Poetry and the Imagination', *Huntington Library Quarterly*, XX (1957), 107–25.

45 Haydn, H., *The Counter-Renaissance*. New York, 1950.

46 Hennig, J., 'Goethe und Bacon', *Modern Language Quarterly*, XII (1951), 201–3.

47 Hesse, M., 'Francis Bacon', in *A Critical History of Western Philosophy*, ed. D. J. O'Connor (New York and London, 1964), pp. 141–52.

48 Hopkins, V., 'Emerson and Bacon', *American Literature*, XXIX (1958), 408–30.

49 Houghton, W., 'The History of Trades: its relation to 17th Century Thought, as seen in Bacon, Petty, Evelyn, and Boyle', *Journal of the History of Ideas*, II (1941), 33–60.

50 James, D. G., *The Dream of Learning*. Oxford, 1951.

51 Jones, R. F., *Ancients and Moderns: A Study of the Rise of the Scientific Movement in Seventeenth Century England* (2nd ed.). Washington, 1961.

51a Jones, R. F., 'Science and Criticism in the Neo-Classical Age of English Literature', in *The Seventeenth Century* (Stanford, 1951, 1965), pp. 41–74.

52 Jones, R. F., 'Science and English Prose Style in the Third Quarter of the Seventeenth Century', *ibid.* pp. 75–110.

53 Jørgensen, S., 'Hamann, Bacon, and Tradition', *Orbis Litterarum*, XVI (1961), 48–73.

54 Keynes, G., 'Bacon and Blake', *TLS*, 8 March 1957, p. 152.

Bibliography

55 Knights, L. C., 'Bacon and the Seventeenth-Century Dissociation of Sensibility', in *Explorations* (London, 1946), pp. 92–111.

56 Kocher, P., 'Francis Bacon on the Science of Jurisprudence', *Journal of the History of Ideas*, XVIII (1957), 3–26.

57 Kocher, P., 'Bacon and his Father', *Huntington Library Quarterly*, XXI (1957), 133–58.

58 Kocher, P., 'Francis Bacon on the Drama', *Essays on Shakespeare and Elizabethan Drama for Hardin Craig*, ed. R. Hosley (London, 1963), pp. 297–307.

59 Krook, D., 'Two Baconians: Robert Boyle and Joseph Glanvill', *Huntington Library Quarterly*, XVIII (1954), 261–78.

60 Larsen, R. E., 'The Aristotelianism of Bacon's *Novum Organum*', *Journal of the History of Ideas*, XXIII (1962), 435–50.

61 Lemmi, C. W., *The Classic Deities in Bacon*. Baltimore, 1933.

62 Lievsay, J. L., 'Tuvill's Advancement of Bacon's Learning', *Huntington Library Quarterly*, IX (1945), 11–32.

63 Lievsay, M., 'Bacon Versified', *Huntington Library Quarterly*, XIV (1951), 223–38.

64 Lilley, S., 'Robert Recorde and the Idea of Progress', *Renaissance and Modern Studies*, II (1958), 1–37.

65 Luciani, V., 'Bacon and Machiavelli', *Italica*, XXIV (1947), 26–40.

66 Luciani, V., 'Bacon and Guicciardini', *PMLA*, LXII (1947), 96–113.

67 McNamee, M., 'Bacon's Concept of Literary Decorum', *St Louis Univ. Studies*, Series A, I (March, 1950), 1–52.

68 Macrae, R., 'Unity of Sciences: Bacon, Descartes, Leibniz', *Journal of the History of Ideas*, XVIII (1957), 27–48.

69 Metz, R., 'Bacon's Part in the Intellectual Movement of his Time', *Seventeenth Century Studies presented to Sir Herbert Grierson* (Oxford, 1938), pp. 21–32.

70 Minkowski, G., 'Francis Bacon und die Academia Naturae Curiosorum', *Fränk. Heimat*, XII, 76–80.

71 Minkowski, H., 'Die *Neue Atlantis* des Francis Bacon und die Leopoldino-Carolina', *Archiv für Kulturgeschichte*, XXVI (1936), 283–95.

72 Minkowski, H., 'Die Geistesgeschichtliche und die Literarische Nachfolge der *Neu-Atlantis* des Francis Bacon', *Neophilologus*, XXII (1937), 120–39, 185–200.

73 Orsini, N., *Bacone e Machiavelli*. Genova, 1936.

74 Patrides, C., 'Bacon and Feltham: Victims of Literary Piracy', *Notes and Queries*, CCIII (1958), 63–5.

75 Prior, M. E., 'Bacon's Man of Science', *Journal of the History of Ideas*, XV (1954), 348–70.

Bibliography

76 Redpath, R. T. H., 'Bacon and the Advancement of Learning', *Pelican Guide to English Literature*, II (London, 1956), 369–85.

77 Righter, A., 'Francis Bacon', *The English Mind*, ed. H. S. Davies and G. Watson (Cambridge, 1964), pp. 7–29.

78 (*a*) Rossi, P., *Francesco Bacone, dalla Magia alla Scienza* (Bari, 1958); (*b*) revised; English translation by S. Rabinovitch, *Francis Bacon: From Magic to Science* (London, 1968).

79 Scott, W. O., 'Shelley's Admiration for Bacon', *PMLA*, LXXIII (1958), 228–36.

80 Sewell, E., *The Orphic Voice*. London, 1961.

81 Snow, V., 'Francis Bacon's Advice to Fulke Greville on Research Techniques', *Huntington Library Quarterly*, XXIII (1960), 369–78.

82 Sommer, I., *Orthographie und Lautlehre in Bacon*. Heidelberg, 1937.

83 Stovall, F., 'Whitman and Bacon', *Philological Quarterly*, XXXI (1952), 27–35.

84 Tarselius, R., '*Would* as Exhortative Auxiliary in Bacon's Prose', *Studier i modern språkvetenskap*, XVIII (1953), 133–44.

85 Tarselius, R., 'For all colours agree in the dark', *Studia Neophilologica*, XXV (1958), 155–60.

86 Taylor, A. E., *Francis Bacon*, in *Proceedings of the British Academy*, XII (1926), 273–94.

87 Thaler, A., 'Browne and the Elizabethans', *Studies in Philology*, XXVIII (1931), 87–117.

88 Thorndike, L., *A History of Magic and Experimental Science*, vols. V–VIII. New York, 1941, 1958.

89 Thorndike, L., 'Bacon and Descartes on Magic', *Science, Medicine and History*, ed. E. A. Underwood (Oxford, 1953), I, 451–4.

90 Tillotson, G., 'Words for Princes', *TLS*, 6 Feb. 1937, and *Essays in Criticism and Research* (Cambridge, 1942), pp. 31–40.

91 Tinivella, G., *Bacone e Locke*. Milano, 1939.

92 Usher, R. G., 'Bacon's Knowledge of Law-French', *Modern Language Notes*, XXXIV (1919), 28–32.

93 Wallace, K. R., *Francis Bacon on Communication and Rhetoric*. Chapel Hill, N.C., 1943.

94 Wallace, K. R., 'Aspects of Modern Rhetoric in Francis Bacon', *Quarterly Journal of Speech*, XLII (1956), 398–406.

95 Wallace, K. R., 'Discussion in Parliament and Francis Bacon', *Quarterly Journal of Speech*, XLIII (1957), 12–21.

96 Wallace, K. R., 'Imagination and Bacon's View of Rhetoric', *Dimensions of Rhetorical Scholarship*. Norman, Oklahoma, 1963.

Bibliography

97 Walters, M., 'The Literary Background of Francis Bacon's Essay "Of Death"', *Modern Language Review*, XXXV (1940), 1–7.

98 Wheeler, T., 'Bacon's Purpose in Writing *Henry VII*', *Studies in Philology*, LIV (1957), 1–13.

99 Whitaker, V. K., *Francis Bacon's Renaissance Milieu*. Los Angeles: William Clark Library, 1962, pp. 29.

100 White, H. B., 'Bacon's Imperialism', *The American Political Science Review*, LII (1958), 470–89.

101 Willey, B., *The Seventeenth Century Background*. London, 1934.

102 Williamson, G., *The Senecan Amble*. London, 1951.

103 Wilson, F. P., *Elizabethan and Jacobean*. Oxford, 1945.

104 Wolff, E., *Francis Bacon und seine Quellen*. Berlin, 1910.

105 Zeitlin, J., 'The Development of Bacon's Essays and Montaigne', *Journal of English and Germanic Philology*, XXVII (1928), 496–519.

Addenda

106 Hill, C., *The Intellectual Origins of the English Revolution* (Oxford, 1965), especially ch. 3, 'Francis Bacon and the Parliamentarians'.

107 Purver, M., *The Royal Society: Concept and Creation*. London, 1967.

108 Nadel, G. H., 'History as Psychology in Francis Bacon's Theory of History', *History and Theory*, V (1966), 275–87.

109 Van Leeuwen, H. G., *The Problem of Certainty in English Thought, 1630–90*. The Hague, 1963.

110 Kargon, R. H., *Atomism in England from Harriot to Newton*. Oxford, 1966.

INDEX

Index

Index

Index